Booktalks and More

Motivating Teens to Read

Lucy Schall

LIBRARIES
U N L I M I T E D
A Member of the Greenwood Publishing Group
Westport, Connecticut • London

Library of Congress Cataloging-in-Publication Data
Schall, Lucy.
    Booktalks and more : motivating teens to read / by Lucy Schall
      p. cm.
    Includes bibliographical references and indexes.
    ISBN 1–56308–982–3
    1. Teenagers—Books and reading—United States. 2. Book talks—United
States. 3. Reading promotion—United States. 4. Best books. 5. Young adult
literature—Bibliography. I. Schall, Lucy.
    Z1037.A1S268   2003
    028.5'5—dc21   2003051650

British Library Cataloguing in Publication Data is available.

Library of Congress Catalog Card Number: 2003051650
ISBN: 1-56308-982-3

First published in 2003

Libraries Unlimited, Inc., 88 Post Road West, Westport, CT 06881
A Member of the Greenwood Publishing Group, Inc.
www.lu.com

Printed in the United States of America

The paper used in this book complies with the
Permanent Paper Standard issued by the National
Information Standards Organization (Z39.48-1984).

10 9 8 7 6 5 4 3 2

Booktalks and More

To James C. Flynn, my father,
and Robert K. Schall, my father-in-law,
who both loved their country,
loved their families, and encouraged
young people to be the best
they could possibly be.

Contents

Acknowledgments

I wish to thank Barbara Ittner, my editor, for her insight and patience and Linda Benson, from VOYA, for continually guiding me to new paths of reading.

The following libraries have provided me with resources as well as staff support: St. Petersburg Public Library in St. Petersburg, Florida; Meadville Public Library and the Lawrence Lee Pelletier Library in Meadville, Pennsylvania; Cochranton Public Library in Cochranton, Pennsylvania; and Rocky River Public Library in Rocky River, Ohio.

Introduction

Booktalks and More continues the search for good books that teenagers enjoy. The first book, *Booktalks Plus*, proved a valuable tool for librarians, media specialists, and teachers, but parents, grandparents, aunts, and uncles discovered that *Booktalks Plus* also helped them communicate with the young people in their families. In fact, many adults told me they were surprised to find young-adult writers so clear, inspiring, and perceptive. Now they make the young-adult section their first library stop even if a young adult isn't around at the time. *Booktalks and More* contains booktalks for teenage books published between 1997 and 2001. These books, which involve suggestions and examples for problem-solving, personal discovery, and learning, relate to each other, to school curricula, and to older works. The summaries, booktalks, and supplementary materials will help librarians, media specialists, classroom teachers, home school instructors, teacher educators, youth workers, or families—any professional or nonprofessional who works with young people—to match teens and books. The related activities will help students and the adults who read with them explore, express, and share their ideas about personal, social, political, and universal concerns.

Like the books in *Booktalks Plus*, the books in *Booktalks and More* explore the journey of life. The chapter topics and subtopics within it address particular aspects of that journey. The books listed within the topics are organized for what a good librarian friend of mine calls shelf browsing. Anyone interested in a particular title will find that the books placed nearby it, within a subtopic, relate by theme, structure, setting, or character. Hopefully the search for one title will lead to the discovery of several more. Chapter 1, "Challenge: We Meet a Powerful World" deals with the confrontations that can show up on anyone's doorstep. Harassment because of appearance or action; problems families create through worn-out customs, poor decision-making, or procrastination; natural disasters or the call of nature's rhythms; national conflicts; and the discovery that spirits from another world may have something to say about our lives all teach us that we need to become powerful too. Consequently, Chapter 2, "Achievement: We Test Coping Skills," talks about the strategies we choose to meet the expectations of our families, peers, schools, neighborhoods, and communities; to seek the spirit within us that will enhance those efforts; to explore the depths of our physical strength for competition and recognition; and to use our minds to figure out what is happening to us. But Chapter 3, "Dedication: We Battle the Forces Against Us," involves the realization that skill is not always enough. In these books, people commit. They use their talents and skills to take a stand in the battle between good and evil; overcome illnesses or nurse others through them; save themselves, loved ones, or even complete strangers from hate and prejudice; and claim independence rather than suffer unhealthy cooperation with harmful family members, some of whom they love very much. Chapter 4, "Legacy: We Are Remembered," tells about the results of life decisions. These books chronicle how one gives back—good or bad—to the world by entertaining it with stories, poems, music, or visual arts; trusting families, friends, and ourselves; exploring new frontiers of earth, sky, and justice; and inspiring others to trust in a future through imagination, life-long habits, investments, or even a small garden seed.

Each booktalk book includes the author, book title, publisher and date of publication, year of publication, number of pages, price, and ISBN. The abbreviation "pa" indicates paperback. An **NF** tag indicates nonfiction. A summary/description accompanies each title. The summary allows the reader to decide quickly the audience to which the book might appeal. The booktalk follows the summary/description and provides a way to present the book, or it might suggest an idea for another presentation. Presenter directions concerning activities related to the booktalk are in italics. Geared to a live audience, the booktalk can be adapted to the user's style or needs. It is short enough to accommodate a school's morning announcements or the school newspaper. The library might want to use the booktalk for public service segments for the local radio station or newspaper, their own newsletter, or a library information Web site. Nonprofit use is permitted and encouraged.

"Related Activities" presents individual and group projects based on the book and works related to the book. The suggestions include discussion topics; writing assignments for journals, longer papers, poems, or creative writing; debates, panel discussions, or presentations—visual, oral, or both. Some activities might even provide a basis for independent studies, portfolios, or senior projects. Activities also suggest alternative groupings for the books. Completion of any of the activities will improve reading, writing, and speaking skills. Any works mentioned in the activities are listed in "Related Works."

"Related Works" lists applicable books within the volume as well as classics, short stories, plays, poems, articles, videos and Web sites. Again, **NF** indicates nonfiction books. These sections will help instructors organize theme units or guide both instructors and parents to works or information sources that speak to particular areas of interest. The index includes authors, titles, and topics for a quick overview of a work's relationship to others mentioned in this volume.

In completing *Booktalks and More,* I consulted award lists, articles, and professional reviews. *VOYA, Booklist, School Library Journal, The ALAN Review,* and *YALSA* (Young Adult Library Services Association) "best" booklists continually remind me of the time, skill, and dedication that teachers, librarians, authors, and scholars devote to keeping teens in a reading community. I would like to thank them all. Their efforts make my reading and writing a pleasure as well.

Challenge: We Meet a Powerful World

Strangers Judge

Neufeld, John. **Boys Lie.**

New York: DK Publishing/Richard Jackson, 1999. 165p. $16.95. ISBN 0-7894-2624-2.

Summary/Description

After he finds out Gina was previously assaulted, a boy she trusts attacks her, a new eighth grader in a California school. The story opens with the description of the initial assault, which took place during the summer in a New York City swimming pool. Subsequent chapters deal with Gina's trauma, the school's rumor mill building the assault into rape, her male classmates coping with their attraction to Gina, the attack she thwarts, and the final rumors she squelches by telling her own story to the entire homeroom. She receives overwhelming support. The attacker, rejected and laughed at, decides to go to a private school. The incident clarifies for her classmates that relationships are built on caring and respect rather than thrill and conquest.

Booktalk

Ask the following questions. Has anyone been involved in a rumor that proved to be false? Has anyone been betrayed by someone they thought was their friend?

If you can answer yes to those questions, you have something in common with Gina. She is the new kid in eighth grade. The boys call her a fox.

Three boys would like to get to know her, and what they can't find out about her they are willing to make up. Each one is sure she wants to love only him. Then the rumors start. Gina has a past. The rumors keep spreading and growing. How can she control what boys will do to her or her reputation? She has to decide soon, because Gina is learning—real fast—that *Boys Lie*.

Related Activities

1. Gina's mother compares passing a rumor to playing the game called Telephone. In the game, one person whispers a story to another. That person passes on what he or she heard and so on. Using at least ten people, whisper a statement or story to one person and allow everyone to pass it on. Then talk about the result in relation to rumor.
2. In *Boys Lie*, Gina defeats Eddie by publicly telling the truth about what happened. In *Speak* (Related Work 1), Melinda waits to tell the truth about the boy who rapes her. Compare the situations presented in the two novels and each girl's reaction. Then discuss the reasons for the different action each girl takes.
3. *Annie's Baby* (Related Work 6), *Painting the Black* (Related Work 4), *Dreamland* (Related Work 3), *Speak* (Related Work 1), and *Boys Lie* all deal with teenage boys harassing and abusing teenage girls. Compare the abusers and abused in the novels. Then write definitions or profiles of both an abuser and a person who is abused.
4. Using your library's resources, including the Internet, research the legal view of sexual harassment in schools. Then discuss how that view applies to *Boys Lie*. You might want to start your research with *Teens on Trial* (Related Work 5).
5. Read "The Poem as Striptease" by Philip Dacey on page 129 of *Poetry After Lunch: Poems to Read Aloud* (Related Work 2). Discuss how the description applies to poetry as well as to any other communication situation. Talk specifically about how it applies to *Boys Lie*.

Related Works

1. Anderson, Laurie Halse. **Speak.** (See full booktalk in chapter 2.) When she sneaks to a drinking party, Melinda Sordino is raped, calls 911, and then is rejected by her peers when the party is raided.
2. Carroll, Joyce Armstrong and Edward E. Wilson, comp. **Poetry After Lunch: Poems to Read Aloud.** (See full booktalk in chapter 4.) **NF** This single-sentence poem, "The Poem as Striptease," focuses on a major problem in *Boys Lie*. The book organizes the poems according to types of food or courses. This poem appears in "Desserts."

3. Dessen, Sarah. **Dreamland.** (See full booktalk in chapter 2.) Caitlin O'Koren loses herself in a controlling boyfriend who supplies her with drugs.
4. Deuker, Carl. **Painting the Black.** (See full booktalk in chapter 2.) A star pitcher feels his ability gives him a license to break rules and harass girls.
5. Jacobs, Thomas A. **Teens on Trial.** Minneapolis, MN: Free Spirit, 2000. 196p. $14.95pa. ISBN 1-57542-081-3. ⓃⒻ Organized in a question-answer format, this book explains cases that apply to teenagers. The chapter "Issue: What if you're sexually harassed at school?" on pages 43 to 49 explains one central case in relation to several others and then suggests action teenagers can take against sexual harassment.
6. Sparks, Beatrice, ed. **Annie's Baby: The Diary of Anonymous, A Pregnant Teenager.** New York: Avon Books, 1998. 245p. $4.50pa. ISBN 0-380-79141-2. Wanting to be popular, a fourteen-year-old girl submits to a star athlete's abuse.

ॐॐ

McNeal, Laura and Tom McNeal. Crooked.

New York: Alfred A. Knopf, 1999. 346p. $16.95. ISBN 0-679-89300-8.

Summary/Description

Fourteen-year-old Clara Wilson's crooked nose makes her think she is too ugly to be popular. Then her best friend, Gerri, decides to join the "in-group." Clara's mother leaves for a teaching job in Spain, and her father starts dating when her parents get a legal separation.

Clara befriends Mrs. Harper, an elderly lady on her paper route, tries out for the school play, stops the show, and attracts two boys. Amos Mackenzie, the son of the milkman, is quiet, intelligent, and shy. Eddie Tripp, the younger half of the notorious Tripp brothers, is jealous, controlling, and threatening.

Amos's life is in turmoil also. Amos's practical joking friend complicates Amos's attempts to date Clara. Amos witnesses vandalism by the Tripps, who beat him up and threaten him. Then his father dies.

When Amos tells Clara about his father's death, they become friends. Jealous Eddie Tripp threatens Amos and his family and tries to date Clara. Popular girls manipulate Amos to make fun of Clara. The couple work through the misunderstandings that result. Finally, the Tripp brothers corner Clara in her home. Charles, the dangerous and dominant brother, attempts to rape her, and Eddie runs away. Amos tries to save her, but the rescue requires Amos, his friend, Clara, and the police.

A year later, Charles Tripp is in jail. Eddie lives out of state with his mother. Amos, his sister Liz, and Clara host Thanksgiving dinner for their combined families, including the former Mrs. Harper and her husband. Clara may now visit and reconcile with her mother in Spain.

Booktalk

Clara Wilson has a crooked nose, and it's throwing her life out of line. She can't trust her friends. She doesn't have enough money for summer camp. Her mother and father can't get along, and she can't find a boyfriend.

But Clara decides to get a life anyway. She focuses on what she can do. She can find some odd jobs to supplement her paper route income. She can get to know quiet Amos Mackenzie a little better. She can try out for a part in the school play, and she can just leave her parents alone.

But any action has a reaction. Suddenly Clara attracts more boys than she can handle. Her acting career makes her a target instead of a star. And when she ignores her parents, she seems to get their constant, annoying attention. Clara's ninth grade year is a wild and *Crooked* ride, but it might get better if she can just look past her nose.

Related Activities

1. Eddie Tripp and Bruce Crookshank both stalk the girls they admire. Discuss how and why the two patterns of behavior are so different in tone.
2. Read *Everything You Need to Know About Dealing with Stalking* (Related Work 5). Also locate the references suggested by the author and any others your librarian might suggest. Then discuss the characters in *Crooked,* the stalkers and the victims, in relation to what you have learned.
3. *Crooked* includes "bad people" who do good things and "good people" who do bad things. Discuss some of the characters' decisions that surprised you. Discuss how these actions or decisions affected your opinion of the characters.
4. Although parents are seen only briefly, they play significant roles. Discuss how the parents in the novel affect the characters' actions.
5. In both *Tightrope* (Related Work 2) and *Crooked,* stalking is a central issue. After reading both novels, compare the stalking described and how it helps the authors accomplish their purposes.

6. Read the poem "Don't Tell Me" by Michael Dugan in *Seeing the Blue Between* (Related Work 3). Compare the speaker's attitude about appearance to Clara's. Then, using the poem as a model, write your own poem about appearance.

Related Works

1. Aydt, Rachel. **Why Me? A Teen Guide to Divorce and Your Feelings.** New York: Rosen Publishing Group, 2000. 64p. (The Divorce Resource Series). $17.95. ISBN 0-8239-3113-7. **NF** Explaining that there is a positive side to divorce, this source tells teenagers to remember they are not the cause, they have the power to help, and they need to develop a relationship with each parent that is separate from their conflict.
2. Cross, Gillian. **Tightrope.** (See full booktalk in chapter 2.) Ashley Putnam discovers that the gang leader who seems to protect her is really her stalker.
3. Dugan, Michael. "Don't Tell Me." In **Seeing the Blue Between: Advice and Inspiration for Young Poets,** compiled by Paul B. Janeczko. Cambridge, MA: Candlewick Press, 2002. 132p. $17.99. ISBN 0-7636-0881-5. **NF** In this humorous poem on page 16, the author lists all the physical problems he has and why the person to whom he is speaking should put a camera away.
4. Stone, Ruth. "The Nose." In **The Invisible Ladder: An Anthology of Contemporary American Poems for Young Readers,** edited by Liz Rosenberg. New York: Henry Holt and Company, 1996. 210p. $16.95. ISBN 0-8050-3836-1. **NF** This analysis of the nose and where it fits in life and the English language begins with the line "Everyone complains about the nose." It would be a good start for discussing Clara's attitude about her own nose. The poem appears on page 166.
5. Wright, Cynthia. **Everything You Need to Know About Dealing with Stalking.** New York: The Rosen Publishing Group, 2000. 64p. (The Need to Know Library). $17.95. ISBN 0-8239-2841-1. **NF** *Stalking* defines stalking, explains the legal definition, profiles different types of stalkers, and explains how to avoid an "engage and enrage" relationship with a stalker.

Peiss, Kathy. Hope in a Jar: The Making of America's Beauty Culture.

New York: Metropolitan Books, 1998. 334p. $25.00. ISBN 0-8050-5550-9. **NF**

Summary/Description

Hope in a Jar records the history of the cosmetics industry in America. Criticized as a commodity controlled by men to exploit women, cosmetics and their popularity actually signaled an increasing desire for independence. Despite society's criticism, beauty products gave women the confidence to enter the working world and even to define their roles in wartime. Women entrepreneurs of all skin colors developed products and systems that improved self-esteem and provided financial success. These businesses established models for consumer education, safety, and marketing. The cosmetics industry and its advertising also heightened the debate about ideal American beauty and its relationship to racism. Kathy Peiss points out that strong political comment and financial prosperity continue to surround the images cosmetics companies create. The book includes several illustrations, extensive footnotes, and a name and topic index. It is a serious historical treatment that will appeal to and surprise adults and older teens.

Booktalk

Ask the group if they can define the words "lady" and "hussy." Their definitions might differ from the 1938 definitions. Clarify that difference.

In 1938, *Mademoiselle* magazine described two lipsticks, one named "Lady" and one named "Hussy." "Hussy" outsold "Lady." The women's revolution was on its way.

Today, a woman doesn't have to define herself as either a lady or a hussy. She can choose from hundreds of shades and colors to suit her purpose, mood, or personality. Does that choice prove a billion-dollar industry controls her, or does it prove she can control how the world sees her?

Does make-up define beauty for us or just make us more aware that everyone has a definition of beauty? What do you think? *Hope in a Jar* has some interesting answers too.

Related Activities

1. After reading *Hope in a Jar,* review the information about Helena Rubinstein, Elizabeth Arden, and Madame Walker. Discuss the public persona each woman developed and how that persona contributed to her success. Choose one of these three women and further research her life. Share your findings with the group.
2. Find advertisements for cosmetics in magazines, newspapers, and television. Describe the promises the advertisements make about people's public and private lives.

3. The following words seem central to the cosmetics industry. Define them. Explain how they are used in each context, and use them in a new context.

    "nascent," pages 44, 53, and 61
    "protean," page 44
    "paradoxical," pages 86, 166, and 203

4. Peiss' historical analysis of our beauty culture has implications for the Women's Liberation movement and the Civil Rights movement. Discuss the relationships you noted and the information that surprised you.

5. The following books demonstrate how a person uses a public persona to direct his or her relationship with the world: *Behind the Mask* (Related Work 5), *Tribute to Another Dead Rock Star* (Related Work 4), *When Zachary Beaver Came to Town* (Related Work 3). Discuss how and why each public person in each of the works focuses on persona.

Related Works

1. Brynie, Faith Hickman. **101 Questions About Your Skin That Got Under Your Skin...Until Now.** Brookfield, CT: Twenty-First Century Books, 1999. 176p. $25.90. ISBN 0-7613-1259-5. **NF** Each chapter deals with a group of related questions about skin, hair, nails, and skin problems.

2. Desetta, Al and Sybil Wolin, ed. **The Struggle to Be Strong.** Minneapolis, MN: Free Spirit, 2000. 179p. $14.95. ISBN 1-57542-079-1. **NF** Two essays, "Beauty Is More Than Skin Deep" by Danielle Wilson on pages 16 to 20 and "I Was a Beauty School Sucker" by Tonya Leslie on pages 36 to 39, tell about the negative side of emphasizing physical appearance.

3. Holt, Kimberly Willis. **When Zachary Beaver Came to Town.** (See full booktalk in chapter 2.) When the town discovers Zachary Beaver is not really the sideshow act he claims to be, they learn a great deal about themselves and those they love.

4. Powell, Randy. **Tribute to Another Dead Rock Star.** (Full booktalk in chapter 3.) Grady Innis Grennan must distinguish between the persona and the real person of his mother, the rock star.

5. Thomas, Jane Resh. **Behind the Mask: The Life of Queen Elizabeth I.** (See full booktalk in chapter 4.) **NF** Thomas explains how Elizabeth maintained her kingdom by assessing and playing to her audiences.

ℭ⅋ℭ

Spinelli, Jerry. Stargirl.

New York: Alfred A. Knopf, 2000. 186p. $15.95. ISBN 0-679-88637-0.

Summary/Description

Looking back on his junior year in high school, Leo Borlock recalls the mystical and mysterious tenth grader named Stargirl who captivated, alienated, and then once again hypnotized him and the rest of the student body. Stargirl, a former home schooler, sings happy birthday to every student in school, leaves treats for her classmates, and intrudes on personal celebrations. She is a cheerleader for her team, the opposing team, and each positive act she sees. At first she is the most popular girl in school, but her eccentric and enthusiastic behavior eventually causes the group to shun her and Leo, who dates her. When Leo explains the importance of "fitting in," Stargirl takes back her real name, Susan Julia Caraway, and imitates every normal behavior she sees. The students continue to shut her out even after she wins the state oratory championship, so she returns to her offbeat personality that embarrasses Leo, dares to go to the prom alone, where she forms a legendary bunny-hop line, and then disappears from the community forever. The story closes with Leo, fifteen years later, reflecting on his mistake in letting her go and still hoping to find the elusive Stargirl.

Booktalk

Susan Julia Caraway is one of the most unusual tenth graders in America. She wears something that looks like a wedding dress on the first day of school. She carries a ukulele on her back in case she needs to sing happy birthday to a classmate. She leaves candy for her homeroom, and she has an office to organize her good deeds. Eleventh grader Leo Borlock thinks he might be in love with her, if she isn't dangerous. She could be an actress planted by the administration, an alien, or a friend's idea of a joke. Whatever, she has turned the high school upside down and inside out. Her classmates don't know whether to clap, boo, whistle, nod, wave, or ignore her. No one has ever seen a *Stargirl* before, and they may never see one again.

Related Activities

1. On page 78, Leo calls Stargirl a "performer—unique and outrageous—on the high school stage." Agree or disagree with his judgment. Draw on specifics from the novel to support your opinion. Would being a performer make her similar to or different from other high school students?

2. Read aloud Archie's words that begin on page 102 with "It's in the morning..." and end on page 103 with "we become ourselves." Discuss what Archie means by his statement and why he is making that statement to Leo. Discuss how that statement might also apply to the characters in *Kit's Wilderness* (Related Work 1).

3. We know very little about Hillari Kimble, but she has a major impact on the story. Discuss what Hillari represents and the motives she might have for her actions.

4. Discuss whether you could be a friend to Stargirl. Explain why or why not.

5. Archie, with his study of paleontology, introduces the idea of ancient instincts versus modern culture. Choose one instinct you feel affects modern culture. Explain the instinct and its effects by using everyday examples. Continue to research the concept of ancient instincts. Discuss how those two ideas develop in the story.

6. In the stories *Stargirl*, *When Zachary Beaver Came to Town* (Related Work 4), and "The Boy Who Called God She" (Related Work 5), a visitor changes lives. After reading all three, describe the visitor and the changes each visitor effects. You might wish to also read "Visitation" in Jerome Stern's *Making Shapely Fiction* (Related Work 6).

Related Works

1. Almond, David. **Kit's Wilderness.** (See full booktalk in chapter 4.) Three friends use ancient stories and patterns to clarify their own places in the world.

2. Brooks, Susan M. **Any Girl Can Rule the World.** Minneapolis, MN: Fairview Press, 1998. 224p. $12.95. ISBN 1-57749-068-1. **NF** In this how-to book for improving oneself and the world, Brooks encourages girls to take risks and overcome obstacles.

3. Creech, Sharon. **The Wanderer.** New York: HarperCollins Publishers/Joanna Cotler, 2000. 305p. $15.95. ISBN 0-06-027730. A group of male cousins and uncles learn to listen to their inner voices and bond as a family by opening themselves to the world of their unusual adopted female cousin and niece.

4. Holt, Kimberly Willis. **When Zachary Beaver Came to Town.** (See full booktalk in chapter 2.) Zachary Beaver, supposedly the fattest boy in the world, inspires the people of a small Texas town to examine their lives.

5. Springer, Nancy. "The Boy Who Called God She." In **I Believe in Water: Twelve Brushes with Religion.** New York: HarperCollins Publishers, 2000. 280p. $24.89. ISBN 0-06-028398-X. A new boy in

a Christian school puzzles his classmates because of his wild hair, polite demeanor, and challenging questions about God.

6. Stern, Jerome. "Visitation." In **Making Shapely Fiction.** New York: Laurel-Leaf Books, 1991. 283p. $6.50pa. ISBN 0-440-21221-9. **NF** Stern describes the structure of the visitation story and its purpose. The entire book defines, describes, and illustrates techniques and organizations used in fiction.

☙❧

McKissack, Patricia. Color Me Dark: The Diary of Nellie Lee Love, The Great Migration North.

New York: Scholastic Incorporated, 2000. 224p. (Dear America). $10.95.
ISBN 0-590-1159-9.

Summary/Description

Eleven-year-old Nellie Lee Love lives in Bradford Corners, Tennessee. When her Uncle Pace returns from World War I, he is beaten so badly that he dies. Knowing racial hate motivated Pace's death, Nellie's brother William, who is also a soldier, refuses to return to Bradford Corners, even to attend the funeral. Nellie's sister Erma Jean, traumatized by Pace's death, can't speak. Uncle Meese persuades Nellie's father, Freeman, to take Erma Jean to Chicago for treatment. Freeman decides to open a branch of the family funeral business in Chicago. The Loves discover Black Pride in Reverend McDonald's Open Mind Church, corruption in city government, better schools and hospitals, and more complicated prejudices. Nellie and her family are caught up in the rioting of "The Red Summer" when their friend Eugene Williams, stoned by whites for floating into the white section, drowns. Nellie's quiet mother joins the Ida B. Wells Club and the Alpha Suffrage Club. William returns to the family, knowing he can earn a living safely. Erma rediscovers her voice when she pleads with her father not to go out into the riot-torn streets, and Nellie's father finally opens his business without paying bribes.

The narrative includes references to James Weldon Johnson, W.E.B. DuBois, Ida B. Wells-Barnett, Madam C.J. Walker, Dr. Daniel Hale Williams, Oscar De Priest, Robert Abbott, and Marcus Garvey. An Epilogue tells what happened to each member of the Love family. The section "Life in America in 1919" includes a Historical Note, pictures and maps, a recipe for Mr. John Cooper's Buttermilk Pie, and the hymn "Lift Ev'ry Voice and Sing," called "The Negro National Anthem." "About the Author" explains how this book came about.

Booktalk

Nellie Lee Love knows a lot about death. Her family owns a funeral business, and World War I has just ended. But when her Uncle Pace is beaten to death because he's black, death looks a lot different. The Love family won't live in Bradford Corners, Tennessee, anymore. They move north, to Chicago. In Chicago, Nellie sees white boys stone an African-American boy, but nobody leaves or moves away. In Chicago, black people fight back with fists, clubs, guns, and knives.

Nellie knows a lot about skin color too. She thinks everybody, white or black, is color-struck enough to prefer light instead of dark skin. But in Chicago she meets Reverend McDonald of the Open Mind Church. He tells her all skin is beautiful, black skin included. She would like to believe him. After all, Nellie Lee Love always did say, like her light-skinned great-grandmother, *"Color Me Dark."* The Loves, dark, proud, and determined, stake their claim to the American Dream. Let Nellie Lee tell you all about it.

Related Activities

1. "Lift Ev'ry Voice and Sing" is included in the Historical Note. Read the hymn aloud. Then read the "Star-Spangled Banner." Compare the two National Anthems. You might want to consider word choice, image, and message in your comparison.
2. Moving to Chicago in 1919, the Love family experiences the "Red Summer." Continue to research African-American history in the year 1919 and share with the group the information you find.
3. Read Claude McKay's poem, "If We Must Die," included in *I, Too, Sing America: Three Centuries of African-American Poetry* (Related Work 3). Discuss the tone of the poem and the context in which it was written. Research McKay's life and how it parallels the lives of the Love family.
4. Paul Laurence Dunbar's "We Wear the Mask," included in *I, Too, Sing America: Three Centuries of African-American Poetry* (Related Work 3) might seem to present a speaker, situation, and tone different from McKay's "If We Must Die." Compare and contrast the two poems. Then research Dunbar's life and time period. Compare the information about Dunbar with the information about McKay.
5. Ask a speaker from the NAACP to speak to your group about its history and its policies. Request issues of the group's publications.
6. Research the history of African-American publications in the United States. Share the information you find and samples of the publications you research with the members of the group.

7. In the Historical Note, McKissack lists several leaders in the African-American experience. Choose one of these leaders and find additional information. Include the Internet in your search. Share the information you find with the group.

Related Works

1. **America's Black Warriors: Two Wars to Win.** Produced by A&E Television Networks, 1998. 50 min. Videocassette. Color. (Special Presentation). $19.95. AAE-40352. The film records the prejudice against black soldiers that has dated from the Revolutionary War and also the respect and glory that the soldiers' bravery deserves.

2. Bacho, Peter. **Boxing in Black and White.** New York: Henry Holt and Company, 1999. 122p. $18.95. ISBN 0-8050-5779-X. **NF** In chapter 3, Bacho talks about Jack Johnson, whose success and defeat in the first two decades of the twentieth century symbolized the struggle to control African-American men, perceived as physically powerful and arrogant. The entire book discusses boxing as a metaphor and safety valve for racial conflict.

3. Clinton, Catherine (prose text) and Stephen Alcorn (illus.) **I, Too, Sing America: Three Centuries of African American Poetry.** Boston, MA: Houghton Mifflin Company, 1998. 128p. $20.00. ISBN 0-395-89599-5. **NF** Both "I Wear the Mask" by Claude McKay and "We Wear the Mask" by Paul Laurence Dunbar appear in the collection. Clinton provides brief biographical and historical notes for each poet.

4. English, Karen. **Francie.** New York: Farrar Straus Giroux, 1999. 199p. $16.00. ISBN 0-374-32456-5. Francie's father has gone to Chicago to work as a Pullman porter. He will send for them when he is able. Sick of the prejudice the family must face, Francie's mother decides to go to Chicago whether he is ready or not. This book concentrates on their decision to leave.

5. Fradin, Dennis Brindell and Judith Bloom Fradin. **Ida B. Wells: Mother of the Civil Rights Movement.** (See full booktalk in chapter 4.) **NF** This biography of a woman often overlooked in African-American history presents Wells as an effective activist who helped end lynching.

6. Peiss, Kathy. **Hope in a Jar: The Making of America's Beauty Culture.** (See full booktalk in chapter 1.) **NF** In recording the history of cosmetics in America, Peiss highlights the African-American entrepreneurs whose businesses gave women financial success and heightened the debate about the American beauty ideal and that ideal's relationship to racism.

ℭℌℭℌ

Myers, Walter Dean. **Monster.**

New York: HarperCollins Publishers, 1999. 281p. $15.95. ISBN 0-06-028077-8.

Summary/Description

Sixteen-year-old Steve Harmon is on trial for murder. If convicted, he could receive the death penalty or a life sentence. He structures the trial and his experiences that relate to the trial into a movie script. The movie script, his personal journal, and comments make up the novel.

Throughout the trial, Steve struggles with peoples' perception of truth more than truth itself. He must convince the police, his fellow prisoners, his attorney, the jury, his parents, and ultimately himself that he is innocent and worthwhile. The prosecuting attorney labels him a monster and tries to associate him, in the jurors' minds, with convicted criminals and other defendants in the case. Steve's defense attorney fights this perception even though she seems to doubt his innocence.

As Steve constructs his play, he includes his life experiences before the trial. These experiences, such as throwing a rock and not admitting it, hanging with the criminals in the street, avoiding gang conflicts, making movies, and watching television with his little brother all suggest his character. The reader builds a verdict along with the jury as Steve, caught up in the judgments of the people around him, begins to see himself as a stranger. Although he is found "not guilty," he cannot judge himself innocent. In the year following the trial, Steve makes a movie of himself to discover his identity. *Monster* intensely explores, in a very public arena, how what others perceive build each person's identity.

Booktalk

Steve Harmon is a *Monster.* He is on trial for felony murder, and winning the trial could mean twenty-five years in prison. Losing the trial could mean losing his life.

Steve Harmon grew up in Harlem and hung out in Harlem. He didn't think James King or Bobo, a couple of street guys, were that bad. They just talked. He didn't even understand what they said most of the time. He didn't know a "getover" meant a robbery, and he didn't know the question "What you got?" was asking about his criminal plans.

Then the police knocked on his door. They put him in jail. He found himself in a courtroom, and he had a defense attorney. How could this happen to him? Should it happen to him? Everyone says he's evil. Maybe they're right. Guilty or not guilty, Steve Harmon will never be innocent again.

Related Activities

1. In his movie, Steve uses several flashbacks. Read these flashbacks aloud. Then discuss the relationship of each flashback to the rest of the novel.
2. Steve's journal is a major part of the novel. Read the journal entries aloud. Discuss the changes in Steve that each entry suggests.
3. Steve concludes that others' perceptions form the perceptions he has of himself. Agree or disagree.
4. Twice in the novel, Steve recalls Mr. Sawicki's advice about telling stories or making movies. Read Mr. Sawicki's advice on pages 19 and 214. How does Steve follow the advice? How does Myers, the author, follow the advice?
5. Act out or film one of the scenes from the novel.
6. Reread Osvaldo's testimony on pages 99 to 109 and Bobo's chicken-dinner testimony on pages 180 and 181. Discuss how these testimonies affect the trial. Especially consider O'Brian's decision to play the cup game with Steve before he testifies.
7. On pages 78 and 79, O'Brian explains how the jury will perceive Steve. She says, "You're young, you're Black, and you're on trial. What else do they need to know?" Later, on page 146, Steve's mother wonders if she should have contacted a black lawyer, and Steve refuses. He believes "It wasn't a matter of race." Discuss why Steve might have come to this conclusion.
8. Read *Harlem* (Related Work 3), also by Walter Dean Myers and Christopher Myers, and *145th Street: Short Stories* (Related Work 4) by Walter Dean Myers. Discuss how these works relate to the novel *Monster.*
9. Read "Just because I love darkness" by Marcel Mendoza on page 4 of *You Hear Me* (Related Work 2). Discuss what the poem has to say about the speaker's identity. How does the speaker's message relate to Steve Harmon?
10. Choose one criminal trial you wish to research or follow. Note the newspaper coverage surrounding the trial. Keep a record of the reports, inferences, and judgments used in the trial and article. Then discuss the perceptions with which the accused must cope.

Related Works

1. Cormier, Robert. **Tenderness.** New York: Bantam Doubleday Dell Publishing Group, Inc., 1997. 229p. $16.95. ISBN 0-385-32286-0. (See full booktalk in *Booktalks Plus,* 2001, on pages 64 to 66.) A young psychopathic serial killer is able to manipulate the press and

gain his freedom. Pursuing more victims, he is ironically accused of a murder he does not commit.

2. Franco, Betsy, ed. **You Hear Me? Poems and Writing by Teenage Boys.** Cambridge, MA: Candlewick Press, 2000. 107p. $14.99. ISBN 0-7636-1158-1. **NF** The poems express the fears, challenges, and joys experienced by teenage boys in the United States.

3. Myers, Walter Dean (poem) and Christopher Myers (illus). **Harlem.** New York: Scholastic Press, 1997. 30p. $16.95. ISBN 0-590-54340-7. (See full booktalk in *Booktalks*, 2001, on pages 241 to 243.) **NF** This illustrated poem celebrates Harlem as an important and natural part of the bigger world.

4. Myers, Walter Dean. **145th Street: Short Stories.** (See full booktalk in chapter 2.) The short stories present both the inspirational and malicious residents of this Harlem neighborhood.

5. Walker, Virginia (text), and Katrina Roechelein (graphics). **Making Up Megaboy.** New York: DK Publishing/Richard Jackson, 1998. 63p. $16.95. ISBN 0-7894-2488-6. (See full booktalk in *Booktalks*, 2001, on pages 82 to 84.) Text and graphics tell the story of a thirteen-year-old boy who shoots a liquor store owner. The boy does not speak. The perceptions of friends, acquaintances, police, and family create the picture of his character.

6. Yearwood, Stephenie. "Popular Post Modernism for Young Adult Readers: *Walk Two Moons, Holes,* and *Monster." The ALAN Review.* (Spring/Summer 2002) 50–53. **NF** On pages 52 and 53, Yearwood explains why *Monster* fits the criteria for post modernism.

⟡⟡

Jordan, Sherryl. **The Raging Quiet.**
New York: Simon & Schuster, 1999. 266p. $17.00. ISBN 0-689-82140-9.

Summary/Description

When Marnie's father has a stroke, 16-year-old Marnie agrees to marry Isake Isherwood, son of the lord of the manor. In exchange, her family will keep their house on the estate. Over twice her age, Isake is a crude, demanding, drinking man who believes the rumors about Marnie's low moral character. He takes her to Torcurra, where they begin to fix a cursed house inherited from his grandmother. After two married nights, Marnie prays that Isake will no longer be attracted to her. That day he dies, and Marnie blames herself.

Marnie finds only two friends in Torcurra: Raven, a deaf boy whom the villagers often whip to drive out his devils and Father Brannan who protects Raven and now Marnie. Marnie and Raven live together in the cottage. Marnie communicates with Raven through hand signs. The villagers perceive Isake's death, Marnie's signs, and Raven's resulting calmness as witchcraft and force a witchcraft trial.

Father Brannan encourages Marnie and Raven to marry. Because of the marriage, the Isherwoods claim the estate. Isake's brother taunts Marnie about losing the house. When he describes a valuable ring given to the grandmother by a king, Marnie realizes Raven found it. They leave the town hoping to find a better life.

This romantic fantasy set in an ancient and magical time deals with problems of ignorance and prejudice. In an Author's Note, Sherryl Jordan explains how she decided on a mythical rather than a specific historical setting.

Booktalk

At sixteen, Marnie receives a marriage proposal. The son of the lord of the manor will give her mother, father, and eleven brothers and sisters a house of their own if she will marry him. But the eager groom, the answer to her mother's prayers, is twice Marnie's age, likes to drink himself into a stupor, and reminds her again and again that she is his property, bought and paid for.

Reluctantly Marnie marries, and the couple travels to Torcurra where the village people believe witches and demons cause every problem and where her husband seeks a hidden treasure. When Marnie's husband dies after two days of marriage, the villagers suspect she killed him. When she befriends and calms Raven, a deaf boy routinely whipped for his evil spirits, they are convinced she is a witch. As the crowd accuses and condemns, Marnie cannot defend herself any better than the speechless Raven. Only Father Brannan, the village priest, can help both Marnie and Raven embrace and conquer the pain that pulls them both from *The Raging Quiet*.

Related Activities

1. Read *Witches and Witch-hunts* (Related Work 3). Meltzer explains the why and how in the history of witchcraft. Continue further research and pay careful attention to ordinary behaviors confused with witchcraft. Share your findings with the group. Discuss how the information applies to *The Raging Quiet*.
2. Raven and Marnie suffer persecution in Torcurra. Discuss why each is a target.

3. In *Homeless Bird* (Related Work 5), *The Raging Quiet,* and *Elske* (Related Work 4), forced marriages and subsequent independence are major issues. Compare how these elements affect each novel.
4. To save herself, Marnie must undergo the test of witchcraft. Discuss what the test adds to the story.
5. Both *The Raging Quiet* and *Tamsin* (Related Work 1) center on true love's triumph over wealth and power. Both use supernatural elements and historical settings different from the average person's experiences. After reading both novels, discuss how those elements pulled or failed to pull you into the story.

Related Works

1. Beagle, Peter S. **Tamsin.** (See full booktalk in chapter 1.) Surrounded by the supernatural elements of her new home, Jennifer Gluckstein helps Tamsin, a 300-year-old ghost, unite with her true love.
2. Levitin, Sonia. **The Cure.** New York: Harcourt Brace and Company, 1999. 184p. $16.00. ISBN 0-15-201827-1. A member of a utopian community is labeled dangerous and deviant because of his love of music. His cure is a time travel to 1348, where he lives as a Jew and is persecuted as an outsider.
3. Meltzer, Milton. **Witches and Witch-hunts: A History of Persecution. ⓝⓕ** (See full booktalk in chapter 3.) Meltzer explains the psychology of witch-hunts and the history related to them. He also explains specific cases in detail.
4. Voigt, Cynthia. **Elske.** (See full booktalk in chapter 2.) Elske escapes a culture that wants to kill her, refuses an arranged marriage, and helps a queen take back her kingdom.
5. Whelan, Gloria. **Homeless Bird.** (See full booktalk in chapter 4.) Pushed into a marriage with a terminally ill boy, Koly eventually builds her own life and selects her own husband.

Families Plan

ℭℨℬℨ

Nolan, Han. **A Face in Every Window.**
New York: Harcourt Brace and Company, 1999. 264p. $16.00. ISBN 0-15-201915-4.

Summary/Description

Grandma Mary dominated her family. Her mentally challenged son married Erin, his childhood friend, who has a hole in her heart.

James Patrick O'Brian is their son. Grandma Mary took care of all of them. When Grandma Mary dies suddenly, Erin (Mam) pursues her dream of winning a house and striking out on her own. She invites people experiencing conflict or change to live in the house. James Patrick, comfortable in the structured life his grandmother provided, resists and resents the "weirdos" his mother forces into his life. He learns, however, to see individuals instead of stereotypes. But JP's greatest change and challenge is accepting his "new" mother.

Believing she has married JP's father for the safety of Grandma Mary's home, Erin has an affair with her doctor, travels with him to Switzerland, and, when she returns home, has his baby. JP must sort out his feelings about his mother, who seems to have abandoned him, and his feelings about his father, who embarrasses him. By the end of the novel, JP, his father and mother, and baby Mary are building a new family, and JP has developed close relationships with the people who shared his house. The situations discussed in the book are for mature audiences, and the discussions of the situations might be considered, by some, to be controversial.

Booktalk

Ask how many people have ever shared a room, a desk, or a work area. Ask them to tell what they liked and what they disliked about the sharing experience.

Before his grandmother dies, fifteen-year-old James Patrick shares nothing. His grandmother, his mentally challenged father, and his mother are all his. Then his grandmother dies. No longer sheltered by Grandma Mary, JP's mother decides to grow up. Because she's thirty-seven, that's a difficult decision for everyone to handle. Then she wins a big new house and invites more and more people to move in with them. JP feels crowded, pushed out, and frustrated. He's not sure he knows his mother, his father, or himself when he's living in a house with *A Face in Every Window.*

Related Activities

1. Reread chapter 1 aloud. Discuss why the narrator begins the novel with this story. Discuss how the story applies to JP's family and the other characters.

2. On page 73 and on page 93, the narrator uses extended metaphors to describe his family. The first is a monster; the second is a ship. Discuss how each reveals his feelings about his family. Develop an extended metaphor you feel would describe JP's family at the end of the novel.

3. "Chaos," "stasis," and "complexity" are central to the ideas in the novel. Write a definition of each. Identify situations in the book that

illustrate each definition. Then find situations outside the novel that illustrate each definition.

4. *When Zachary Beaver Came to Town* (Related Work 3) and *A Face in Every Window* both deal with negative stereotypes. Discuss how each author uses those stereotypes to accomplish the novel's purpose?

5. Discuss JP's judgments about each of the characters, as well as the reports and inferences behind the judgments.

Related Works

1. Coville, Bruce. **Odder than Ever.** New York: Harcourt Brace and Company, 1999. 146p. $16.00. ISBN 0-15-201747-X. Each story centers on a person trying to find a place in society.

2. Fraustino, Lisa Rowe, ed. **Dirty Laundry: Stories About Family Secrets.** New York: Viking Press, 1998. 181p. $16.99. ISBN 0-670-87911-8. "The Secret of Life, According to Aunt Gladys," by Bruce Coville, deals with a family member who wishes to have a sex change. "Popeye the Sailor," by Chris Crutcher, explains how abuse, never discussed, leads to more abuse. "Something Like...Love," by Graham Salisbury, explores the true meaning of love.

3. Holt, Kimberly Willis. **When Zachary Beaver Came to Town.** (See full booktalk in chapter 2.) The summer Toby Wilson's mother leaves to find herself, Toby discovers a new world in his small town and family.

4. Klebanoff, Susan and Ellen Luborsky. **Ups & Downs: How to Beat the Blues and Teen Depression.** 🕮 (See full booktalk in chapter 3.) This book explains how teenagers in difficult situations can learn to make decisions that will improve their attitudes and lives.

5. Powell, Randy. **Tribute to Another Dead Rock Star.** (See full booktalk in chapter 3.) Grady Innis Grennan must decide if he wishes to defend the memory of his famous mother and her lifestyle or become part of the more stable but more rigid home of his mentally challenged half-brother.

ᑯᕀᑐᕀ

Levitin, Sonia. Clem's Chances.
New York: Orchard Books, 2001. 208p. $17.95. ISBN 0-439-29314-6.

Summary/Description

Clem's father went west over a year ago. His mother and sister are dead from the fever. Fourteen-year-old Clem cannot maintain the house and farm by himself, so the Warren family takes him in. Clem does the lion's share of the work and suffers abuse from the Warrens and their sons. Molly Warren, the daughter, and Clem develop a close relationship, and when he heads west to find his father, she stays loyal.

After being unfairly thrown out of a saloon job, Clem signs up with the Pony Express. He also befriends and works for Libby, a widow on a nearby farm who sells food to the Express station and travelers. Clem learns Libby met his father when her husband was dying and his father failed to bring the doctor he promised. Libby also tells Clem his father headed for San Francisco, not the gold fields as he had told Clem. When robbers shoot a Pony Express rider, Clem volunteers to carry the mail. Clem finally finds his father and discovers him to be a vain, self-centered man who never intended to return or contact his family. Clem uses his art talent to get a job with a lithographer, vowing to reunite with all the people who helped him on the journey and bring Molly Warren to live with him.

Alluding to *Oliver Twist* throughout the novel, Levitin weaves a coming-of-age story that requires Clem, in his journey, to sort through the prejudices of his family, town, and country.

Booktalk

After Clem's father leaves to seek his fortune in the gold fields and Clem's mother and sister die of fever, Clem is left alone with his "future." That future seems to be hunger, hard work, and abuse, but fourteen-year-old Clem soon finds that "one thing leads to another," and what happens next might be better. He decides to head west to find his father. But to find his father, he must discover himself. Is he an untrustworthy thief, a loyal friend, an animal slayer, an animal trainer, a daring Pony Express rider, a scholar, or an artist? Who are the people he can trust? Who are the girls he loves? What do love and trust mean, anyway? And in the end, will the wild frontier or his own decisions defeat him? *Clem's Chances* might not be very good, but maybe it's how he takes the chances, instead of the chances themselves, that really matters.

Related Activities

1. Reread the first chapter. Discuss what Clem reveals about himself and his family. Discuss how Levitin uses that chapter to prepare us for the rest of the novel.
2. Throughout the novel, Clem identifies with Oliver in *Oliver Twist*. After reading *Clem's Chances*, read *Oliver Twist*. Discuss the similarities and differences between the two boys and their situations. In the discussion, consider each author's use of coincidence and the differences between the two endings.

3. In his journey, Clem compares people's opinions and his own experience. Cite several instances in the novel where the opinions of others and Clem's experiences contradict or conflict. Discuss how these contradictions aid Levitin's purpose.
4. In *Clem's Chances, Sunshine Rider: The First Vegetarian Western* (Related Work 4), and *The Great Turkey Walk* (Related Work 5), a young man must confront his father's weakness. Discuss how each young man deals with the father-son relationship.
5. Gabriel is a major figure in Clem's life, although he does not appear in most of the story. Explain how Gabriel and the life experiences he shares affect Clem. Further research the lives of African freemen before and during the Civil War and the dangers they faced. Share your findings with the group and explain how the information enhances or supports the story.

Related Works

1. Calabro, Marian. **The Perilous Journey of the Donner Party.** (See full booktalk in chapter 1.) **NF** While traveling with the Mormons, Clem mentions the importance of preparation so other travelers will not repeat the mistakes of the Donner Party whose leadership, journey, failure, and survival Calabro describes.
2. Cox, Clinton. **Come All You Brave Soldiers.** New York: Scholastic Incorporated, 1999. 182p. $15.95. ISBN 0-590-47576-2. (See full booktalk in *Booktalks Plus*, 2001, pages 155 to 157.) **NF** Gabriel's great-great-grandfather, a slave of George Washington, won his freedom by fighting in the Revolutionary War for one year. Cox discusses the injustices against Africans who fought in the Revolutionary War.
3. Dickens, Charles (text) and Don Freeman (illus.) **Oliver Twist.** New York: William Morrow and Company, 1984. 442p. $20.00. ISBN 0-688-12911-0. Originally published in 1867, this story about an innocent orphan, abused by society, tells how the orphan eventually discovers his family, who rescue him. Encouraged by Oliver's story, Clem seeks someone who will save him, but helps others and saves himself instead.
4. Hardman, Ric Lynden. **Sunshine Rider: The First Vegetarian Western.** New York: Laurel-Leaf Books, 1998. 343p. $4.99pa. ISBN 0-440-22812-3. Wylie Jackson discovers that John Boardman, the trail boss whom he has always admired, is his real father.
5. Karr, Kathleen. **The Great Turkey Walk.** (See full booktalk in chapter 2.) Simon Green must prevent his dishonest father from stealing the turkeys Simon is taking west.

6. Rinaldi, Ann. **Mine Eyes Have Seen.** New York: Scholastic Press, 1998. 275p. $16.95. ISBN 0-590-54318-0. (See full booktalk in *Booktalks Plus,* 2001, pages 243 to 245.) Annie Brown, John Brown's fifteen-year-old daughter, tells about the summer of preparation for Brown's raid on Harper's Ferry, the raid for which Gabriel prepared but in which he did not participate.

ᑕ᛫ᑐ

Namioka, Lensey. **Ties That Bind, Ties That Break.**
New York: Delacorte Press, 1999. 154p. $15.95. ISBN 0-385-32666-1.

Summary/Description

In 1925, nineteen-year-old Ailin meets her former fiancé when he comes to her husband's restaurant for real Chinese food in America. Their meeting causes her to reflect on her life, which began in China.

When she is five, Ailin is the indulged youngest child in a wealthy Chinese family. Even though she is to be betrothed, she is allowed to keep her feet unbound. Her fiancé's mother insists that Ailin's feet should be bound and breaks the engagement. Her seven-year-old fiancé proudly tells Ailin about his experiences in public school. When Ailin is nine, her father allows her to attend. Miss Gilbertson, her English teacher, discovers Ailin's aptitude for languages. Ailin's father dies, and Ailin's uncle forbids her to go to school, but Miss Gilbertson continues to tutor her. Because of Ailin's questioning attitude, her big feet, and her education, Ailin's uncle arranges for her to be a concubine. When she objects, he says her other choices are becoming a nun or a poor farmer's wife. Ailin, through Miss Gilbertson, secures a nanny job with the Warners, American missionaries. She finds herself between two worlds. One world considers her defiant and untraditional. The other considers her heathen. The Warners return to America, and sixteen-year-old Ailin goes with them. On the voyage, she meets twenty-six-year-old James Chew, her future husband. Hearing how much Ailin has risked, he challenges tradition by opening his own restaurant. He marries Ailin. Ailin discovers that Americans respect hardworking women, and she stands on her two strong feet.

Booktalk

If you have ever spent a day in spiky high heels, you can feel for women who bind their feet for beauty. But high heels are not permanent, and bound feet are. Slowly the bindings curl and break the toes until only an ugly wedge remains. These upper-class ladies totter through their lives and make decisions as small as their steps.

When Ailin is five years old and sees the pain she will face, she refuses to have her feet bound. Her father agrees. After all, China is changing. Women will be freer, perhaps even educated, but now big feet will not allow a teenaged Ailin to marry into a wealthy family. When her father dies, Ailin can't even stay in her own family. Her large feet carry her on daring journeys—one to a new country—where Ailin learns about *Ties that Bind, Ties that Break.*

Related Activities

1. Ailin mentions the Opium War of 1839 and the Boxer Rebellion. Using your library's resources, research those two conflicts and share your findings with the group. Discuss how these historical events relate to the novel.
2. On page 55, the Second Sister tells the story of the silkworm. On page 56, Ailin interprets it. Discuss the story and Ailin's interpretation. Explain its relationship to the entire novel and your own experience.
3. On page 66, Ailin encounters Hanwei and then begins to ponder the tradition of bound feet that has separated them. She cannot answer the questions "Who started it?" and "Why is it so important?" Choose a tradition you question. Using research, try to answer those same two questions about it.
4. On page 111, Ailin realizes she is like a bamboo shoot that is too tough to eat. Compare yourself to a plant and explain the appropriateness of your comparison.
5. Prejudice as well as tradition challenge Ailin. Explain the prejudices and how she deals with them. How are these prejudices similar to or different from prejudices you have encountered?
6. On page 123, Ailin uses the word "miasma" to describe her "third-class section" on the ship. Define the word. Explain what it communicates about her living situation.

Related Works

1. Jordan, Sherryl. **The Raging Quiet.** (See full booktalk in chapter 1.) Despite the prejudices that surround them, a young widow and her good friend, a deaf man, fall in love and marry.
2. Osborne, Mary Pope. **Standing in the Light: The Captive Diary of Catharine Carey Logan.** New York: Scholastic Incorporated, 1998. 184p. (Dear America). $10.95. ISBN 0-590-13462-0. Catherine Carey Logan is captured by the Lenape nation and caught between the traditions and beliefs of two different cultures.
3. Staples, Suzanne Fisher. **Shiva's Fire.** New York: Frances Foster Books/Farrar Straus Giroux, 2000. 276p. $17.00. ISBN 0-374-

36824-4. Given special gifts, a young girl decides to use them instead of being intimidated by the rules of her culture.

4. Whelan, Gloria. **Homeless Bird.** (See full booktalk in chapter 4.) A young woman forced into an arranged marriage builds a new and independent life after becoming a widow.

5. Yep, Lawrence. **Lady of Ch'iao Kuo: Warrior of the South.** New York: Scholastic Incorporated, 2001. 224p. (The Royal Diaries). $10.95. ISBN 0-439-21598-6. Knowing the cultures of her own Hsien tribe and the Chinese, Princess Redbird leads the war against the Dog Heads and becomes a strong ruler and voice for peace.

ᘓᘔ

Powell, Randy. **Run If You Dare.**

New York: Farrar Straus Giroux, 2001. 185p. $16.00. ISBN 0-374-39981-6.

Summary/Description

In this coming-of-age novel, fourteen-year-old Gardner Dickinson decides he won't emulate his father but will get a specific direction in life. At forty-nine, the father loses his job and refuses to help around the house or look for work in the middle of a booming Seattle economy. Gardner's exhausted mother works long hours in a job with no benefits. Lacy, Gardner's eighteen-year-old sister, works at a pizza shop, helps around the house, and goes to school. Lacy points out to Gardner that since their father lost his job, each family member is going in a different direction and that Gardner needs to be more independent and helpful. She also believes that because of their heredity, no one in the family can ever be rich and successful.

Gardner examines his own habits, such as taking out library books but not reading them, keeping a messy room, and talking about getting in shape instead of working out. He recognizes he is copying his father's "one of these days" attitude and decides to read, clean, compete, and work. He becomes more self-directed when his father confides that he has lost all his dreams and wants to run away from the family to pursue them. By the end of the novel, even though his father takes a job, Gardner does not believe he will keep it and concludes that everyone should follow his or her own path by working hard and achieving as much as possible even if it means leaving the familiar territory of friends and family.

Booktalk

Gardner Dickinson is a lot like his dad. They both like to hang onto stuff and pile it all around them. They're always looking forward to what they'll do "one of these days." And they think that just kicking back, talking, and enjoying themselves is a great way to spend the day—everyday. Then Gardner's dad loses his job, and looking for a job seems like too much effort. That means Gardner's mom has to work twice as hard as his father ever did. His sister Lacy decides to go to work, too, and that leaves Gardner to decide if being a chip off the old block is such a good idea—especially when the old block confides that both his old job and the family didn't really have anything to do with his dreams. Will Gardner someday wind up like his dad, sitting in a dark room and dreading his forty-ninth birthday? Or will Gardner take charge of his life and meet the challenge he decides to give his dad: *Run If You Dare*?

Related Activities

1. On page 15, Gardner quotes the messages his father shared with motivational speakers. Discuss why Gardner's father was unsuccessful in following his own advice. Be sure to consider "river rafting in Costa Rica" (page 22). Ask your librarian to help you identify three popular motivational speakers. After reading their materials, explain to the group how their advice is the same or different.
2. As in *Tribute to Another Dead Rock Star* (Related Work 4), Powell makes religious belief a major role in *Run If You Dare*. Discuss how religion in each novel helps Powell accomplish the novel's purpose.
3. Aidan Skeepbo, Sophie Beam, and Annie Harris are minor characters in the novel. Discuss what each character contributes to Gardner's transformation.
4. In chapter 5, Gardner describes his room. He concludes from the mess around him that he is just like his father. Read the chapter again. Using it as a model, describe your own room and interpret what your room reveals about you.
5. In chapter 17, Gardner writes a poem about a boy. It makes Gardner and his classmates think about the boy's position in life. Read the poem and the fictional class's reaction to it. Discuss how the poem supports the story. Then, using it as a model, write another poem about an ordinary object and the person who owns it.
6. Read the last paragraph of the novel. Discuss why Gardner changes "Here Come the Dickinsons" to "Here Are the Dickinsons." Discuss also the significance of the concluding sentence.

Related Works

1. Covey, Sean. **The 7 Habits of Highly Effective Teens.** (See full booktalk in chapter 4.) **NF** Covey outlines seven positive habits that

will help both teens and adults. Examples from teenagers are included.

2. Efaw, Amy. **Battle Dress.** (See full booktalk in chapter 2.) Raised in a dysfunctional family, the main character decides to take on the challenge of a military academy.

3. Peck, Robert Newton. **Cowboy Ghost.** New York: HarperCollins Children's Books, 1999. 200p. $15.95. ISBN 0-06-028168-5. (See full booktalk in *Booktalks Plus*, 2001, pages 15 to 16.) Titus MacRobertson proves himself on a cattle drive and faces down a father who has always considered him too small to count.

4. Powell, Randy. **Tribute to Another Dead Rock Star.** (See full booktalk in chapter 3.) The main character rebels against the rules of his half-brother's Christian home.

5. Wallace, Rich. **Playing Without the Ball.** New York: Alfred A. Knopf, 2000. 213p. ISBN 0-679-98672-3. After a year living independently over Shorty's Bar, seventeen-year-old Jay McLeod decides to enter a local community college and surround himself with as many stable people as possible.

CO KO

Nolan, Han. **Dancing on the Edge.**
New York: Puffin Books, 1997. 244p. $4.99pa. ISBN 0-14-130203-8.

Summary/Description

Sixteen-year-old Miracle McCloy was born after her mother was hit and killed by an ambulance. Her grandmother, her father's mother, tells Miracle that the birth portends Miracle's special powers. During one of her grandmother's séances, Miracle's father, a literary prodigy, disappears—or as her grandmother says, "melts." Harassed by the people in town, the family moves in with Miracle's eccentric Grandfather Opal even though her grandmother and grandfather are divorced. As her grandparents fight, Miracle becomes more strange and withdrawn. She wears her father's robe, cuts her hair like his, and throws herself into wild dances that bruise her body. Feeling responsible for her mother's death and her father's disappearance, she believes they are trying to return through the spirit world. After a tornado destroys her grandfather's house and her grandfather suffers a heart attack, Miracle moves in with her Aunt Casey, her mother's sister. Her aunt leaves her husband and pursues a degree. Once again, Miracle is ignored. She tries to melt herself with fire, but discovers she burns. Casey extends Miracle's hospital stay for psychiatric treatment. Miracle learns her mother and father did not love each other. Her mother, a dancer, did not want a baby and probably committed suicide. Her grandmother dominated Miracle's father and tried to dominate Miracle. Casey discerns that the self-absorbed family has ignored Miracle. When Miracle's grandmother tries to kidnap her from the home, Miracle convinces her to let her go and then returns to build a new life with her grandfather and Aunt Casey.

Booktalk

Miracle McCloy believes she is disappearing. In fact, she suspects she never was born.

But her grandmother tells Miracle she's special. Not many girls were born after their mother died, and no one Miracle knows ever had a father, a real prodigy, who just melted away one night. But if her grandmother knows all about magic, why do they have to run away? Why isn't Miracle safe from the people who throw mud and insults at her? Why does her grandmother avoid Miracle's questions? As her life twists and turns through spells, storms, stories, and lies, Miracle finds the answers to her life, *Dancing on the Edge.*

Related Activities

1. Miracle comments that Kafka's "The Metamorphosis" (Related Work 3) is one of her father's favorite stories. After reading the short story, discuss why you think her father liked it and how it applies to the novel as a whole.

2. Miracle names her bicycle Etain. She explains the history of the name on page 64. Discuss how the name applies to the story.

3. Miss Emmaline Wilson sings "Amazing Grace" (Related Work 5), and Miracle comments that the hymn expresses how she (Miracle) feels about herself. Read the words of the hymn. Discuss what parts of it apply to Miracle. Continue to examine hymns and their origin. Choose a hymn you feel defines your life and explain your choice.

4. Miracle writes a story about a ballerina. Read her summary of it on pages 119 and 120. Discuss how the story relates to the rest of the novel.

5. When Miracle begins casting love spells, she discovers truths about love and magic. Discuss what those truths are.

6. Miracle identifies with the first verse of Emily Dickinson's poem "I'm Nobody! Who are you?" (Related Work 1) She does not consider the second verse, however. Read the second verse and discuss how it affects the meaning of the poem.

7. Nolan uses the last paragraph of each chapter as a kind of dramatic signpost that signals Miracle's thinking and feelings. Read the last

paragraph or two from each chapter. Then explain how those paragraphs map Miracle's illness and recovery.

8. During one of the sessions, Dr. DeAngelis says, "Miracle, you're fourteen. You know the difference between fact and fantasy. You know what's real and what isn't." Discuss whether you agree with the doctor. Be sure to consider the meaning of "real."

Related Works

1. Dickinson, Emily. "I'm Nobody! Who are you?" In **The Poems of Emily Dickinson: Variorum Edition, Vol. 1,** edited by R.W. Franklin. Cambridge, MA: The Belknap Press of Harvard University Press, 1998. 534p. $38.75, 3 vol. ISBN 0-674-67622-X. **NF** The second verse changes the poem's tone to a positive one as the speaker concludes that being public is merely playing "To an admiring bog"—not a great achievement. The poem's manuscript is dated about 1861. It appears on page 279.

2. Fraustino, Lisa Rowe. **Dirty Laundry: Stories About Family Secrets.** New York: Viking Press, 1998. 181p. $16.99. ISBN 0-670-87911-8. The stories deal with secrets that could help or destroy family members.

3. Kafka, Franz. Stanley Corngold, trans., ed. **The Metamorphosis.** New York: W.W. Norton & Company, 1996. 218p. (A Norton Critical Edition). $7.95. ISBN 0-393-96797-2. Harassed and abused, a young man awakes to find he has become a cockroach. This edition includes an introduction by Corngold, the story, background and context, criticism, and a selected bibliography. The story was first published in 1946.

4. Lovelace, James and Laura Howell Smith. "The Motherless Daughter: An Evolving Archetype of Adolescent Literature." *The ALAN Review.* (Winter 2002) 16–20. **NF** The article discusses *Dancing on the Edge* and six other young-adult novels in the context of grieving the loss of a mother.

5. Newton, John. "Amazing Grace." In **Sing Joyfully**. Carol Stream, IL: Tabernacle Publishing Company, 1997. 683p. $10.95. ISBN 0-916642-39-9. **NF** Miracle feels that "Amazing Grace" is a defining song for her. The hymn is number 343.

⟆⟅

Berg, Elizabeth. Joy School.

New York: Ballantine Books, 1997. 208p. (Ballantine Reader's Circle). $11.95. ISBN 0-345-42309-7.

Summary/Description

Thirteen-year-old Katie is an army brat. She and her father just moved to a new town. Katie's mother is dead. Her older sister, Diane, who does not get along with their father, is back in Texas, married and pregnant. Cherylanne, Katie's best friend, writes Katie letters about high school love life, and Katie must slowly build new relationships and a healthy independence in this new and not-so-friendly town. Greg and Marsha, the twins next door, harass her. Cynthia O'Connell, an only child, will be her friend if Cynthia and Katie follow all of Mrs. O'Connell's rules. Taylor Sinn, charming and beautiful, will be Katie's friend if Katie shoplifts and experiments with boys. But Katie's most exciting friend is Jimmy, the twenty-three-year-old service station manager, around whom she builds romantic fantasies.

With the advice of Ginger the housekeeper, Father Compton, and Cherylanne, Katie develops her beliefs about sex, fairness, and morality. She makes the twins respect her, helps Cynthia become more independent, and tells Taylor Sinn "no." She sees Ginger and her father become romantically involved and Diane and her husband drift apart. Although the love-troubled Cherylanne assures Katie that Jimmy will leave his wife for the love of a thirteen-year-old, Katie must accept that Jimmy loves his wife, sees Katie as a friend, and will be moving away to earn a better living for his family. At the end of the novel, Katie throws away the lucky stone Jimmy gave her for her birthday and realizes she will search for it again in the spring. The book includes some strong language and mature situations, but both are appropriate in the novel's context. The Ballantine Reader's Circle edition includes "A Conversation with E. Berg," and "Reading Group Questions and Topics for Discussion."

Booktalk

Katie's mother is dead. Katie and her father have moved to a new town. Her older sister's new baby will make thirteen-year-old Katie an aunt, and now Katie has found her true love. She's having new experiences, meeting new people, and handling a bunch of mixed feelings. The new housekeeper is nice, but she might want to take the place of Katie's mother. The baby will be fun, but her sister doesn't seem too happy about it. Her new friends are exciting but a little frightening, and—oh yes—her true love is married with children. Katie has to learn quite a bit, and the *Joy School* finals come up sooner than she thinks.

Related Activities

1. In *Joy School*, Jimmy gives Katie a lucky stone. Choose an object that is important to you because of its luck or because of the person who

gave it to you. Describe what it looks like, how you got it, and what it means to you.

2. *Saying It Out Loud* (Related Work 1), *Bad* (Related Work 2), and *Joy School* involve three similar elements: a mother's death, a strict father's distance, and a teenage love. Compare the relationship of these elements in the novels.

3. *Joy School* and *Alone at Ninety Foot* (Related Work 4) both deal with friendships and peer pressure. Each main character must turn to a woman who is not her mother and who might marry her father. Compare how each author handles these elements to accomplish the purpose of the novel.

4. "Birches" (Related Work 3) by Robert Frost is alluded to in the novel. After reading the poem, explain its relationship to the story.

5. Even though Diane rarely appears in the story, she presents a significant force. Discuss Diane's role in Katie's life and her function in the novel.

6. As Katie becomes more assertive, her life improves. Research definitions and applications of assertiveness and aggressiveness. Share your information with the group and explain how your definitions apply to the actions of the other characters as well.

Related Works

1. Abelove, Joan. **Saying It Out Loud.** New York: DK Publishing /Richard Jackson, 1999. 136p. $15.95. ISBN 0-7894-2609-9. Knowing her mother is dying, sixteen-year-old Mindy must also deal with her father's coldness and his refusal to talk about the death.

2. Ferris, Jean. **Bad.** (See full booktalk in chapter 2.) Because of her father's coldness, sixteen-year-old Dallas Carpenter turns to a destructive peer group to give herself a sense of belonging.

3. Frost, Robert. "Birches." In **Robert Frost: Collected Poems, Prose, & Plays.** Poems selected and notes written by Richard Poirier and Mark Richardson. New York: The Library of America, 1995. 1036p. $35.00. ISBN 1-883011-06-X. New York: Simon and Schuster, 1942. **NF** Frost's poem, which appears on pages 117 to 118, talks about taking chances, seeking challenges, and learning to love.

4. Holubitsky, Katherine. **Alone at Ninety Foot.** (See full booktalk in chapter 3.) After her mother commits suicide and her father starts dating again, fourteen-year-old Pamela Collins must find where she fits with family and friends.

5. Klebanoff, Susan and Ellen Luborsky. **Ups & Downs: How to Beat the Blues and Teen Depression.** (See full booktalk in chapter 3.) **NF** This self-help book distinguishes the difference between sadness and depression and suggests ways to deal with each.

CR20

Klass, David. **You Don't Know Me.**

New York: Frances Foster Books/Farrar Straus Giroux, 2001. 262p. $17.00. ISBN 0-374-38706-0.

Summary/Description

Fourteen-year-old John lives with his mother and her boyfriend, who secretly abuses and degrades him. As John sarcastically describes himself as surrounded by hostile, indifferent, or misguided strangers, the narrative's tone ranges from humorous to poignant. John and his friend compete for the same trophy date, a spoiled and pampered girl who uses boyfriends to infuriate her father. John perceives his challenging algebra teacher as torturing and his caring music teacher as out of touch. He retreats into the nonexistent world of the Lashasa Palulu, an African tribe.

When John's mother leaves to care for a dying aunt, John's problems escalate. First, John borrows money from the boyfriend's bureau for a date with the beautiful Gloria. When he must flee her house minus some clothes and money, John confronts his mother's furious boyfriend, who forces him to load and unload stolen televisions all night to pay him back. At school, John blurts out a cruel nickname he has created for his math teacher and discovers she is a fragile and dedicated person whom he has crushed. He is suspended from school. The boyfriend whips him with a belt as punishment. During his suspension, a girl he has ignored pleads with him to take her to the school dance. He accepts, but when he returns home after the dance, the boyfriend tries to whip him again. John fights back. Through the efforts of John's music teacher, who has been watching the house, the boyfriend is arrested for assault and theft. Recovering from the vicious beating, John discovers that his mother, teachers, and friends care for him.

Booktalk

John's mother has a boyfriend. He lives in John's house, and when Mom isn't looking he "WHOPS" John on the back of the head. Most of the time John's eyes see red and yellow, and his ears ring. His house is a war zone, and school isn't much better. His friends are getting arrested. The algebra teacher wants to torture him. The administration has sentenced him to wrestle a live tuba in the school orchestra, and the girl he loves won't give him a second look. No wonder his real father named him after a toilet. Life is so bad that fourteen-year-old John makes up an African tribe, the Lashasa Palulu, whose customs can solve all his problems. But he can't live with the tribe—because they don't exist. He can't stay at home—because he really doesn't have one. He can't tell anyone what his life is like or he might not stay alive. He must keep the dirty secret and say to everyone in his threatening world, *"You Don't Know Me."*

Related Activities

1. John's sarcastic voice is funny—up to a point. Discuss where you think the tone of the narrative shifts. Explain your choice. Discuss why the tone changes.
2. At the end of the novel, John realizes he has not perceived his world accurately. What mistakes has he made? Discuss why he has made them.
3. Irony is a major tool for Klass. Using library references as well as a standard dictionary, define it. Explain how Klass uses irony in the novel.
4. Read the first chapter, "who I am not" and the last chapter, "who I am." Discuss how these two chapters unify the novel.
5. Read again the "Epilogue, Whatever that Means" on pages 260 and 261. Do you feel the epilogue is necessary? Support your answer with specifics from the novel.
6. Read "The Whipping"(Related Work 5) by Robert Hayden. Discuss what the speaker does, the speaker's reaction, and possible reasons for that reaction. Be sure to refer to the text of the poem. How does this picture of violence relate to *You Don't Know Me?*

Related Works

1. Brooks, Martha. **Being with Henry.** New York: DK Publishing /Melanie Kroupa, 2000. 216p. $17.95. ISBN 0-7894-2588-2. In contrast to John's mother, sixteen-year-old Laker Wyatt's mother chooses her third husband over her son.
2. Buchanan, Jane. **Hank's Story.** (See Booktalk in chapter 2.) Targeting a younger audience, *Hank's Story* tells about the abuse orphaned Hank Donohue endures and finally escapes.
3. Carroll, Sissi. "An Interview with Author/Screen Writer David Klass." *The ALAN Review.* (Spring/Summer 2002) 5–9. **NF** Klass talks about his family, his dual career in Hollywood, young-adult novels, and the writing process that produced *You Don't Know Me.*
4. Coville, Bruce. "The Metamorphosis of Justin Jones." In **Odder Than Ever.** New York: Harcourt Brace and Company, 1999. 146p. $16.00. ISBN 0-15-201747-X. Abused by his Uncle Rafe, Justin flees to a forever-safe place where he could stay the same. He elects instead to return to the real world so that one day he can help children like himself. The story appears on pages 127 to 141.
5. Hayden, Robert. "The Whipping." In **Poetry After Lunch,** compiled by Joyce Armstrong Carroll and Edward E. Wilson. (See full

booktalk in chapter 4.) **NF** The speaker witnesses the whipping of a boy and reflects on a shared experience and the attacker's motivation. The poem appears on page 101.

6. Pines, Ana Angélica. "No One Spoke Up for Irma." In **The Struggle to Be Strong,** edited by Al Desetta and Sybil Wolin. Minneapolis, MN: Free Spirit, 2000. 179p. $14.95. ISBN 1-57542-079-1. **NF** Although an entire neighborhood witnesses a mother abusing her daughter, no one reports it because they feel they should mind their own business. The essay appears on pages 141 to 146.

7. Williams, Carol Lynch. **The True Colors of Caitlynne Jackson.** New York: Delacorte Press, 1997. 168p. $14.95. ISBN 0-385-32249-6. Two physically and emotionally abused sisters, abandoned by their mother, finally demonstrate to the world how badly they have been treated.

Na, An. A Step from Heaven.

Asheville, NC: Front Street, 2001. 156p. $15.95. ISBN 1-886910-58-8.

Summary/Description

Young Ju, a Korean immigrant, relates her family's entry to and life in the United States. The story, a series of essays based on the author's experience, begins when Young Ju is three years old and ends when she is about eighteen. The three-year-old Young Ju believes she and her family are going to heaven, but when they arrive, she discovers that America is *A Step from Heaven.* Her father's drinking and abuse, her mother's denial, and her culture's strictness travel with them. Young Ju develops the toughness she needs to succeed, help her parents assimilate, and supervise her younger brother. In the process, she becomes American and persuades her mother to resist her husband's brutality. Finally, the mother and two children elect to stay in the United States, and the father returns to Korea. The essays begin with "Sea Bubble," in which Young Ju's father gently teaches her to love the ocean waves, and end with "A Family of Dreamers," in which Young Ju realizes her brutal father at one time was a gentle and loving man. The Epilogue reflects on how her mother's rough and calloused hands enabled the children to have the smooth hands of good education and well-paid jobs.

Booktalk

America is a magic word. When Young Ju's parents say it, everyone smiles. Their fighting and angry words stop. Then her mother tells Young

Ju they will all go there. As they leave Korea and rise into the sky, Young Ju is sure America is the heaven her grandmother told her about. But America is *A Step from Heaven,* such a big step that the small girl wonders if she can ever climb it. Her parents tell her she must study hard, ignore the American girls who would like to be her friends, take care of her brother while her parents work, and keep silent about her father—his drinking, his beatings. America tells her she has choices. Young Ju knows she must bring these two countries together in her head and her heart. But she wonders what she will lose when she tries.

Related Activities

1. In the opening chapter "Sea Bubble," Young Ju speaks to an adult who is coaxing her into the ocean waves. In the last chapter, "A Family of Dreamers," Young Ju and the reader find out that the person is her father. After reading the opening chapter a second time, discuss how and why the author waits to reveal the identity.
2. "Hands" is the epilogue rather than the last chapter. Discuss why the author made that choice.
3. Much of the novel deals with the Korean family structure. Ask your librarian to help you find out more about Korean families. Share your information with the group. Then compare it to the structure of an American family.
4. Choose an incident from your own childhood. Using An Na's essays as models, try telling about the event through your eyes at the time it happened.
5. Ask at least three other people to read *Split Image* (Related Work 3) and *A Step from Heaven.* Compare Laura Li and Young Ju. Discuss your reactions to the two novels.

Related Works

1. Budhos, Marina. **Remix: Conversations with Immigrant Teenagers.** New York: Henry Holt and Company, 1999. 145p. ISBN 0-8050-5113-9. **NF** Teenagers who have come to the United States share their experiences. The story of "Lucy" on pages 21 to 29 tells how a Korean girl makes up for her physical appearance with high achievement and how the discrepancies of the two cultures have driven her to think about suicide.
2. Frank, E. R. **Life Is Funny.** (See full booktalk in chapter 2.) The character Sonia is caught in the pressure between two cultures.
3. Glenn, Mel. **Split Image: A Story in Poems.** New York: Harper-Collins Publishers, 2000. 159p. $15.95. ISBN 0-688-16249-5. **NF** Laura Li is required to keep the Chinese traditions and also suc-

ceed in the American culture. The conflicts she experiences result in suicide.

4. Kay, Philip, Andria Estepa, and Al Desetta. **Things Get Hectic: Teens Write About the Violence That Surrounds Them.** New York: Touchstone Books, 1998. 182p. $13.00. ISBN 0-684-83754-4. **NF** In the section "Home Is Where the Hurt Is—Abuse," letters and essays discuss the violence that occurs in the home and what that violence does to families.

5. Lee, Cherylene. "Hollywood and the Pits." In **Help Wanted: Short Stories About Young People Working,** compiled by Anita Silvey. New York: Little, Brown, 1997. 174p. $15.95. ISBN 0-316-79148-2. A fifteen-year-old entertainer previously known as the Chinese Shirley Temple decides she must seek another future as her career winds down. She builds her decision on her experiences and observations while she pursues her archeological interests in the Le Brea Tar Pits. The story appears on pages 117 to 128.

Nature Prevails

ぱ

Adams, Simon. **Titanic.**

New York: DK Publishing, Inc., 1999. 59p. (Eyewitness Books). $15.95. ISBN 0-7894-4724-X. **NF**

Summary/Description

Packed with colored pictures of the people and things that were part of and related to the Titanic, this fascinating record of the tragic disaster describes and illustrates the ship's construction, appointments, captain, crew, passengers, accommodations, and destruction. Captions for each picture piece together the historical information within the context of the period. A name and item index shows how specific names or items relate to more than one chapter. This would be an excellent book to use when beginning a unit on the Titanic, historical tragedies, or the lifestyle of the early twentieth century.

Booktalk

Ask how many people in the group have heard about the Titanic. Most people will probably be familiar with the movie. Then ask them to take a quiz about the Titanic.

1. In which country was the Titanic built? (Northern Ireland, p.10)

2. What was the name of the Titanic's sister ship? (RMS Olympic, p.10)
3. What was the name of the ship that rescued the survivors of the Titanic? (The Carpathia, p.23)
4. Who was the wealthiest man on board? (John Jacob Astor IV, p.26)
5. Who was the captain of the ship? (Captain Edward Smith, p.20)

As you answer the questions, show the pages of pictures on which the answers appear. Then pass the book around the room.

Each of us might know these facts about the *Titanic*, the ship that was supposedly unsinkable, but the ship still holds some mysteries. Did some people really predict the disaster? Why did the captain ignore the warnings he received? Because of its construction, would the ship have sunk even if it hadn't hit an iceberg? Read *Titanic* and see if you can figure out the answers that go far beyond simple facts.

Related Activities

1. Construct and complete your own version of the simulation game described in the August, 2000 issue of *VOYA* (Related Work 2).
2. Richard Peck, author of *Ghosts I Have Been* (Related Work 5), and several speakers in the four-videocassette A&E documentary *Titanic* (Related Work 6) are members of the Titanic Historical Society of America. Ask your librarian to help you find out more about that society and share your information with the group.
3. Using Adam's *Titanic*, Kupperberg's *The Tragedy of the Titanic* (Related Work 3), and the A&E documentary (Related Work 6) as references, discuss how Peck based his story on fact.
4. Peck, in *Ghosts I Have Been* (Related Work 5) describes Blossom's vision of the Titanic and her encounter with Julian and his aristocratic parents. After reading *Titanic, Heroine of the Titanic: The Real Unsinkable Molly Brown* (Related Work 4), and *Ghosts I Have Been* (Related Work 5), describe the meeting Blossom might have had with Molly Brown—either real or supernatural. Indicate, through description and dialogue, what they might have had in common.
5. After completing activities one through four, list the reasons that both the building and sinking of the *Titanic* remain significant historical events.

Related Works

1. Bredeson, Carmen. **The Challenger Disaster: Tragic Space Flight.** Berkeley Heights, NJ: Enslow Publishers, Inc., 1999. 48p. (American Disasters). $18.95. ISBN 0-7660-1222-0. **NF** As the Titanic defined sea disasters at the beginning of the century, the Challenger defined tragedy in space flight at the end of the century and

generated extensive investigation to find the causes. Bredeson's book is a record of the shock, the flight, and the subsequent investigation.

2. Cannon, Holly L. and Susan M. Blackman. "Reenacting the Titanic: A Simulation Game Teaches Lifelong Lessons." *VOYA*. August, 2000: 176 and 177. **NF** The article describes a two-day simulation activity for eighth graders. The deck each student occupied and the student's survival was determined by the amount of information he or she knew about the Titanic. Students gained insight into the unfairness of the class system and the importance of preparation and cooperation. E-mail Smblrb@aol.com for more information.

3. Kupperberg, Paul. **The Tragedy of the Titanic.** New York: Rosen Publishing Group, 2003. 48p. (When Disaster Strikes!) $17.95. ISBN 0-8239-3679-1. **NF** This description of the disaster places the Titanic in the context of the Gilded Age and mechanical progress. An extensive bibliography of the sources used, suggestions for further reading, and a list of Web sites provide material for continued research.

4. Landau, Elaine. **Heroine of the Titanic: The Real Unsinkable Molly Brown.** (See full booktalk in chapter 4.) **NF** This nonfiction account describes the real-life Molly (Margaret) Brown, a wealthy socialite with working class roots who fought for the rights of women and workers.

5. Peck, Richard. **Ghosts I Have Been.** New York: Viking Press, 1977. 214p. $20.00. ISBN 0-670-33813-3. Blossom Culp's second sight joins her to a small boy deserted by his aristocratic parents during the Titanic disaster.

6. **Titanic.** Produced by A&E Television Networks, HEARST/ABC /NBC, 1994. 200 min. Videocassette. Color. $19.95. AAE-12900. The four-tape documentary analyzes the controversial construction, disaster, rescue, and salvage of the Titanic.

ぐ╲

Calabro, Marian. **The Perilous Journey of the Donner Party.**

New York: Clarion Books, 1999. 192p. $20.00. ISBN 0-395-86610-3. **NF**

Summary/Description

Driven by "land fever" and the mindset of "Manifest Destiny," a group that became known as the Donner Party left prosperous lives in the Midwest to settle in California. Calabro points out that their fatal mistake was their reliance on one source of information: *The Emigrant's Guide to Oregon and California* by Lanford Warren Hastings. Hastings had made only one trip west. The party relied on his advice over the warnings of those who had lived in and explored the region. Calabro describes the trip from its hopeful and confident beginning of elaborate wagons and luxurious supplies through its bad habits of procrastination and continued misplaced trust and to a horrible deterioration of morale and health that resulted in cannibalism. She then describes the rescue of the survivors, their lives in California, the Donner memorials, and the effects this tragedy had on the Donner Party descendants. In addition to the main text, the book includes The Journey of the Donner Party map, a Members of the Donner Party roster that also lists nicknames and approximate ages of the participants, the full text of Virginia Reed's letter that narrates Virginia's survival experience, a chronology based on Frank Mullen Jr.'s *The Donner Party Chronicles*, a Roster of the Dead with dates of death listed where known, a bibliography of Books for Young Readers, a list of Web sites, a full bibliography for research sources, and a topic and name index with illustration pages in bold print.

Booktalk

Every day you take a journey. How do you prepare for it? *The Perilous Journey of the Donner Party* tells a story of love, hope, hate—even the grim reality of cannibalism. But it also explains how so many good people, through poor planning, procrastination, and misplaced trust, found themselves in such a bad situation. The Donner Party's story is important, not because of the people who were lost but because of the lessons that come from those losses. It's a story not only of defeat but also of triumph. What went wrong? Why did some people get out and others perish? Why did some survivors go on to live happy lives while others destroyed themselves? The answers apply in the twenty-first century as surely as they applied in the nineteenth. Planning on trying something new and exciting this week? First, take time to read about the Donner Party.

Related Activities

1. The Donner Party relied on one source of information that proved to be inaccurate. After reading Calabro's account, list what you learned about evaluating a source of information.
2. Choose one of the books, videos, or Web sites listed on pages 181 to 183. Review it and share the additional information you find with the rest of your group. Ask your librarian to help you find additional sources. Ask each member of your group to do the same.

3. Compare the Donner Party's preparation and purpose with that of the Lewis and Clark expedition. Discuss the factors that accounted for the failure of the one and the success of the other. You might wish to start with page 44 of *The Saga of Lewis and Clark* (Related Work 5) and page 21 of *The Perilous Journey of the Donner Party.*

4. Read Virginia Reed's letters on pages 165 to 171. Discuss what her letters reveal about her and her experiences.

5. After reading *The Journal of Douglas Allen Deeds: The Donner Party Expedition* (Related Work 4), cite examples of how Philbrick used the facts of the Donner expedition to tell his story.

Related Works

1. Durbin, William. **The Journal of Sean Sullivan, Transcontinental Railroad Worker.** New York: Scholastic Incorporated, 1999. (My Name Is America). $10.95. ISBN 0-439-04994-6. When Sean Sullivan joins his father to work on the Transcontinental Railroad, he records his life in the camps within its social and political context. The Donner Party disaster emphasized the need for a national railroad if Manifest Destiny were to become a reality.

2. Gregory, Kristiana. **The Great Railroad Race: The Diary of Libby West.** New York: Scholastic Incorporated, 1999. 201p. (Dear America). $10.95. ISBN 0-590-10991-X. Libby's father is a reporter who wishes to record the railroad race that will open the Western frontier.

3. Hite, Sid. **Stick and Whittle.** New York: Scholastic Press, 2000. 208p. $16.95. ISBN 0-439-09828-9. Stick and Whittle meet in their Western journeys, become partners, and defeat the bad guys. The characters' attitudes toward "luck" or "divine intervention" as well as the reference to Manifest Destiny as "man-infested-destiny" reveal how thinking affects results, whether those results are normal or bizarre.

4. Philbrick, Rodman. **The Journal of Douglas Allen Deeds: The Donner Party Expedition.** New York: Scholastic Incorporated, 2001. 160p. (My Name Is America). $10.95. ISBN 0-439-21600-1. In this fictional account, an orphan, Douglas Allen Deeds, travels with the Breen family, becomes part of The Forlorn Hope rescue mission, refuses cannibalism, and survives to become a wealthy gold miner in partnership with Edward Breen.

5. Schmidt, Thomas and Jeremy Schmidt. **The Saga of Lewis and Clark: Into the Uncharted West.** (See full booktalk in chapter 4.) **NF** This very successful journey initiated by Thomas Jefferson reinforced the idea of Manifest Destiny and prepared pioneers for Westward expansion.

ℭℨ℞ℨ

Paulsen, Gary. Brian's Return.

New York: Delacorte Press, 1999. 117p. $13.50. ISBN 0-385-32500-2.

Summary/Description

Brian of *Hatchet, The River,* and *Brian's Winter* decides the wilderness is his home. After his return to civilization, he gradually isolates himself from his peers. Carl, a bully and school athlete, attacks Brian and two companions. Brian reacts as he would have in the wilderness and beats Carl senseless. He is arrested and referred to a counselor, Caleb Lancaster, who advises him to visit the Cree family who rescued him in *Brian's Winter.* Securing a bush flight that will bring him within one hundred miles of his destination, Brian encounters more nature emergencies and a wilderness man named Billy. After speaking with Billy, Brian dreams about him and decides Billy is guiding him to a life in the wilderness also. When he approaches the Smallhorns, the Cree family he intended to visit, he decides he will come back later. The closing sentence, "He would follow his medicine," promises Brian's life will be a constant discovery of self in relation to nature.

Booktalk

You met him in *Hatchet.* You read about his winter adventure in *Brian's Winter.* You saw him save a life in *The River.* Now, in *Brian's Return,* Brian is back in civilization with pizza, chocolate, movies, parties, dates, television, friends, family, and school. Is he happy? Not really. He is living in the suburbs, but the wilderness is living inside him. In a wild rage, Brian almost kills one of his classmates. Brian survived nature's harsh challenges and the media limelight, but he doesn't know if he or the people he loves can survive the person he has become. Then he meets a blind man, Caleb Lancaster, who can see deep into Brian's heart. With Caleb's help, Brian decides to find the wisdom to follow his own "medicine."

Related Activities

1. Read Robert Frost's "The Road Not Taken" (Related Work 1). Discuss how that poem applies to Brian's decision to return to the wilderness.
2. Brian calls himself an "animal-boy." Discuss whether you feel that name is accurate and whether it should be considered a positive or negative label.
3. In both *Touching Spirit Bear* (Related Work 2) and *Brian Returns,* a fight sends the main character into the wilderness. Reread the fight

scene in each novel. The *Touching Spirit Bear* fight scene begins on page 7 in chapter 1 with the words "Later, after school…" and ends with "got away with it." The *Brian Returns* fight scene appears on pages 9 through 11 in chapter 2, beginning with the words "In that instant…" and ending with the chapter. Explain what each fight reveals about the character.

4. After reading all four books in the *Hatchet* series (Related Works 4, 5, 6 and *Brian's Return*), discuss Brian's final decision. Discuss or write about whether you agree with his decision.

5. Paulsen's *The Transall Saga* (Related Work 3) is a science fiction survival story in which the main character becomes a hero in another world, returns to the earthly world, and studies to become a successful scientist, a hero of a different kind. Compare Mark Harrison's journey and adjustment in *The Transall Saga* with Brian's journey and adjustment in *The Hatchet* and the sequels that conclude with *Brian's Return.* Ask your librarian to help your find several different definitions of heroism. Apply them to these two works.

Related Works

1. Frost, Robert. "The Road Not Taken." In **Poetry After Lunch,** compiled by Joyce Armstrong Carroll and Edward E. Wilson. Spring, TX: Absey & Co., 1997. 164p. $17.95. ISBN 1888842-03-2. **NF** Encountering a fork in the road, a traveler decides to take the path "less traveled." The poem is on page 64.

2. Mikaelsen, Ben. **Touching Spirit Bear.** (See full booktalk in chapter 2.) A young boy has a last chance in the juvenile system when he is sentenced to an island for a year and encounters the tough love of nature and his parole officer.

3. Paulsen, Gary. **The Transall Saga.** New York: Delacorte Press, 1998. 248p. $15.95. ISBN 0-385-32196-1. (See full booktalk in *Booktalks Plus*, 2001, pages 192 and 193.) This supernatural survival story forces the main character to descend into the unknown and emerge as a hero better able to cope with the real world.

4. Paulsen, Gary. **Brian's Winter.** New York: Delacorte Press, 1996. 133p. $15.95. ISBN 0-385-32198-8. This "what if" sequel to *Hatchet* extends Brian's stay to the winter months. When Brian finds a Cree family to rescue him, he begins to discover that life in the wilderness might be his way of life.

5. Paulsen, Gary. **Hatchet.** New York: Puffin Books, 1987. 195p. $4.95pa. ISBN 0-14-032724-X. This survivalist novel, the first in the series, includes the plane wreck, survival test, and rescue that teach Brian to be a man.

6.   Paulsen, Gary. **The River.** New York: Delacorte Press, 1991. 132p.
     $15.00. ISBN 0-385-30388-2. In this sequel to *Hatchet,* a govern-
     ment psychologist asks Brian to return to the wilderness so they can
     record for others the things that helped Brian survive. This time,
     Brian must save not only himself but also the psychologist.

Ryan, Pam Muñoz. Esperanza Rising.
New York: Scholastic Press, 2000. 272p. $15.95. ISBN 0-439-12041-1.

Summary/Description

Esperanza Ortega is born into privilege and affluence. When she is
thirteen, bandits kill her father, and her two greedy uncles take over
the family's finances. After Esperanza's mother refuses a marriage proposal from one of the uncles, he burns their home and crops. The mother
then pretends to accept his proposal, but flees with Esperanza and the
housekeeper's family to the United States. Here their lives are dictated
by the hardships of the Great Depression. They all work and live in a
company camp. Esperanza works instead of giving orders and learns how
little so many have. When her mother becomes critically ill from Valley
Fever, Esperanza earns enough to pay the rent and hospital bills. She
deals with the prejudice against Mexicans, her own prejudices against
former servants, and the strikers who threaten her livelihood but must
have better wages.

   In contrast to Esperanza, sixteen-year-old Miguel, the housekeeper's
son, sees this move to America as a step up. In America, if he works hard
enough, he can become someone. He helps Esperanza learn to work,
and they develop a closeness that would have been impossible in Mexico.
Eventually he returns to Mexico to bring back Esperanza's grandmother,
a task Esperanza could not achieve. The book deals with Mexican Repatriation, a policy adopted in 1929 to send Mexican workers back to Mexico. The workers picked up in these "sweeps" included American citizens
who looked Mexican, and the actions were used to control strikes and
free jobs for the unemployed. The fruit that dominates the action and the
characters' lives titles each chapter. An Author's Note explains how the
author's grandmother inspired the story. The note also explains the
story's historical context.

Booktalk

In Mexico, thirteen-year-old Esperanza spends her time deciding on her
favorite dress, lining up her beautiful porcelain dolls, and giving her ser-

vants orders. Then bandits kill her father, and her uncles seize all the family money. She and her mother must flee to the United States, where she will spend her time taking care of real babies, cooking meals, and sweeping floors. Here she is another Mexican, the last hired and the first fired. No one thinks she is pretty, smart—or determined. Remembering her grandmother's words "Do not ever be afraid to start over," she will someday rule over a great family, just as she always planned. This time people, not numbers, will make her wealth. This time nature's rhythms, not social status, will guide her. No one will see Esperanza defeated for long. They will see only *Esperanza Rising*.

Related Activities

1. Esperanza learns to listen to the rhythms of nature instead of the artificial labels people use to organize the world. As you read the book, list the people and events that teach her the power and hope of nature.
2. *Esperanza* centers on the Mexican Repatriation policy of 1929. Further research that policy and the immigration laws governing Mexico. Share your findings and your feelings about the policy with the group.
3. Esperanza and her family confront the American culture, but Esperanza must also learn about the culture of people within her own country. Discuss what she learns about each world and how those lessons change her.
4. Ryan ties each chapter to a crop of fruits or vegetables. Tell an experience of your own that centers on something you eat.
5. In *Out of the Dust* (Related Work 3), fourteen-year-old Billie Joe tells about living through the Dust Bowl of the Great Depression. Esperanza's family comes to the United States during the same event. After reading *Out of the Dust* and *Esperanza Rising*, compare the destruction and rebirth each girl experiences.
6. Read the story "The Bubble Gum Pink House" by Viola Canales (Related Work 1). How does the story, like *Esperanza Rising*, treat people who celebrate nature as opposed to those who value status?
7. Like *Esperanza*, *My Own True Name* (Related Work 5), a collection of poems by Pat Mora, is organized with natural images. Three poems in the collection—"1910," "Border Town: 1938," and "Immigrants"—express the difficulties of moving from one culture to another. After reading these poems, compare these difficulties to those described in *Esperanza*.

Related Works

1. Canales, Viola. **Orange Candy Slices and Other Secret Tales.** Houston, TX: Piñata Books, 2001. 122p. $9.95pa. ISBN 1-5585-

332-4. This collection of short stories describes the lives of Hispanics. Like Esperanza, their hopes and dreams are universal. "The Bubble Gum Pink House," on pages 38 to 45, centers on a disagreement over house colors inspired by nature and property values.

2. Copley, Robert E. **The Tall Mexican: The Life of Hank Aguirre All-Star Pitcher, Businessman, Humanitarian.** Houston, TX: Piñata Books, 2000. 159p. $9.95pa. ISBN 1-55885-294-8. **NF** Like Esperanza's family, the Aguirre family came to America and started over, first as migrant workers. Aguirre, born at the beginning of the depression, combined his athletic career and business skills to help thousands of Hispanic Americans in Detroit who also were once part of the migrant circuit.

3. Hesse, Karen. **Out of the Dust.** New York: Scholastic Press, 1997. 227p. $4.99pa. ISBN 0-590-37125-8. (See full booktalk in *Booktalks Plus*, 2001, pages 30 to 32.) Fourteen-year-old Billie Joe tells her story in a series of poems. Having lost her mother to an accidental fire and her father to grief, she struggles with a new and bleak life, but she learns about her own ability to survive.

4. Johnston, Tony. **Any Small Goodness: A Novel of the Barrio.** New York: Blue Sky Press, 2001. 128p. $15.95. ISBN 0-439-18936-5. Hoping to improve their lives, Arturo's family moves to the barrio of Los Angeles. Arturo discovers that holding onto the generosity of his own heritage and identifying the good people to emulate from every heritage will help him live successfully.

5. Mora, Pat (poetry), and Anthony Accardo (illus.). **My Own True Name: New and Selected Poems for Young Adults.** Houston, TX: Piñata Books, 2000. 81p. $11.95. ISBN 1-55885-292-1. **NF** The titles "Blooms," "Thorns," and "Roots" organize the poems, some of which are written in both English and Spanish. The poems cited in activity 7 appear on the following pages: "1910," page 30; "Border Town: 1938," page 31; "Immigrants," page 36.

☙❧

Philip, Neil, ed. In a Sacred Manner I Live: Native American Wisdom.
New York: Clarion Books, 1997. 93p. $20.00. ISBN 0-395-84981-0. **NF**

Summary/Description

*I*n a Sacred Manner I Live is a collection of Native American pictures, poems, songs, and speeches from 1609 to 1995. The collection reflects a great respect for nature and language. Keeping this respect means living "in a sacred manner." A caption describes each picture, and a short explanation describes the author and context of each passage. The book as a whole demonstrates the great cultural clash that was bound to occur between the Native Americans and the white settlers.

Booktalk

White settlers staked their own claim to land that Native Americans believed belonged to no one. Today, the descendants of those settlers are learning that although Native Americans' weapons were not powerful, their wisdom is. These songs and speeches say that all may enjoy the gifts of land, language, and spirit and all are responsible for preserving them. *In a Sacred Manner I Live* tells and shows the lives of men and women who lived their beliefs and who inspire us today to return to the life of earth, trust, and faith.

Related Activities

1. Using historical reference resources in your area, research one aspect of the Native American nations that lived there: their spiritual beliefs, family structures, or names. Share your findings with the group.
2. Each day read one passage from *In a Sacred Manner I Live*. In your journal, write the value or values the passage expresses.
3. List the values that are prominent in the passages. Find modern messages from the print and non-print media that either parallel or conflict with those values.
4. Use two copies of *In a Sacred Manner I Live*. Create a display with the pictures and passages from the book along with the material gathered from activities 2 and 3.
5. *Bone Dance* (Related Work 2); *Standing in the Light* (Related Work 6); *Echohawk* (Related Work 3); *The Turtle Clan Journey* (Related Work 4); and *The Girl Who Chased Away Sorrow: A Diary of Sarah Nita, a Navajo Girl, New Mexico, 1864* (Related Work 8) all deal with the meeting of the Native American and white cultures. After reading these novels, discuss the results of that blend. Consider what divides and unites the two groups.
6. The Native American passages use metaphors involving mother, teacher, and blanket as well as personification to explain nature's relationship to man. List as many instances of metaphor and personification in the passages as you can. Then, using the information from activity 3, employ metaphor and personification to express the way a society you are familiar with perceives nature.

Related Works

1. Aronson, Marc. **Art Attack: A Short Cultural History of the Avant-Garde.** New York: Clarion Books, 1998. 192p. $20.00. ISBN 0-395-79729-2. **NF** This history of modern art combines the visual and musical. The index heading "Native Americans" guides readers to the relationship between the avant-garde and art formerly seen as primitive or inferior.

2. Brooks, Martha. **Bone Dance.** (See full booktalk in chapter 1.) The spirits of an Indian burial ground and the visions the characters share bring together two very different young people.

3. Durrant, Lynda. **Echohawk.** New York: Clarion Books, 1996. 181p. $14.95. ISBN 0-395-74430-X. Four-year-old Jonathan Starr is captured and adopted by the Mohicans, whom he grows to love and respect.

4. Durrant, Lynda. **The Turtle Clan Journey.** (See full booktalk in chapter 3.) When the white man's disease destroys their tribe, Echohawk (Jonathan Starr) and his father and brother must travel to the Ohio Valley. All three of them must face hostile nations, and Jonathan must face being returned to the white world.

5. Neihardt, John G. (text) and Standing Bear (illus.). **Black Elk Speaks: Being the Life Story of a Holy Man of the Oglala Sioux.** Lincoln, NE: University of Nebraska Press, 1979. 299p. $15.89. ISBN 0-8032-3301-9. **NF** Black Elk tells the full story of his life and the failure he feels in not fulfilling his vision. The work was published originally in 1932.

6. Osborne, Mary Pope. **Standing in the Light: The Captive Diary of Catharine Carey Logan.** New York: Scholastic Incorporated, 1998. 284p. (Dear America). $10.95. ISBN 0-590-13462-0. A young girl captured by the Indians discovers a satisfying life she must give up when "rescued" by white men.

7. Stefoff, Rebecca. **Tecumseh and the Shawnee Confederation.** New York, Facts on File, 1998. 138p. (Library of American Indian History). $25.00. ISBN 0-8160-3648-9. **NF** This portrait of Tecumseh explores the importance of oratory in the Native American world and more fully explains the cultural differences that caused the Native Americans and the newcomers to clash.

8. Turner, Ann. **The Girl Who Chased Away Sorrow: A Diary of Sarah Nita, a Navajo Girl, New Mexico, 1864.** New York: Scholastic Incorporated, 1999. 182p. (Dear America). $10.95. ISBN 0-590-97216-2. The book tells about the Navajo march to Fort Sumner and the abuse and misunderstanding resulting from cultural prejudices.

Nations Conflict

ॸॣ॔ॶ

Rinaldi, Ann. **Amelia's War.**

New York: Scholastic Press, 1999. 272p. $15.95. ISBN 0-590-11744-0.

Summary/Description

In August of 1861, Amelia Grafton sees DeWitt Clinton Rench shot in the back because he joined the Southern army. Amelia reports the incident to Mr. Dechart, who owns the local newspaper. His editorial leads to his arrest for "Southern leanings," and Amelia, feeling responsible for this arrest, decides never to get involved in the war again. Because she lives in Hagerstown, Maryland, a town constantly beset by Union and Rebel forces, her task is formidable. People who do get involved surround her. Amelia's father, a local storeowner, makes money from the war, but also keeps the town going with goods and fair prices. Her mother, a Union supporter but not a Yankee, works in the hospitals. Her brother Wes and his girlfriend, Jimmy Pearl Beale, join the Union army. Her best friend, twelve-year-old Josh, Mr. Dechart's son, tries to keep an accurate record of the war and produce a newspaper. When Amelia's uncle, General McCausland, marches on the town and declares he will burn it if not given a $200,000 ransom, Amelia secretly changes the numbers to $20,000 and helps her father, the town treasurer, save the town. She doubts she has done the right thing, and she can tell no one else about it. *Amelia's War* includes a Prologue that establishes Amelia's family and social context, an Epilogue that tells what happened to family and friends after the war, and an Author's Note that explains how Rinaldi constructed the story from fact and fiction. A Bibliography suggests further reading.

Booktalk

When the Civil War begins, Amelia Grafton doesn't think about making choices. She sees a Rebel soldier shot in the back before he even goes to war, and she thinks she must tell someone. That someone owns the local paper, and when he decides to write an editorial about it, he goes to prison for "Southern leanings." Before the war, expressing an opinion was no crime, but this Civil War has changed the rules, and because Amelia lives in Maryland, the rules change with every band of Yankees and Rebels that take the town. Amelia is Union, but not Yankee. She has friends and family who fight for the North and for the South. Anything she does could hurt someone she loves. But finally, if she doesn't act, her entire family and town might be destroyed. She won't be able to end the Civil War, but she *can* try for some victories in *Amelia's War*.

Related Activities

1. Read the Author's Note. Here Rinaldi explains how she used fact to construct the story. Referring to the Bibliography at the end of *Amelia's War* and additional information from the library collection, find facts or actual situations that would be appropriate for a novel or short story.
2. Read Josh's viewpoints about newspapers in chapter 2. Begin with "That's what words are all about" and end with "That's not what this country is supposed to be all about, Amelia." Discuss Josh's viewpoints.
3. Choose a political issue. Ask each person in the group to find an article about that issue and identify the point of view the article presents. Discuss the facts, inferences, and judgments presented in each article. Organize a class debate on the issue.
4. Amelia Grafton's father in *Amelia's War* says, "You make a choice and you pay for it the rest of your life." Cite specific choices, positive and negative, that you have observed. Then discuss whether the statement could also be "You make a choice and you benefit from it the rest of your life."
5. When Amelia says she won't be permitted to see her aunt during the summer, Josh replies, "Guess you came home last time with too many seditious ideas." Find the meaning of seditious, and discuss why that term would be important during wartime.

Related Works

1. **Civil War Journal II: Volume 5.** Produced by A&E Networks, HEARST/ABC/NBC, 1994. 100 min. Videocassette. Color. $14.95. AAE-1211. "Women at War," the second half of the video, explains the contributions women made and the hardships they endured during the Civil War.
2. Damon, Duane. **When This Cruel War Is Over.** Minneapolis, MN: Lerner Publishing Group, 1996. 88p. $19.95. ISBN 0-8225-1731-0. **NF** Damon's short nonfiction account explains how the Civil War split families. It states and outlines the difference between slavery supporters and union supporters.
3. Hesse, Karen. **A Light in the Storm: The Civil War Diary of Amelia Martin.** New York: Scholastic Incorporated, 1999. 176p. $10.95. ISBN 0-590-56733-0. The war causes Amelia's parents—one who supports the North and one who supports the South—to end an already unhappy marriage.

4. Hite, Sid. **Stick and Whittle.** New York: Scholastic Press, 2000. 208p. $16.95. ISBN 0-439-09828-9. In chapter 14 of *Amelia's War,* "For Once They Named a Battle Right," Amelia discusses the battle called "The Wilderness" with the town doctor. Her brother Wes was wounded there, and the doctor notes that only "the lucky ones" got out. In this Western journey of two good friends, the Battle of the Wilderness plays a central part in Stick's thinking, and Whittle helps Stick talk through the memories that haunt him.

5. McGlinn, Jeanne M. **Ann Rinaldi: Historian & Storyteller.** Lanham, MD: The Scarecrow Press, Inc., 2000. 94p. (Scarecrow Studies in Young Adult Literature, No. 2) $29.50. ISBN 0-8108-3678-5. **NF** Although McGlinn briefly summarizes *Amelia's War* in the Afterword, the Rinaldi themes McGlinn identifies apply to *Amelia's War* also.

6. Rinaldi, Ann. **Girl in Blue.** New York: Scholastic Incorporated, 2001. 320p. $15.95. ISBN 0-439-07336-7. Fifteen-year-old Sarah Louisa runs away from abuse and a forced marriage to join the Union army. When her disguise is discovered, she is offered an opportunity to be a Pinkerton agent.

Bagdasarian, Adam. Forgotten Fire.

New York: DK Publishing, Inc., 2000. 273p. $17.95. ISBN 0-7894-2627-7.

Summary/Description

Vahan Kenderian recounts the terrible physical and emotional journey he is forced to take between 1915 and 1918 as the youngest son in a well-respected and prosperous Armenian family during the Armenian holocaust. Twelve-year-old Vahan flees his home and watches his family disappear and die as the Turks, allied with the Germans in World War I, slaughter the Armenian population. He endures hunger, violence, molestation, desertion, grief, and the constant fear of his own imminent death. Once sheltered and pampered, he learns to assess whom he can love, trust, and fear as he serves the highest Turkish officials and tries to protect the downtrodden. Based on the memoirs of the author's greatuncle, Vahan's journey, eventually ending in an orphanage in Constantinople where he is reunited with his only surviving sister, is an expansion of Bagdasarian's short story "The Survivor." A brief foreword explains this little-known chapter in Armenian/Turkish history, and a map traces Vahan's trek.

Booktalk

Ask how many people in the group have heard of the Holocaust. Ask them to explain what it was.

When we hear the word holocaust, we usually think of Hitler's World War II Germany where millions of Jews lost their lives. Few of us even know about another holocaust in which two-thirds of the Armenian population of Turkey suffered and died. *Forgotten Fire* tells the story of one boy, Vahan Kenderian, who found himself trapped in that tragedy.

Growing up in a wealthy, respected, and well-educated family, twelve-year-old Vahan assumes he will always have happiness, money, and respect. His family ignores rumors of a massacre in Adana. Then the Turkish police come to take his father away. Still the family is certain the authorities will correct this mistake, and their father will come home tomorrow. But there is no mistake. All Armenians will be killed or driven out of Turkey. Now Vahan learns about the bad times, the fires of life his father told him would turn him to steel. For the next three years, he must survive alone in that fire—hungry, thirsty, and afraid, with only his own head, heart, and hands to guide him.

Related Activities

1. On page 245 of *Passage to Ararat* (Related Work 1), Arlen reports the question Hitler asked Hermann Goering before invading Poland: "Who still talks nowadays of the extermination of the Armenians?" Discuss what this question suggests about each citizen's and each country's responsibility in relation to studying history and other cultures?

2. What other pogroms have been carried out in history? Choose one. Research that one persecution and share your findings with the group.

3. Vahan hears from his father about "fires of life." List the fires Vahan faces. Discuss how each confrontation with danger or persecution makes him stronger.

4. Identify a fire of life you or someone you know has encountered. Explain the result.

5. On page 5, Vahan says, "Time and destiny were my allies, the twin magicians of my fate." Discuss that statement in reference to Vahan's position and the subsequent events that affect him.

6. After the discussion suggested in activity 4, write a personal essay in which you react either to the original statement or to an opinion from one of the members of the discussion group.

Related Works

1. Arlen, Michael. **Passage to Ararat.** New York: Viking Press, 1982 (reissue edition). 293p. $11.88pa. ASIN 0140063110. **NF** In search-

ing for his Armenian heritage, Arlen discusses the history of the Armenian/Turkish relationship. He graphically describes the holocaust upon which *Forgotten Fire* is based and the factors that caused it to be ignored and forgotten by the rest of the world.

2. Hiçyilmaz, Gaye. **Smiling for Strangers.** New York: Farrar Straus Giroux, 2000. 152p. $16.00. ISBN 0-374-37081-8. Fourteen-year-old Nina must flee Bosnia to seek an uncertain home in England after her family is taken away or killed.

3. **The Inquisition.** Produced by A&E Television Networks, 1999. 100 min. Videocassette. Color. $29.95. AAE-40486. This documentary shows how Ferdinand used heresy as an excuse to attack the Conversos who flourished in the Christian world to which they converted. Their success paralleled that of the Armenians during World War I.

4. Meltzer, Milton. **Witches and Witch-hunts: A History of Persecution.** (See full booktalk in chapter 3.) **NF** In chapter 10, Meltzer explains how history and culture supported Hitler's witch-hunt. The explanation can apply also to the Armenian situation from World War I.

5. Simoen, Jan and John Nieuwenhuizen (trans.). **What About Anna?** New York: Walker, 2001. 254p. $16.95. ISBN 0-8027-8808-4. A young girl who thinks her brother died in the Bosnian war discovers that he has been in hiding after denouncing his father, a major force in the Muslim persecution.

Hughes, Dean. Soldier Boys.
New York: Atheneum Publishers, 2001. 162p. $16.00. ISBN 0-689-81748-7.

Summary/Description

Teenagers Dieter Hedrick, a German, and Spencer Morgan, an American, want to prove their manhood in battle. In alternating chapters, the historical novel traces their military journeys to the Battle of Bastogne. Dieter, the dedicated and decorated member of Hitler's Youth, rejects his family's indifference to the war and denies his responsibility in the disappearance and death of friends. Dieter's patriotic zeal gets him into battle. He is matched with the war-weary, middle-aged Schaefer who tells him Hitler is evil and their battle is futile. Spencer Morgan, a Mormon, delays his promise to be a missionary so he can fight in World War II. Too young to enlist on his own, he pressures his father to sign the enlistment papers, joins the Paratroopers, and dreams about returning as a hero to his hometown and the girl he admires. Dieter is wounded at Bastogne and cries out for his protector, Schaefer. Hearing Dieter's cries and horrified when an American soldier kills a German medic who might have saved Dieter, Spencer dies in an attempted rescue. Dieter, realizing the American soldier wanted to help him, is saved by the men who killed Spencer. Dieter begins to rethink his dedication and decides to examine German propaganda. Spencer, in giving up his own life instead of taking another, completes his original missionary promise and proves his courage.

Booktalk

Spencer Morgan lives in Utah. He is fifteen when the Japanese bomb Pearl Harbor. By the time he is sixteen, he is afraid that if he doesn't sign up soon, he'll miss the war completely. He'll never be able to show people in his Mormon community, especially the beautiful LuAnn, how brave he is.

Dieter Hedrick lives in Germany. Hitler gave him a medal for outstanding leadership in the Hitler Youth. Dieter knows, even though some say he is too young, that he can make a bigger contribution on the front lines than by digging ditches. He can help win the war for Germany.

Both Spencer and Dieter will get their chances for glory soon—at Bastogne in the Battle of Bulge, one of the toughest and bloodiest battles of World War II. Seasoned soldiers fall and die. Gunfire and exploding bombs surround them. On different sides, these *Soldier Boys* might find themselves fighting the same enemy—themselves.

Related Activities

1. Read the paragraph on page 92 of *All Quiet on the Western Front* (Related Work 8) that begins "He is right…" and ends with "we believe in this war." Discuss how this paragraph spoken by a German soldier about World War I applies to *Soldier Boys*.

2. Pages 223 to 233 in *All Quiet on the Western Front* (Related Work 8) describe a soldier's first hand-to-hand kill in battle and his reaction to that kill. Find instances in *Soldier Boys* where Spencer and Dieter react to death. Discuss what each incident and their reaction to it tells about them.

3. For Dieter, Corporal Schaefer is the voice of truth. Dieter rejects that voice, yet Schaefer continues to protect Dieter, and Dieter calls Schaefer's name when wounded. Discuss their relationship and Schaefer's function in the novel.

4. Discuss what other elements of the story would have been different if Schaefer or Spencer had lived.

5. Two poems by Bertolt Brecht, "War Has Been Given a Bad Name" and "To My Countrymen," talk about the German participation in World War I and World War II. Both appear in *War and the Pity of War* (Related Work 7). Read each poem. Discuss the point Brecht makes in each poem. Discuss how each poem relates to *Soldier Boys*.

6. Further research the Battle of Bastogne and the Battle of the Bulge. Share your findings with the group and discuss why these particular confrontations were appropriate for Hughes's purpose.

Related Works

1. Brokaw, Tom. **The Greatest Generation.** New York: Random House, 1998. 412p. $24.95. ISBN 0-375-50202-5. **NF** The World War II experiences include those of several men involved in the Battle of the Bulge.

2. Chan, Gillian. **A Foreign Field.** Toronto, ON: Kids Can Press Ltd., 2002. 192p. $16.95. ISBN 1-55337-349-9. Chan combines narrative, letters, and nightmares to tell the love story of a sixteen-year-old English soldier and a fourteen-year-old Canadian girl who meet when he is sent to Canada to train for the Royal Air Force.

3. Giblin, James Cross. **The Life and Death of Adolf Hitler.** New York: Clarion Books, 2002. 246p. $21.00. ISBN 0-395-90371-8. **NF** Pages 207 to 209 describe Hitler decorating a small boy who subsequently falls asleep.

4. LaMachia, John. **So What Is Patriotism Anyway?** New York: Rosen Publishing Group/Rosen Central, 2000. 48p. (A Student's Guide to American Civics). $17.95. ISBN 0-8239-3098-X. **NF** This definition of patriotism uses Adolph Hitler and his followers as a negative example of patriotism and nationalism.

5. Müller, Melissa. **Anne Frank: The Biography.** Translated by Rita and Robert Kimber. New York: Henry Holt and Company, 1998. 330p. $14.00pa. ISBN 0-8050-5997-0. **NF** This biography, told in the political and social context of Anne Frank's time, explains how a society was led to support the persecution of the Jews. It also explores the irony of war that dictates one person is saved and another destroyed.

6. Osborne, Mary Pope. **My Secret War: The World War II Diary of Madeline Beck.** New York: Scholastic Incorporated, 2000. 192p. (Dear America). $10.95. ISBN 0-590-68715-8. Thirteen-year-old Madeline Beck is an enthusiastic war supporter on the home front until her father, a Navy career officer, is critically wounded.

7. Philip, Neil, ed., and Michael McCurdy (illus.). **War and the Pity of War.** New York: Clarion Books, 1998. 96p. $20.00. ISBN 0-395-

84982-9. (See full booktalk in *Booktalks Plus*, 2001, pages 44 to 46.)
NF In this anthology of war poems, "War Has Been Given a Bad Name" is on page 65 and "To My Countrymen" is on page 70.

8.   Remarque, Erich Maria. **All Quiet on the Western Front.** New York: Fawcett Crest, 1975. 296p. $4.95pa. ISBN 0-449-21394-3. This anti-war story, set in World War I and first published in 1928, is told by a young German soldier pressured to go to war and disillusioned by what he sees. He is killed one month before the Armistice.

9.   Tunnell, Michael O. **Brothers in Valor: A Story of Resistance.** New York: Holiday House, 2001. 260p. $16.95. ISBN 0-8234-1541-4. This historically based novel describes the efforts of a resistance group organized by Mormon teenagers within Germany. It highlights the coercion and persuasion used in the Hitler Youth organizations.

Ung, Loung. First They Killed My Father: A Daughter of Cambodia Remembers.

New York: HarperCollins Publishers, 2000. 239p. $23.00. ISBN 0-06-019332-8. **NF**

Summary/Description

Loung Ung's nonfiction narrative begins when the Khmer Rouge take over her city. She is five years old, and with her six brothers and sisters, enjoys a comfortable middle-class life. After the invasion, the family drives, walks, and rides in transport trucks to country villages and government camps where they suffer beatings, humiliation, and starvation. They try to keep their identities secret and the family together, but over the months and years of occupation, the older children are sent to other work camps, and both parents are executed as threats to the government. When the Vietnamese invade the country, the surviving brothers and sisters reunite and make their way to a refugee camp. The oldest son marries and decides to take Loung with him and his wife to Thailand, and eventually America. Loung visits Cambodia to reunite with family members. She now works as a spokesperson for Campaign for a Landmine-Free World. The resources listed for further information are Campaign for a Landmine-Free World and The Cambodian Genocide Program.

Booktalk

Loung is five years old. Everyone in her Cambodian city admires her beautiful Chinese mother, and she thinks her father must be related to the gods. Her six brothers and sisters share her good life that includes lots of delicious food, beautiful clothes, antique jewelry, a comfortable apartment, and even a television. But this is 1975. The Khmer Rouge invade her city. They drive the people out, burn their homes, declare money useless, and kill anyone who challenges them. The family must run and hide or die. For the next four years, Loung and her family suffer constant hunger, abuse, and fear. They might die if anyone discovers they are educated city people and have Chinese blood. They trust only each other, but even a look or sigh can betray a forbidden thought or feeling. The Khmer Rouge separate Loung from her family and tell her the only path to a new life is through their powerful and righteous plan, but Loung always remembers, even as they offer her food and promise her safety—*First They Killed My Father.*

Related Activities

1. Using the library and the Internet, research the landmine problem in our world today and identify the countries most affected by the problem. Share the information you find with the group.
2. Using your library and the Internet, continue to research the Khmer Rouge regime. Share your findings with the group.
3. Loung's name in Chinese means dragon. Research the meaning of the dragon in the Chinese culture. Discuss how Loung's name proved to be appropriate or inappropriate.
4. The Khmer Rouge regime had "ethnic cleansing" as one of its major goals. Contact The Cambodian Genocide Program for more information about Cambodian ethnic cleansing. Construct a display that will inform others about it.
5. Maurya Simon's poem "Standing Between Two Ideas" appears in page 153 of *The Invisible Ladder* (Related Work 5). After reading the poem, discuss the ideas presented about fate and free will. Then write a paragraph or a poem in which Loung Ung responds to the poem also.

Related Works

1. Budhos, Marina. **Remix: Conversations with Immigrant Teenagers.** New York: Henry Holt and Company, 1999. 145p. ISBN 0-8050-5113-9. **NF** Interviews with teenagers who talk about their past and their lives in the United States make up the book. In the interview "Sorianyi" on pages 44 to 51, a young Cambodian girl born when her mother was running from the Khmer Rouge tells about coming to live with her father in the United States.
2. Davis, Terry. "In the Valley of Elephants." In **On the Edge: Stories at the Brink,** edited by Lois Duncan. New York: Simon & Schuster

Books for Young Readers, 2000. 211p. $17.00. ISBN 0-689-82251-0. In the panic of flight from Communist troops, a Laotian mother accidentally kills her baby. The story is set in 1975 and appears on pages 197 to 209.

3. **Return to the Killing Fields.** Produced by Kurtis Productions and A&E Television Networks, 2000. 50 min. Videocassette. Color. (Investigative Reports). $19.95. AAE-17833. This documentary compares the reign of the Khmer Rouge to the Nazi Holocaust. It explains its roots, development, and fall as well as Cambodia's reluctance to persecute those responsible for it.

4. Meltzer, Milton. **Witches and Witch-hunts: A History of Persecution.** (See full booktalk in chapter 3.) **NF** Although the Cambodian conflict is not mentioned, many of the attitudes that drove the Khmer Rouge and their followers are.

5. Simon, Maurya. "Standing Between Two Ideas." In **The Invisible Ladder: An Anthology of Contemporary American Poems for Young Readers,** edited by Liz Rosenberg. New York: Henry Holt and Company, 1996. 210p. $16.95. ISBN 0-8050-3836-1. **NF** The poem questions how much of what happens to us is part of our fate or subject to our free will.

෴

Osborn, Shane with Malcolm McConnell and adapted for young people by Michael French.
Born to Fly: The Heroic Story of Downed U.S. Navy Pilot Lt. Shane Osborn.
New York: Delacorte/Random House, 2001. 183p. $15.95. ISBN 0-385-72999-5.

Summary/Description

Beginning at the end, the prologue describes how Osborn's routine mission becomes an international incident. The prologue's last sentence, "I was a navy pilot—a role I had been preparing for my entire life," anticipates a narrative that explains how emotional, physical, and mental toughness helped him achieve his career dream and, in an encounter with "one aggressive Chinese pilot," land his plane and face the anger and interrogation of the Chinese government. Although the later chapters of his account use technical and military language, Osborn's positive attitude, high standards, and work ethic are the focus. He copes with his parents' divorce, new schools, academic challenges, blended families, jobs he hates, a life-threatening accident, and some disappointing assignments. He is a team player who meticulously follows military guidelines while respecting his own judgments and everyone else's contributions. The book includes a map of the observation area, pictures of Osborn's life, and a glossary of aviation terms.

Booktalk

What does it take to be a hero? Maybe just doing your best every day. Shane Osborn wanted to become a navy pilot. While other guys were out having a good time, he studied planes, math, politics, and military training. Taking jobs other people didn't want made him tough. Doing them well helped him learn about cooperation and satisfaction. He didn't believe all his hard work, hope, and determination were unusual. They were simply the right things to do.

Then, a few critical minutes on April 1, 2001, prove him right. Eye to eye with a Chinese pilot who wants to push Osborn's crew and plane out of the sky, he suffers a hit. The Chinese pilot goes down. Osborn and his twenty-three crewmembers might have less than an hour to live. Thinking fast and working together, they land the plane. But landing is only the beginning. Faced with intense interrogation and possible disgrace, they begin a journey more dangerous and exciting than they ever imagined— a journey that ends in a hero's homecoming. Doing the job he was given and doing it right turns out to be a flight into history for navy pilot Shane Osborn, a man who believes he was *Born to Fly*.

Related Activities

1. The incident involving Osborn's EP-3E received extensive coverage. Research the coverage of one news source. Discuss the source's reporting and editorial comments in relation to Shane Osborn's perceptions.
2. Many events in Osborn's life could have discouraged him from becoming a navy pilot. Identify these events and how Osborn coped with them. What do his reactions to adversity reveal about his character and attitude?
3. Choose one of Osborn's qualities that you would like to emulate. Explain your reasons with specifics.
4. On page 173, Shane describes the medals awarded to him and fellow crewmembers. Research the meaning and appearance of these medals in relation to other military awards. Share your information with the group through a display or oral presentation.
5. In the novel *Battle Dress* (Related Work 2), the main character successfully completes the West Point Beast. This fictional account that focuses on a female character dealing with simulated problems

might be considered much different from the Shane Osborn account. Discuss the similarities you find between the two and what each work communicates about military life.

Related Works

1. Benson, Peter L., Judy Galbraith, and Pamela Espeland. **What Teens Need to Succeed: Proven Ways to Shape Your Own Future.** Minneapolis, MN: Free Spirit Publishing, 1998. 360p. $14.95. ISBN 1-57542-027-9. Osborn emulates the qualities that Benson, Galbraith, and Espeland describe.
2. Efaw, Amy. **Battle Dress.** (See full booktalk in chapter 2.) Andi Davis discovers that the harsh and demanding West Point initiation program develops a discipline and pride that the pointless abuse she received from her dysfunctional family could not.
3. Menez, Gene. "Scorecard." *Sports Illustrated* (April 23, 2001) 271. **NF** The article discusses the Olympic committee's fear that the United States would exert pressure to keep China from hosting the Olympic games. It cites previous blunders and two previous boycotts.
4. Schindenette, Susan, Maureen Harrington, Kelly Williams, Vickie Bane, and Macon Morehouse. "Born to Fly: The Right Man in the Tight Spot, Navy Pilot Shane Osborn enjoys a hero's welcome for saving his plane and his crew." *People Weekly* (April 30, 2001) 521. **NF** This article presents a personal profile of Osborn.
5. Thompson, Mark. "Plunge and a Tough Choice: Going Nose to Nose in the Sky." *Time* (April 23, 2001) 41. **NF** This description of Osborn's choices and accomplishments includes high praise from former pilots President Bush and Secretary of Defense Rumsfeld.

びわ

Cameron, Sara in conjunction with UNICEF. Out of War: True Stories from the Front Lines of the Children's Movement for Peace in Colombia

New York: Scholastic Press, 2001. 224p. $15.95. ISBN 0-439-29721-4. **NF**

Summary/Description

In *Out of War,* nine teenagers, members of the UNICEF-related Children's Movement for Peace in Colombia, tell about their attempts to seek peace in the Colombian civil conflict. Uprooted and abused by violence, each young adult tells about discovering the peace movement and applying its principles to their personal lives, families, neighborhoods, communities, country, and the world. Ranging from fifteen to nineteen years old, these young men and women, who have inherited a forty-year war, use their own resources to spread the message that violence, revenge, and physical punishment will destroy rather than build unity and cooperation. Some have been asked to share their message with international conferences, but each believes that any hope for peace lies in the hearts of Colombian children who must learn to overcome the violence, hate, and poverty in their own homes and neighborhoods. In the essay "Where Are We Now?," Cameron explains the current status and difficulties of the Children's Movement for Peace. An Author's Note explains Cameron's journey in writing the book. Resources lists Web sites and addresses that will help interested readers learn more about the Movement.

Booktalk

Ask how many people in the group are afraid of violence in their schools, homes, and neighborhoods. Discuss some of the ways they have seen people cope with violence.

In *Out of War*, nine teenagers share their experiences with violence. They all live in Colombia, a country in South America (*show a map of Colombia*) that has suffered a civil conflict for over forty years. Their family members and friends have been shot and killed. Their homes have been destroyed. Most have little or no money. Many of their schools are too dangerous to attend. They are all struggling, not only to survive but also to spread a message of peace. Each speaker is part of the Children's Movement for Peace in Colombia. Some have traveled to foreign countries and spoken to world leaders and Nobel Prize winners. Some are still trying to stop the violence in their own homes. All are winners, not victims, and all are committed to a family, neighborhood, and country in which each person can live peacefully and productively. And their efforts are making a difference. If you share their goals, you should read what they have to say. And if you wish, you can explore more action for peace with the Web sites and addresses Sara Cameron lists at the back of her book. You might even discover you have made some contributions to world peace that began right in your own heart and home.

Related Activities

1. Although the United States is not in a civil war, we are experiencing a great deal of conflict in our schools and communities. Research instances of violence in the United States today and the methods being used to deal with it. You might wish to start with *Kids and Guns* (Related Work 5) and *Gangs: Opposing Viewpoints* (Related Work 3).

2. Contact one of the organizations listed at the end of the book. Ask them for information about peace-making activities and organizations. Compare the information you receive with the information you gathered in activity 1.

3. In "Some Serious Déjà Vu: War Stories" from *Things Get Hectic: Teens Write About the Violence that Surrounds Them* (Related Work 4), the essays talk about violence in the United States that parallels the violence in other countries. Choose one of the essays. Read it and explain how the problems described parallel the situations included in *Out of War.* Discuss what those parallels suggest about violence and violent situations.

4. In *Voices from the Streets* (Related Work 1), the many stories emphasize that positive role models help young people direct their lives. Write a definition of role model. Give an example of a person you would consider a role model. Then discuss how the lack of role models complicates the problem in Colombia.

5. Using your library sources, research the political history of Columbia. Find out as much as possible about the country's government over the past twenty years. Share your information with the group and explain the political issues that complicate the peacekeeping efforts of Columbia's youth.

Related Works

1. Atkin, Beth S. **Voices from the Streets: Young Former Gang Members Tell Their Stories.** Boston, MA: Little, Brown, 1996. 131p. $17.95. ISBN 0-316-5634-0. **NF** Former gang members explain why they became involved in gangs and how they were able to leave them. The necessity of positive role models is heavily emphasized.

2. Carmi, Daniella. **Samir and Yonatan.** New York: Arthur A. Levine Books, 2000. 192p. $15.95. ISBN 0-439-13504-4. Surrounded by the Israeli/Palestinian conflict, two boys find peace by living in a computer world they can control.

3. Egendorf, Laura. **Gangs: Opposing Viewpoints.** San Diego, CA: Greenhaven Press, 2001. 170p. (Opposing Viewpoints Series). $23.00. ISBN 0-7377-0510-8. **NF** People from all walks of life discuss elements that encourage violent behavior.

4. Kay, Philip, Andria Estepa, and Al Desetta. **Things Get Hectic: Teens Write About the Violence That Surrounds Them.** New York: Touchstone Books, 1998. 282p. $13.00. ISBN 0-684-83754-4. **NF** In a series of personal essays, teenagers describe the violence they see and experience in their homes, neighborhoods, and countries.

5. Schwarz, Ted. **Kids and Guns.** New York: Franklin Watts, 1999. 128p. $24.00. ISBN 0-531-11723-5. **NF** After reviewing some of the most recent "kid" shootings, Schwarz gives a history of guns in the United States and maintains that communities refusing to discuss violence and media projecting inaccurate images of violence are the most responsible for it.

Supernatural Forces Intrude

සා

Beagle, Peter S. Tamsin.
New York: ROC, 1999. 275p. $21.95. ISBN 0-451-45763-3.

Summary/Description

This ghostly/coming-of-age novel focuses on nineteen-year-old Jennifer Gluckstein, who is living in the present day, and nineteen-year-old Tamsin Willoughby who died three hundred years ago. Jennifer's mother remarries when Jennifer is thirteen. They move to Dorset, England, and live on a haunted estate managed by her stepfather. Here she discovers boggarts, a pooka, the billy-blind, the ghost cat, Miss Sophia Brown, and the ghost of Tamsin. Tamsin lived on the estate during the Bloody Assizes. She loved Edric the musician, but Lord Chief Justice Jeffreys, the judge of the Assizes, loved her. He arranged for Edric to forever flee a band of ghost riders called the Wild Hunt while the Justice relentlessly pursued Tamsin, even in the grave. Unwittingly, Jennifer has allied herself with the Old Lady of the Elder Tree, who makes Jeffreys the object of the Wild Hunt and allows Edric to unite with Tamsin.

As Jennifer, with the help of her family and friend, tries to figure out how to save Tamsin, she must confront her own hostile feelings toward her mother, father, stepfamily, and peers. Because she is insecure and self-conscious, she fights every person and suggestion until she realizes she can effect change and help others. Jennifer writes her story when she is nineteen. Looking back at her thirteen-year-old self, she sees her mistakes and insecurities and realizes that Tamsin and the spirits helped her rid herself of her own ghosts as much as she helped Tamsin. Some might consider Jennifer's language and actions during her maturing process to be objectionable, but her final perception of herself is instructive and funny.

Booktalk

Jennifer Gluckstein isn't very pretty, popular, or nice. But she has her reasons. Her skin is driving her crazy. She has to make an appointment to see her own father, and now her mother is getting married. Pretty bad. Then she finds out she and her mother will have to move to England so her stepfather can take a new job and his sons can stay in the same school. That's worse. Then she learns that the *new* house is run down, cold, and—well, haunted. Jennifer confronts a new family, a new school, a new country, and the afterlife all at the same time. This world of pookas, boggarts, and billy-blinds is scary, but not as scary or fascinating as the transparent Tamsin who lived three hundred years ago and now wants Jennifer to help her find eternal love.

Related Activities

1. Tamsin calls Roger Willoughby, the first owner of Stourhead Farm, a Prodigious Romantic. Explain what she might mean by this label and how it might apply to the other characters in the novel.
2. Tony explains Monmouth's Rebellion and the Bloody Assizes on pages 88 to 91. Further research this period of history, particularly the notorious Lord Chief Justice Jeffreys, and find additional historical accounts that support the fictional work *Tamsin.*
3. In *Tamsin, Bone Dance* (Related Work 1), *The Other Shepards* (Related Work 2), *Spellfall* (Related Work 4), and *The Taker's Stone* (Related Work 5), the author uses supernatural events to help the main character clarify his or her relationship with parents. Ask five people to read one of the novels and then discuss the author's use of the supernatural in each novel.
4. Jennifer Gluckstein tells her story when she is nineteen. The story happens when she is thirteen. Choose one scene from the novel. Rewrite it from the point of view of thirteen-year-old Jennifer.
5. List all the supernatural and natural characters that enter Jennifer's life. Explain how each changes her.

Related Works

1. Brooks, Martha. **Bone Dance.** (See full booktalk in chapter 1.) A young girl who inherits a piece of land from her father finds her life transformed by the spirits that haunt it.
2. Griffin, Adele. **The Other Shepards.** (See full booktalk in chapter 1.) Two sisters meet the sister who died before they were born, and the encounter frees them from their parents' overwhelming grief.
3. Peck, Richard. "Waiting for Sebastian." In **Dirty Laundry: Stories about Family Secrets,** edited by Lisa Rowe Fraustino. New York: Viking Press, 1998. 181p. $16.99. ISBN 0-670-87911-8. Charlotte, a young girl, commits suicide when her brother's body is brought

home from the war. Her ghost now haunts the room of a guesthouse. The story appears on pages 80 to 87.

4. Roberts, Katherine. **Spellfall.** (See full booktalk in chapter 3.) Natalie Marlins discovers her family is tied to the supernatural and a war between good and evil.

5. Russell, Barbara Timberlake. **The Taker's Stone.** (See full booktalk in chapter 3.) After snatching a red stone, fourteen-year-old Fischer finds himself saving the world from the forces of evil and gaining his father's respect.

ෆ෩

Lubar, David. **Hidden Talents.**

New York: Tom Doherty Associates, 1999. 213p. $16.95. ISBN 0-312-86646-1.

Summary/Description

At age thirteen, Martin Anderson has been expelled from several schools and now is beginning his last chance at Edgeview Alternative School. He insults and alienates his teachers and classmates, infuriates his father, and confuses his mother. Only his sister understands him. When he enters Edgeview, he meets supernatural talents who don't realize their own powers and some violent bullies.

Martin makes friends with the supernaturals. Torchie, Martin's roommate, seems to set fire to anything he touches. Cheater can read minds. Lucky can find anything anyone else has lost. Trash can make objects fly across the room. Flinch can see into the future. When Mr. Briggs, the science teacher, shows his class how to structure experiments, Martin takes the opportunity to confirm his suspicions that his friends are good people who have never learned to control their powers. He persuades them to turn negatives into positives, and they identify Martin's ability to perceive a person's greatest dreams and deepest fears. Combining their unusual talents in a positive way, Martin and his group outsmart and defeat the sneaky Bloodbath bullies who terrorize the weaker boys.

Martin also discovers that the Edgeview staff is at risk. The teachers and administration are transfers or rejects, and the school might close because of finances. When the evaluation team asks to speak to Martin as the sample student, he realizes he can choose to insult the team or manipulate them into loving him. He speaks as truthfully as possible. When he gives his recommendations, the board enacts his reforms. They support the teachers, send the bullies away, and introduce an evaluation process that allows students to return to their regular schools. Martin learns to recognize and use insult, constructive criticism, manipulation, and positive reinforcement. He returns to his own school and family and encourages his friends to do the same.

Booktalk

Martin Anderson is a small kid with a big mouth. When he finds himself living in the dilapidated Edgeview Alternative School, he knows it's his last chance to figure out how to get along. His chances aren't too good. On the first day, he insults all his teachers. He rooms with Torchie, a nice guy who sets fires but says he never carries matches. Lester Bloodbath, the school bully, wants to kill Martin. The principal thinks electric shock would do him some good, and his parents don't seem to want him home. Then Martin notices some things. When objects fly across the room, Trash, accused of throwing them, hasn't touched them. Cheater, accused of cheating, is really very smart, and Lucky, accused of stealing, can find anything that's lost. Are these people criminals or something more than human? Amazing things happen when Martin takes a break from fighting the world and, instead, tries to discover its *Hidden Talents*.

Related Activities

1. Define the word paranormal. Then research one instance of paranormal behavior. Report your findings to the group.
2. Identify a negative quality or power of a person you know. Suggest how that quality or power could be turned into a positive. Repeat the process with a negative quality or power of your own.
3. *Hidden Talents* uses letters, notes, writing assignments, and poems to support the narrative. Write a letter Martin will receive from one of his Edgeview friends in ten years.
4. Choose one of the characters on the staff at Edgeview. Write the final evaluation that person might have written about Martin.
5. On page 5, Martin describes his welcome to Edgeview. Read that description. Discuss the tone it sets. Then describe Edgeview five years later. Explain the tone your description sets and how that description anticipates the changes in the school.

Related Works

1. Ferris, Jean. **Bad.** (See full booktalk in chapter 2.) Living in a girls' rehabilitation unit, sixteen-year-old Dallas Carpenter realizes her behavior will determine how successful her life will be.
2. Galloway, Priscilla. **Snake Dreamer.** (See full booktalk in chapter 2.) A young girl discovers how to control the mysterious powers of the snakes and snake dreams that haunt her.

3.   Packer, Alex J., Pamela Espeland, ed., and Jeff Tolbert (illus.). **How Rude! The Teenagers' Guide to Good Manners, Proper Behavior, and Not Grossing People Out.** (See full booktalk in chapter 2.) **NF** In an entertaining manner, Packer explains how to handle life situations—whether dealing with insults or a friend's pressure to take drugs.
4.   Rowling, J.K. **Harry Potter and the Sorcerer's Stone.** New York: Arthur A. Levine Books, 1998. 341p. $17.95. ISBN 0 439-06486-4. Until Harry discovers his wizard talents and finds a school to help him direct them, he lives a sad life with relatives who don't want him.
5.   Thesman, Jean. **The Other Ones.** (See full booktalk in chapter 3.) A young girl discovers she has supernatural powers that can help her friends, but also realizes that accepting them will mean she will be considered odd or different.

ʊʐ

Heneghan, James. The Grave.
New York: Farrar Straus Giroux/Frances Foster Books, 2000. 245p. $17.00.
ISBN 0-374-32765-3.

Summary/Description

Tom Mullen was abandoned in a toy department when he was a baby. At thirteen and three quarters, he has lived in several Liverpool foster homes. He has roomed with and protected the intellectually challenged Brian for three years in an abusive foster situation. A mass grave recently uncovered on the school ground fascinates Tom. Exploring at night, he falls into the grave and time-travels from 1974 Liverpool to 1847 Ireland where he saves Tully Monaghan, his double, from drowning. While in Ireland, Tom grows close to the Monaghan family. He helps them fight their landlord, secure food during the potato famine, and nurse their sick. Tom returns to 1974 only because of football and his coaches, especially the fatherly Coach Greensleeves. Eventually Tom's life with the Monaghans takes him to the mass grave in Tom's schoolyard, the grave that started his journey. Tom realizes he has traveled full circle, that he will return to 1974 to care for Brian, and that he will change his name to Monaghan. As he leaves, Hannah gives him the Claddagh ring Tully carved for her, a match to the ring he carved for their mother. When Tom explains his travel to his football coach, the coach shows him the matching Claddagh ring. Greensleeves is the name of his landscaping business, but his real name is Monaghan. The coach is Tom's father, who reveals that Tom, then named Jason, was kidnapped. Coach Monaghan and his wife want Tom and Brian to live with them, and through *The Grave*, Tom has found his life.

The language is sometimes strong, but quite appropriate. An Author's Note at the end of the novel explains the factual base for the story.

Booktalk

By 1974, Tom Mullen has lived in foster homes all over Liverpool, but his favorite home is a grave that takes him to Ireland, 1847. In this time and country he has few clothes and little food, but he does have a family, the Monaghans. Beaten down by high taxes and the potato famine, they need Tom to fight for them, even steal for them. But Tully Monaghan doesn't feel so good about this stranger who breathes the very life back into him, fights with the moves of a circus performer, and fastens clothes with a magical fastener called a zipper. This Tom, who could pass for Tully's twin, might be a sheeog, a "grinning goblin," a visitor from *The Grave* that has come to take Tully's mind, life, and maybe his very soul.

Tom thinks being abandoned by his mother when he was a baby, being abused in foster homes, and losing everyone he has ever loved have started working on his mind. Who are these people he has never met but wants to join? Why can he get along with them when he fights with everyone else? Tom finds the answers and his life in *The Grave*.

Related Activities

1. On page 132, Hannah explains the symbolism of the Claddagh ring. Discuss how the novel develops each theme the ring represents.
2. Discuss the significance of Mr. Feinberg's song, "I Get Along Without You Very Well."
3. Research the Irish potato famine of 1847 that is used as a backdrop for the novel. Note the reasons for it and how it reduced the population by death and emigration.
4. Research Irish mythology. Share with the group one story about the spirits, fairies, and leprechauns that would have captured people's imaginations at that time.
5. Irony and coincidence seem to dominate the book. Find examples of each, and discuss how they strengthen or weaken the story.

Related Works

1. Baptiste, Angi. "How I Graduated." In **The Struggle to Be Strong**, edited by Al Desetta and Sybil Wolin. Minneapolis, MN: Free Spirit, 2000. 179p. $14.95. ISBN 1-57542-079-1. **NF** The speaker explains how keeping a positive attitude helped her get along in a foster

home. Her interview in this collection of survival stories appears on pages 106 to 109.

2. Bennett, Cherie and Jeff Gottesfeld. **Anne Frank and Me.** (See full booktalk in chapter 3.) An affluent schoolgirl time-travels as a Jew to 1942 France and discovers she is part of history.

3. Levitin, Sonia. **The Cure.** New York: Harcourt Brace and Company, 1999. 184p. $16.00. ISBN 0-15-201827-1. When a citizen of a futuristic utopia time-travels as a Jew to Germany at the time of the Black Death, he finds his life purpose.

4. McCaughrean, Geraldine. **The Stones Are Hatching.** New York: HarperCollins Publishers, 1999. 230p. $15.95. ISBN 0-06-028765-9. Set after World War I, the story, steeped in Irish mythology, tells the story of a young man's battle against evil and his resulting reunion with his father.

5. Wilde, Lady. "The Famine Year." In **The Penguin Book of Irish Verse**, 2nd ed, edited by Brendan Kennelly. London: Penguin Books, 1988. 470p. $6.95. ISBN 0-14-058526-5. **NF** The poem describes the overwhelming suffering and death that resulted in men deserting their families and the necessity of mass graves. It appears on pages 232 to 234.

Griffin, Adele. **The Other Shepards.**

New York: Hyperion Books for Children, 1998. 218p. $14.95. ISBN 0-7868-0423-8.

Summary/Description

Eleven-year-old Geneva and thirteen-year-old Holland Shepard live in the shadow of two brothers and a sister who were killed in an automobile accident before Geneva and Holland were born. These angels shape the girls' identities. Bad dreams and groundless fears plague Geneva. Rituals help Holland control her own life. When Annie appears, their lives change. Annie is hired to paint designs on the kitchen walls. She allows the girls to help, listens to their stories about the death of their siblings without shock, introduces them to new adventures, and encourages them to take risks. These risks include inviting Holland's new boyfriend to the house. When Mrs. Shepard comes home and discovers the boyfriend kissing Holland in Holland's bedroom, mother and daughter clash. Holland begins to challenge the memory of the angel siblings.

Finally, Holland and Geneva decide to take a secret trip to Saint Germaine, the site of the accident. The Shepards rent their cottage to

the Hubbards, longtime family friends who were like second parents to
the other Shepard children. Annie accompanies them on the trip and
then disappears just before the Hubbards arrive. As the Hubbards welcome and entertain them, the girls find the joy and love they wished for
in their own parents.

When Geneva and Holland return home, they find that their parents
have been discussing Annie with their psychiatrist. The parents believe
she was an imaginary friend who appeared as a result of the girls' unhap-
piness. The girls believe she was Elizabeth, the sister who died and returned to share with them her own love of life. She has shown them how
to move on.

Booktalk

Mr. and Mrs. Shepard have six children. Geneva and Holland live at
home. Brett has a wife and a new baby. The other three, Kevin, John, and
Elizabeth, are dead, killed in a single accident before Geneva and Holland were born. The dead Shepards, *The Other Shepards,* control the
house. They were the perfect children, nothing like the problem-filled
Geneva and Holland. *The Other Shepards,* not Geneva and Holland,
were the children their parents hugged and called nicknames. But finally
Geneva and Holland meet Annie, one person who finds them more interesting than the other Shepards' accident. She's fun, mysterious—even
dangerous. Who is she? Why is she there? And will the Shepards ever be
the same?

Related Activities

1. Discuss the following question: Is Annie an imaginary friend or the
    angel sister Elizabeth? List specifics from the text that support your
    answer.
2. How do Geneva and Holland try to get control of their lives? Which
    of their techniques are most successful?
3. Read the paragraph at the bottom of page 126 that begins "The prob-
    lem with living…" and ends on page 127 with "our own unhaloed
    heads." Restate the paragraph in your own words. Then write a para-
    graph in which you react to what Holland has said and the compar-
    isons she has chosen to express her ideas.
4. On pages 148 and 149, Holland talks about her parents and life in a
    "haunted" house. What does she reveal about her parents, herself,
    and everyone's difficulty in relating to death, especially an untimely
    one? Continue to research the process of grieving after loss or death.
    Apply your information to the characters in the novel and share your
    analysis with the group.

5. Read the paragraph on page 213 that begins "Being older… ." What does the speaker reveal about herself and her relationship with her parents?
6. After reading *The Heavenly Village* (Related Work 5), write a chapter that describes Elizabeth/Annie's life there.
7. Both *Signs and Wonders* (Related Work 1) and *The Other Shepards* use imaginary friends. How does the friend in each work aid the novel's purpose?

Related Works

1. Collins, Pat Lowery. **Signs and Wonders.** New York: Houghton Mifflin Company, 1999. 176p. $15.00. ISBN 0-395-97119-5. Fourteen-year-old Taswell writes her most confidential thoughts to Pim, her imaginary friend, until her new stepmother invites her to join their family in a real way.
2. Giddens, Sandra and Owen Giddens. **Coping with Grieving and Loss.** New York: The Rosen Publishing Group, 2000. 122p. (Coping). $17.95. ISBN 0-8239-2894-2. **NF** The book focuses on loss, grieving, and mourning.
3. McGlinn, Jeanne M. **Ann Rinaldi: Historian & Storyteller.** Lanham, MD: The Scarecrow Press, 2000. 94p. (Scarecrow Studies in Young Adult Literature, No. 2). $29.50. ISBN 0-8108-3678-5. **NF** In "Emerging as a Whole Person" on pages 77 to 79 within this analysis of Rinaldi's work, McGlinn points out that Anne Brown must stop trying to win her father's approval if she is to become an adult. As in *The Other Shepards*, the conflict in the parent/child relationship centers on the death of a sibling.
4. Rinaldi, Ann. **Mine Eyes Have Seen.** New York: Scholastic Press, 1998. 275p. $16.95. ISBN 0-590-54318-0. (See full booktalk in *Booktalks Plus*, 2000, pages 243 to 245.) As Annie Brown acts as a lookout for her father John Brown, she also works out the relationship with her father that is influenced by the death of her younger sister.
5. Rylant, Cynthia. **The Heavenly Village.** New York: The Blue Sky Press, 1999. 95p. $15.95. ISBN 0-439-04096-5. (See full booktalk in *Booktalks Plus*, 2001, pages 52 to 54.) This small book describes a village made up of people who have died unexpectedly and still have business to complete on earth.
6. Wong, Janet S. "OK." In **Behind the Wheel: Poems About Driving.** New York: Simon & Schuster/Margaret K. McElderry Books, 1999. 44p. $15.00. ISBN 0-689-82531-5. **NF** "OK" addresses the problem that no one wants to be preached to, but when behind the wheel, each person has the power to kill someone. The poem appears on page 26.

Ćʃʔʒ

Brooks, Martha. Bone Dance.

New York: Laurel-Leaf Books, 1997. 179p. $4.50pa. ISBN 0-440-22791-7.

Summary/Description

Alexandra Marie Sinclair lives in the city. Lonny LaFreniére lives in rural Manitoba. Alexandra lost her grandfather and father. Lonny lost his biological mother and father. Visions haunt both of them. Suddenly they meet through a piece of land. Alexandra's father, Earl McKay, bought a piece of land from Lonny's stepfather. He committed himself to building a cabin on it and then leaving it and $17,000 to his daughter Alex, essentially $1,000 for every year of her life. The land contains Medicine Bluff, an Indian burial ground. When Lonny is eleven, he and his friend Robert Lang dig up bones in the burial ground. Even though his parents tell him to simply put them back, he continues to dig and hide them. Lonny's mother dies two days later, and the spirits of the mound and the guilt haunt him. Alex and Lonny meet when Alex comes to see her inheritance. Closure for both begins when Lenny gives Alex a letter from her dead father. They share the strange dreams and visions each has experienced, all related to the land. A vision transformed the life of Alex's father, also. Final closure comes when they scatter the ashes of Alex's father over the land.

Booktalk

As an introduction to the booktalk, ask the group the following questions and briefly discuss their answers. What do dreams mean? Is it possible to learn from dreams? Do we control them or do spirits from the other side control them?

Seventeen-year-old Alex Sinclair is having dreams and visions she can't explain or share. So is Lonny LaFreniére. They've never even met. How can their experiences be so similar? When Alex inherits the land that haunts them, they find out. Suddenly death controls life as the *Bone Dance* rhythms draw them into each other's worlds as well as the spirit world. Joy, regret, mystery, anger, and love all sing in their lives now. They must listen carefully to each song and each other. Then they may sing new songs and dance new dances. Gifts from the dead may be the best and most frightening gifts of their lives.

Related Activities

1. Read Earl McCay's letter to Alex (pages 146 to 150). Discuss what the letter reveals about McCay. Discuss how it ties to other elements of the novel.

2. Choose a friend or family member you have not seen for a while. Write a letter that explains how you feel about them and how they fit into your life.

3. Read "Land Cannot Be Sold," "Land Is More Valuable Than Money," and "The True Teacher" from *In a Sacred Manner I Live: Native American Wisdom* (Related Work 5). Discuss what each passage reveals about the speaker's perception of the land.

4. Read either "Behold this Day" on p. 16 of *In a Sacred Manner I Live: Native American Wisdom* (Related Work 5) or chapter 3, "The Great Vision," in *Black Elk Speaks* (Related Work 3). Discuss Black Elk's vision of what the good or right world should be.

5. In chapters 12 and 13 of Part One and in chapter 2 of Part Two of *Bone Dance*, dreams are central. Reread the dreams and explain how they influence each character's perception.

6. Discuss how the perceptions in activities 3 and 4 relate to the mystical power of land and nature in *Bone Dance* and the character perceptions discussed in activity 5.

7. Further research the spiritual beliefs of Native Americans. You might wish to start by reading *In a Sacred Manner I Live: Native American Wisdom* (Related Work 5) and *The Great Mystery: Myths of Native America* (Related Work 4).

Related Works

1. McDonald, Joyce. **Swallowing Stones.** (See full booktalk in chapter 2.) The Ghost Tree, inhabited by the spirit of the Lenape, brings together a boy who accidentally killed a man and the victim's daughter.

2. Mikaelsen, Ben. **Touching Spirit Bear.** (See full booktalk in chapter 2.) A juvenile delinquent discovers answers to his anger in the rhythms of nature and Indian beliefs.

3. Neihardt, John G. and Standing Bear (illus.). **Black Elk Speaks: Being the Life Story of a Holy Man of the Oglala Sioux.** Lincoln, NE: University of Nebraska Press, 1979. 299p. $15.89. ISBN 0-8032-3301-9. **NF** Black Elk explains his life in relation to the visions he was given to interpret. The book was originally published in 1932.

4. Philip, Neil. **The Great Mystery: Myths of Native America.** (See full booktalk in chapter 2.) **NF** In this volume Philip explains the common motifs of Native American beliefs and then examines the spiritual beliefs of specific tribes.

5. Philip, Neil. **In a Sacred Manner I Live.** (See full booktalk in chapter 1.) **NF** The passages "Land Cannot Be Sold," "Land Is More Valuable Than Money," and "The True Teacher" address the importance of land and people's relationship to it.

6. Vanasse, Deb. **Out of the Wilderness.** New York: Clarion Books, 1999. 165p. $15.00. ISBN 0-395-91421-3. Fifteen-year-old Josh Harris lives with his father and older half-brother, Nathan, in the Alaskan wilderness. Nathan has withdrawn farther and farther from civilization in his worship of nature. Josh eventually saves Nathan from an attacking mother bear but decides that civilization rather than Nathan's romantic vision of nature promises a happier and healthier future.

Achievement:
We Test Coping Skills

Trying to Meet Expectations

Dessen, Sarah. **Dreamland.**

New York: Viking Press, 2000. 250p. $15.99. ISBN 0-670-89122-3.

Summary/Description

Caitlin O'Koren believes she cannot take the place of her perfect sister who rebelled and ran away. Caitlin isn't as pretty, smart, or popular. When Caitlin becomes a cheerleader to please her mother, she knows she isn't being true to herself. To assert her identity, she begins dating Rogerson Biscoe, a mysterious, rebellious, rich, abused, abusive, possessive, and brilliant young man who pulls her away from her studies, friends, and family and into a world of aimless roaming, lying, and drugs. When her parents and friends finally see her bruises and figure out why she is chronically half-asleep and unfocused, they realize how they failed to protect and help her. Rogerson is arrested, and Caitlin enters a recovery center where she learns to value herself as a person and understand how her sister Cassandra and Rogerson influenced her life.

Booktalk

Caitlin O'Koren isn't as pretty, as smart, or as perfect as her older sister. Even though she makes cheerleader, she knows she really doesn't belong in that group. She isn't the preppy her parents want, and she isn't the free spirit her friends want. Then along comes Rogerson Biscoe, and she finds her niche—Rogerson's girlfriend. She is in her *Dreamland.* But slowly her love dreams become nightmares, and Caitlin might not be able to wake up—ever.

Related Activities

1. Read "The Song of J. Alfred Prufrock" by T.S. Eliot (Related Work 2). Explain how the poem is central to the novel.
2. Caitlin's interest in photography leads her to examine the faces of the portraits she takes and her assumptions about what she sees. Discuss how photography helps Caitlin figure out her life. In the discussion, consider the paragraph beginning on page 184 with "My favorite picture…" and ending on page 185 with "none of them were looking that closely at me."
3. Define the term unreliable narrator. How reliable a narrator is Caitlin?
4. Further research relationship violence. You might wish to start by reading *Everything You Need to Know About Relationship Violence* (Related Work 6). After completing your research, make up a list of questions you still have about relationship violence. Invite an abuse counselor to talk to your group. Ask the counselor the questions you have composed.
5. In *Annie's Baby: The Diary of Anonymous, A Pregnant Teenager* (Related Work 5), Annie submits to an abusive relationship. Compare Annie and Caitlin. Discuss how two different girls in very different situations find themselves with similar problems.

Related Works

1. Burgess, Melvin. **Smack.** New York: Henry Holt and Company, 1996. 327p. $16.95. ISBN 0-8050-5801-X. Abused and aimless teenagers form their own family and slowly deteriorate in the world of drugs.
2. Eliot, T.S. "The Love Song of J. Alfred Prufrock." In **The Classic Hundred Poems: All-Time Favorites, 2nd ed.,** edited by William Harmon. New York: Columbia University Press, 1998. 360p. $19.95. ISBN 0-231-11259-9. **NF** Prufrock fears his acceptance and is overwhelmed and drowned by his fears and the pressures around him. Eliot's background, the poem, and its discussion appear on pages 232 to 238.
3. Myers, Walter Dean. **145th Street.** (See full booktalk in chapter 2.) In "A Story in Three Parts" on pages 117 to 138, a young drug addict must decide to save himself or die.

4. O'Dell, Katie. "Ringing True: The Authentic Voice of Sarah Dessen." *VOYA*. (June 2002) 100–102. **NF** The author discusses why she wrote *Dreamland*. A book discussion guide appears on page 102.
5. Sparks, Beatrice, ed. **Annie's Baby: The Diary of Anonymous, A Pregnant Teenager.** New York: Avon Books, 1998. 245p. $4.50pa. ISBN 0-380-79141-2. Fourteen-year-old Annie submits to an abusive relationship with a high school football star so she will be popular.
6. White, Katherine. **Everything You Need to Know About Relationship Violence.** New York: Rosen Publishing Group, 2001. 64p. (The Need to Know Library). $17.95. ISBN 0-8239-3398-9. **NF** White explains how to identify relationship violence and what to do about it.
7. Williams-Garcia, Rita. "About Russell." In **Dirty Laundry: Stories About Family Secrets,** edited by Lisa Rowe Fraustino. New York: Viking Press, 1998. 181p. $16.99. ISBN 0-670-87911-8. The narrator's older brother, who is an enthusiastic learner, gradually slips into poverty and mental illness, but his family can't help him.

Anderson, Laurie Halse. Speak.

New York: Farrar Straus Giroux, 1999. 198p. $16.00. ISBN 0-374-37152-0.

Summary/Description

In the August before her ninth grade year, Melinda Sordino goes to a party that includes high school seniors and drinking. Andy Evans, a football player, rapes her. When she calls 911, the police bust the party but do not discover the rape. Melinda becomes a social leper. She hides in the janitor's closet rather than attend class. Her grades drop. Although her parents, principal, and guidance counselor pressure her to talk about her poor performance, she will not *Speak*.

Melinda's recovery centers on a teacher and two classmates. Mr. Freeman, her art teacher, assigns each student an image to develop in different styles. Melinda's image is a tree. Her interpretations bring her closer to a former friend, Ivy, who struggles with a clown image. Ivy encourages Melinda to trust her talent and assures her that Andy Evans is a predator. Melinda's lab partner, David Petrakis, helps Melinda express herself when he confronts their bullying and bigoted social studies teacher. Melinda, strengthened by the support, tells her ex-best friend Rachel, who is now dating Evans, about the rape. When Andy becomes too aggressive at the prom, Rachel realizes Melinda is telling the truth and walks off the floor. Andy is humiliated. On the last day of school, he tracks down Melinda in the janitor's closet, beats her up, and tries to rape her again. Melinda fights, screams, and is rescued and vindicated. She finally completes a tree image that expresses her feelings and tells her story to Mr. Freeman.

Booktalk

Read "The First Ten Lies They Tell You in High School" on pages 5 and 6 and "Ten More Lies They Tell You in High School" on page 148. Ask how many people agree with the list.

Melinda Sordino's report card might be full of Ds and Fs, but her lists show she has learned a lot about high school. She can also identify all the groups, such as the "Jocks," "The Big Hair Chix," and the "Shredders." And she knows the groups really boil down to two groups: the predators and the prey. Right now she is the prey, and the predators are doing some heavy hunting. She tries to hide, even from herself, but neither she nor her friends can forget that drinking party last summer, and her life is spinning out of control. Nothing will go away, and nothing will get better until Melinda decides to *Speak*.

Related Activities

1. In "Code Breaking" on pages 100 to 102, Melinda describes a discussion about symbolism in *The Scarlet Letter* (Related Work 3). Discuss the significance that *The Scarlet Letter* and the class discussions hold for Melinda. Identify the symbolism and imagery Laurie Halse Anderson uses in *Speak*. You might start by discussing the importance of the seeds, the tree, and the frog.
2. Both *Heroes* (Related Work 2) and *Speak* center on a hidden rape committed by a popular and handsome man. Discuss the significance of the rape in each novel.
3. On page 33, in the paragraph beginning "The musical would be easy…," Melinda describes how she uses nonverbal behavior to communicate. After reading the paragraph, write a paragraph about your own or a friend's nonverbal behavior. Using your library's resources, continue to research nonverbal behavior and its importance in communication. Explain in an essay or presentation how that information affects your own communication.
4. Discuss the many symbols Merryweather High uses to identify itself during Melinda's school year. Discuss what these changes demonstrate about the power and importance of symbols and images. Then relate your conclusions to Anderson's use of the tree.

5. Anderson, in an interview for *VOYA* (Related Work 4), states that Melinda, the main character from *Speak,* is an unreliable narrator and then explains that, as an author, Anderson considers every first-person speaker to be an unreliable narrator. After reading *Speak,* agree or disagree with Anderson's assessment of Melinda.

Related Works

1. Bode, Janet. **Voices of Rape.** New York: Franklin Watts, 1998. rev. ed. 160p. $25.00. ISBN 0-531-11518-6. **NF** The book discusses several rape situations and several points of view about rape. Chapter 7 expresses the views of a serial rapist.
2. Cormier, Robert. **Heroes.** (See full booktalk in chapter 2.) Francis Joseph Cassavant joins the service and tries to kill himself after he fails to prevent the rape of his friend. Finally he decides to confront the rapist, a former personal hero.
3. Hawthorne, Nathaniel. **The Scarlet Letter.** Philadelphia, PA: Courage Books/Running Press, 1991. 201p. (Courage Classics). $4.98. ISBN 1-561-38036-9. The story explains the guilt and double standard involved in an adulterous affair between a young wife and her minister. The first edition was published in 1850.
4. Hill, Christine M. "Laurie Halse Anderson Speaks: An Interview." *VOYA.* (December 2000) 325–327. **NF** Laurie Anderson explains how she began writing young-adult fiction, how she developed *Speak,* and how the *Speak* writing process differed from the writing process of *Fever, 1793.* She also discusses Melinda as an unreliable narrator.
5. Holmes, Stewart W. "Perceptions and Descriptions." In **Classroom Exercises in General Semantics, 2nd ed.,** edited by Mary S. Morain. Concord, CA: International Society for General Semantics, 1996. 184p. $18.00pa. ISBN 0-918970-43-1. **NF** The exercise combines the problems of expression and communication with art, a central technique in *Speak.* The exercise would be interesting to use with *Speak.*
6. Sparks, Beatrice. **Annie's Baby: The Diary of Anonymous, A Pregnant Teenager.** New York: Avon Books, 1998. 245p. $4.50pa. ISBN 0-380-79141-2. Annie's abusive relationship with Danny, a star football player, leads to rape and motherhood at fourteen.

ᎯᏋᎯᎵ

Karr, Kathleen. **The Great Turkey Walk.**
New York: Sunburst, 2000, 197p. $4.95pa. ISBN 0-374-42798-4.

Summary/Description

In 1860, fifteen-year-old Simon Green, who failed third grade four times, lives with an aunt, uncle, and cousins who wish he would go away. Miss Rogers, his teacher, suggests he should leave school and "spread his wings." With Miss Rogers's money, he buys one thousand turkeys to walk across country to Denver and sell. He hires an alcoholic mule skinner, Bidwell Peece, and Peece's dog Emmett to help him. On their way, they acquire Jabeth Ballou, a runaway slave, and Elizabeth Hardwick, with whom Simon falls in love. Simon's adventures include moving the turkeys across rivers and negotiating with Indians who are more educated than most white men he has known. His greatest challenge comes when he meets his father. Samson Green deserted Simon when Simon was a baby and now wants Simon's turkeys. Simon, Jabeth, Bidwell, and the Indians foil Samson's plan and save the turkeys. Because Simon bought the turkeys for twenty-five cents each and sells them for six dollars apiece in Denver, he pays all his bills and realizes a handsome profit. Bidwell, Jabeth, and Elizabeth are so close to Simon and each other that they use their shares from the turkey sales for Simon's next venture, a turkey farm.

Booktalk

The year is 1860. Simon Green has failed third grade three times. Everybody thinks Simon is pretty simple. He is pretty lonesome too. His mother died. His father left him. His aunt, uncle, and greedy cousins don't want him around. This life wouldn't look very promising to most people, but Simon figures out, because his Aunt Maybelle calls him *"peabrained,"* that he probably fits in with birds better than with people. Miss Rogers, his teacher, suggests he should leave school and "spread his wings," so Simon decides to buy some turkeys, a thousand of them, for twenty-five cents each. He'll drive them to Denver and sell them for five dollars each. Miss Rogers thinks it's such a good plan that she invests her life savings in Simon's turkeys. Suddenly Simon has both turkeys and people ready to do whatever Simon says, and he starts out on *The Great Turkey Walk* that will change his life and lots of other lives along the way.

Related Activities

1. In *The Great Turkey Walk, Sunshine Rider: The First Vegetarian Western* (Related Work 1) and *Clem's Chances* (Related Work 4), young men experience a Western adventure that proves their strengths and forces them to face fathers who have left them. Discuss how each author uses these elements to accomplish the novel's purpose.

2. In this story, Miss Rogers is a very minor character with an over-whelming impact. Explain the role she plays in both failing Simon and investing her life savings in his venture.

3. All the characters Simon encounters have disabilities or disadvantages. List the disability or disadvantage each has. Then list the strengths of each character. Discuss what might be Karr's purpose in bringing these people together.

4. Simon's father, Samson, is a villain in the tradition of the Duke and the Dauphin in Mark Twain's *Huckleberry Finn* (Related Work 5). After reading both *Huckleberry Finn* and *The Great Turkey Walk*, compare how the main characters deal with these dishonest adults.

5. Simon is the simple classic character who proves to be wise. Samson is the physically strong character whose moral character makes him weak. Discuss how and why Karr makes Simon's confrontation with Samson a major part of the novel.

6. In both *The Great Turkey Walk* and *The Boxer* (Related Work 3), Kathleen Karr includes a father who has deserted his family and then attempts to take advantage of his own son's success. Compare the father figures in each novel and what each contributes to the novel's purpose.

7. Both *The Great Turkey Walk* and *Stick and Whittle* (Related Work 2) center on good people who help each other. Discuss what each of these humorous books has to say about trust and friendship.

8. Continue to research the habits of turkeys. Explain how Karr based her story on turkey facts. Present any additional information you find about turkeys that could have complicated Simon's journey. Write another scene for the book that includes those complications.

Related Works

1. Hardman, Ric Lynden. **Sunshine Rider: The First Vegetarian Western.** New York: Laurel-Leaf Books, 1998. 343p. $4.99pa. ISBN 0-440-22812-3. A comic cattalo named Roselle that Wylie Jackson promises to deliver for his friend and an array of colorful human characters force Wylie into manhood when he signs up for a cattle drive with a man whom he doesn't know is his father.

2. Hite, Sid. **Stick and Whittle.** New York: Scholastic Press, 2000. 208p. $16.95. ISBN 0-439-09828-9. This humorous western adventure set in 1872 lets the least likely heroes save the day, get the girls, bag the money, and build a true friendship.

3. Karr, Kathleen. **The Boxer.** (See full booktalk in chapter 2.) When John Woods becomes a successful fighter—as Johnny "the Chopper" Woods—his father, who deserted the family, returns to share in the wealth.

4. Levitin, Sonia. **Clem's Chances.** (See full booktalk in chapter 1.)
    After his mother dies, Clem heads west to find the father who left to
    search for gold. His journey matures him and proves to him that his
    father is selfish and exploitive.
5. Twain, Mark. **Adventures of Huckleberry Finn.** New York: Ran-
    dom House, 1996. 418p. $25.00. ISBN 0-679-44889-6. Like Simon,
    Huckleberry must decide whom he can trust. Huckleberry Finn's
    coming-of-age story was originally published in a different form in
    1885 by Charles L. Webster and Company.

ℭℨℕℨ

Mikaelsen, Ben. Touching Spirit Bear.
New York: HarperCollins Publishers, 2001. 241p. $15.95. ISBN 0-380-97744-3.

Summary/Description

Fifteen-year-old Cole Mathews faces jail time for brutally beating a
fourteen-year-old schoolmate who informed on him to the police.
With a long history of trouble, Cole believes he can continue to beat the
system. This time the charges are serious, but his parole officer, a Tlingit
Indian, offers him a Circle of Justice alternative common in the officer's
native culture. Cole will live on an isolated Alaskan island for a year. A
Tlingit elder will monitor him, but Cole will be responsible for his food,
shelter, and maintenance. Thinking he can trick the system again, Cole
burns the cabin and supplies given to him and tries to swim away from
the island. He cannot escape; when he encounters a spirit bear, a large
white bear that usually does not appear on these islands, he attacks it.
The bear mauls him. Knowing he is close to death, Cole starts to rethink
his life and is rescued by the Tlingit elder just in time.

Six months later, Cole returns to the island even though his Keepers'
Circle, made up of the people who determine his sentence, doubt his quick
conversion. The Tlingits stay with him on the island, requiring him to rebuild the cabin himself and establish a specific daily routine. Eventually
Cole realizes his own healing is tied to his victim's. He asks his schoolmate to
come to the island, where they begin the road to peace and understanding.

Booktalk

*Ask students if they feel jail time will reform a criminal or make him
worse. Ask what alternatives to jail time they might suggest.*

After almost killing a schoolmate in a brutal beating, Cole Mathews
decides he will accept an alternative sentence over jail. His parole officer,
a Tlingit Indian, thinks Cole might benefit more from living alone on a

remote Alaskan island for a year than sitting in jail. Actually, Cole plans to accept the alternative sentence and then get out of it. At fifteen, he has manipulated the fools in the system for years. Islands don't have bars or guards; escape will be a snap. But Mother Nature proves to be tougher than any parole officer, judge, or prison guard as she hands back, with a vengeance, anything Cole tries to dish out. A mysterious white bear seems to be her mighty messenger, and Cole discovers that *Touching Spirit Bear* leads him to the most difficult sentence of all.

Related Activities

1. Using your library's resources, research alternative sentencing programs. Include Circle of Justice in your research. Choose one of these programs to explain to the group.
2. Garvey and Edwin use several demonstrations and illustrations to explain principles of living to Cole. The cake, the walk on the line, the stick, the hot dog, the rock, and the pool all teach an aspect of being human. Review each demonstration. Explain which holds the most significance for you and why.
3. In the Keepers' Circle, holding a feather gives a person the right to speak without interruption. In your next discussion, try that same system. Discuss your feelings about the process and the result.
4. Edwin and Garvey give Cole a second chance but also exercise a great deal of tough love. List the things they do to teach Cole to be a responsible human being.
5. Compare Brian of *Hatchet* (Related Work 2) by Gary Paulsen with Cole of *Touching Spirit Bear.* Each character has some of the same experiences in and out of the wilderness. Why do their reactions bring different results?
6. *Hatchet* (Related Work 2) has three sequels. Describe the sequel or sequels for *Touching Spirit Bear* that you would like to read. Send your suggestions to Ben Mikaelsen, care of HarperCollins Publishers.

Related Works

1. Myers, Walter Dean. **Monster.** (See full booktalk in chapter 1.) In this story of a young man's trial, the accused—labeled a monster by the prosecuting attorney—writes a movie script in which he explores how the term might apply to him.
2. Paulsen, Gary. **Hatchet.** New York: Puffin Books, 1987. 195p. $4.95pa. ISBN 0-14-032724-X. In this first book in the series, a young man confronts and respects nature rather than defying it. See full booktalk of *Brian's Return*, the final sequel, in chapter 1.

3. Philip, Neil. **The Great Mystery: Myths of Native America.** (See full booktalk in chapter 2.) **NF** Philip explains the stories of each region and discusses how they overlap. In the chapter titled "The Arctic," Philip explains that the Native Americans of that region believe the bear was created to teach man fear.

4. Schmidt, Thomas and Jeremy Schmidt. **The Saga of Lewis and Clark: Into the Uncharted West.** (See full booktalk in chapter 4.) **NF** The authors describe the expedition's encounter with grizzly bears, an animal respected and feared by the Indians.

5. Vanasse, Deb. **Out of the Wilderness.** New York: Clarion Books, 1999. 165p. $15.00. ISBN 0-395-91421-3. This story about two brothers who live in the wilderness is framed by two bear encounters. The first separates the brothers because the younger tries to shoot a charging bear. The second shows that the older brother's dedication to nature has grown into a mental illness that will kill him.

ᘓᘔ

Dessen, Sarah. Keeping the Moon.
New York: Viking Press, 1999. 228p. $15.99. ISBN 0-670-88549-5.

Summary/Description

Nicole Sparks (Colie) is fifteen years old. Her mother, Kiki Sparks, is a fitness and weight loss expert who helped her lose forty-five pounds. Because her mother is traveling, Colie will spend the summer with her single, overweight, eccentric Aunt Mira. The thin Colie still lacks confidence, and although at first she dreads staying with her aunt, her summer experiences teach her to face the bullies in her exclusive neighborhood and school. Norman, a hippie type who lives with Colie's aunt, meets Colie at the train station. Norman's car-dealer father has rejected Norman's artist career choice. Norman works at the Last Chance Restaurant with Isabel and Morgan, the waitresses who persuade Colie to work with them. She learns that the almost too confident but gorgeous Isabel was also a high school misfit and that the wise Morgan, not so wise in her love life, has opened herself to an exploitive relationship with a two-timing minor league ballplayer. When Caroline Dawes, Colie's next-door neighbor and main persecutor, shows up at the restaurant and makes fun of Colie, Isabel teaches Colie how to fix her hair, make-up, and attitude. Norman becomes even more solicitous, eventually asks her to pose for a portrait, and becomes her first boyfriend. By the end of the summer, Colie has learned the importance of mutual caring and respect. Some mature situations and strong language are part of Colie's experience.

Booktalk

Nicole Sparks is model thin and has a successful mom who can tell her how to stay that way. She lives in an exclusive neighborhood and goes to an exclusive school. Nicole and her mom were not always so physically and financially fit. Once they were too fat and too poor. Sometimes Nicole longs for those days because she and her mom were always together. Now Mom is traveling, and Nicole is supposed to spend the summer with her eccentric laugh-at-her-not-with-her aunt, a boy who looks like a refugee from a hippie colony, and two girls who are tough enough to chew her up and spit her out. In *Keeping the Moon,* Nicole must not only survive what promises to be a disaster summer but also find out who Nicole Sparks really is.

Related Activities

1. The following novels include bullies. Describe the bully in each story and why each is important to the author's purpose: *Keeping the Moon, Speak* (Related Work 1), *Alone at Ninety Foot* (Related Work 5), *Hidden Talents* (Related Work 6), *Bad* (Related Work 4), *Name Me Nobody* (Related Work 11), and *The Other Ones* (Related Work 9). Continue to research what constitutes a bully and how to deal with one. Contribute that information to the class discussion.
2. Read pages 192 and 193. Discuss why Dessen chose to include Norman's story about the lunar eclipse and why she uses a phrase from that story for the book's title.
3. In the novel, Aunt Mira is considered the town joke. Discuss how readers perceive her.
4. Read the paragraph that begins "My body had changed…" on page 6. At the end of the summer, do you think Colie would come to the same conclusion?
5. Successful parents sometimes present problems for their children. Discuss how the parents' success functions in each of the following novels: *Keeping the Moon, Zack* (Related Work 2), *Someone Like You* (Related Work 3), *Speak* (Related Work 1), *Tribute to Another Dead Rock Star* (Related Work 8), and *When Zachary Beaver Came to Town* (Related Work 10).

Related Works

1. Anderson, Laurie Halse. **Speak.** (See full booktalk in chapter 2.) Brutalized and raped by a popular football player, Melinda Sordino finds herself rejected and despised by the entire school until she has the courage to *Speak.*
2. Bell, William. **Zack.** New York: Simon & Schuster, 1999. 192p. $16.95. ISBN 0-689-82248-0. Although his parents think their son

has no ambition, Zack Lane doesn't work because he doesn't think he can meet their high standards.

3. Dessen, Sarah. **Someone Like You.** (See full booktalk in chapter 4.) Halley rebels against her dominant mother's take-charge personality.

4. Ferris, Jean. **Bad.** (See full booktalk in chapter 2.) Dallas Carpenter finds out that caving into her friends is a good way to wind up in jail or dead.

5. Holubitsky, Katherine. **Alone at Ninety Foot.** (See full booktalk in chapter 3.) Intimidated by the "popular" group, Pam Collins, with the help of her father's new girlfriend, learns to stand up for herself.

6. Lubar, David. **Hidden Talents.** (See full booktalk in chapter 1.) Martin Anderson discovers that he and his friends can overcome the bullies if they combine their supernatural talents in positive ways.

7. O'Dell, Katie. "Ringing True: The Authentic Voice of Sarah Dessen." *VOYA.* (June 2002) 100–102. **NF** Dessen discusses the popularity of *Keeping the Moon.* A book discussion guide appears on page 102.

8. Powell, Randy. **Tribute to Another Dead Rock Star.** (See full booktalk in chapter 3.) While honoring his famous rock star mother, Grady Innis Grennan must decide if he can live with his step-brother's family who are against everything for which she stood.

9. Thesman, Jean. **The Other Ones.** (See full booktalk in chapter 3.) Bridget Raynes discovers that the different people in her town have supernatural powers.

10. Holt, Kimberly Willis. **When Zachary Beaver Came to Town.** (See full booktalk in chapter 2.) When Toby Wilson's mother moves to Nashville to make it big in country western music, Toby begins a summer that forces him to explore people's lies and dreams.

11. Yamanaka, Lois-Ann. **Name Me Nobody.** New York: Hyperion Press, 1999. 227p. $14.99. ISBN 0-7868-0452-1. Emil-lou Kaya submits to abusive boyfriends and intimidating rumors until she figures out that each person has the right to be accepted for who they are.

ᘓᘔ

Frank, E. R. **Life Is Funny.**

New York: DK Publishing/Richard Jackson, 2000. 263p. $17.95.
ISBN 0-7894-2634-X.

Summary/Description

*L*ife Is Funny spans six years. The lives of eleven teenage speakers intertwine. Their contact ranges from romance to friendship and to brief and barely noticed encounters. In each section, designated by the year, teenage speakers describe their worlds—how they feel about themselves, the people around them, and the challenges they face. Bright and beautiful young people learn to deal with addicted, absent, and abusive parents, low and high family expectations, and the physical characteristics of race and beauty that give them breaks or obstacles. In some cases, adults help them, but for the most part, they help each other. The situations discussed involve sex, self-mutilation, and drug use. The language is often graphic. A mature reader is required, and the situations and their discussion might offend certain audiences.

Booktalk

Is life funny or should people just laugh instead of cry? Eleven teenagers in Brooklyn don't think all the votes are in on that question. China, Ebony, and Grace have a friendship that has to survive China's brains, Ebony's emotional problems, and Grace's good looks. Eric doesn't seem to get along with anybody, so his school puts him in a special class. Keisha can't go to bed at night without worrying about her brother breaking into her room. Fellow students accuse Sonia of being a terrorist, but she struggles every day just to survive in two different cultures. Gingerbread and Sam, smooth and savvy, know all about being biracial. Drew is the man with the money, but he and his mother better duck when his father shows up. All these people are neighbors. Their lives overlap, intertwine, and sometimes just brush by, yet they think they are alone with their problems. If they only knew—they might think *Life Is Funny* after all.

Related Activities

1. Mrs. Giles uses poetry to describe her mood, situations, or people. Collect poems or parts of poems in a journal and briefly explain how each selection applies to or touches your life.
2. Sonia in *Life Is Funny* and Laura Li in *Split Image* (Related Work 2) both must balance a life in two cultures. Compare the problem each girl faces and how each chooses to cope with her problem.
3. Both *Life Is Funny* and *You Don't Know Me* (Related Work 3) deal with family violence. Compare the situations described in the two works.
4. Grace in *Life Is Funny* and Gina of *Boys Lie* (Related Work 5) both deal with good looks. Compare the two girls, their attitudes, and their opportunities. Discuss each author's attitude toward good looks.
5. In *Life Is Funny*, both Ebony and Grace cut or mutilate themselves. In *Cut* (Related Work 4), a girl tells her story of self-mutilation, treatment, and recovery. Choose either Ebony or Grace. Write one page from the girl's diary that expresses her feelings about cutting or her feelings about getting treatment.

Related Works

1. Budhos, Marina. **Remix: Conversations with Immigrant Teen-agers.** New York: Henry Holt and Company, 1999. 145p. ISBN 0-8050-5113-9. **NF** On pages 62 to 88, three interviews with Muslim girls living in America today—Farida from Bangladesh, Nubaisha from Pakistan, and Ashrat from Afghanistan—reveal the tensions and rebellions produced by living in two cultures. Their conflicts parallel Sonia's problems in *Life Is Funny.*
2. Glenn, Mel. **Split Image: A Story in Poems.** New York: Harper-Collins Publishers, 2000. 159p. $15.95. ISBN 0-688-16249-5. **NF** Overwhelmed by trying to meet the expectations of Eastern and Western cultures, Laura Li commits suicide.
3. Klass, David. **You Don't Know Me.** (See full booktalk in chapter 1.) When his mother allows her abusive boyfriend to move in with them, a young boy suffers the abuse in silence and retreats into a fantasy world.
4. McCormick, Patricia. **Cut.** (See full booktalk in chapter 3.) Feeling as if she is disappearing, a teenage girl begins to cut herself to confirm she is alive but learns she has to take responsibility for a positive life.
5. Neufeld, John. **Boys Lie.** (See full booktalk in chapter 1.) Entering eighth grade, Gina, who is physically well developed, learns to handle her good looks and the rumors they create.

ःःः

Holt, Kimberly Willis.
When Zachary Beaver Came to Town.
New York: Henry Holt and Company, 1999. 227p. $16.95. ISBN 0-8050-6116-9.

Summary/Description

Toby Wilson lives in Antler, Texas. His father raises and sells worms. His mother left for Nashville, Tennessee, to make it big in the country western world. Toby's best friend, Cal McKnight, has three brothers and sisters: Wayne, serving in Vietnam; Kate, the never noticed sister; and Billie, another older brother. The McKnights, the family Toby prefers over his own, grow cotton, and the family works together to make their farm a success. Toby has a crush on the most beautiful girl in town, Scarlett Stalling, but Scarlett asks Toby to take care of Tara, her little sister, while Scarlett dates the tough and mean Juan.

Into this community comes Zachary Beaver, who at 643 pounds, claims to be the "fattest boy in the world." At first, Zachary is considered a freak. His manager/guardian leaves for Paris to find another sideshow act. Zachary stays in Antler, and Myrtle Mae (the spinster librarian), Ferris (the alcoholic owner of the bowling alley), Kate, and the sheriff all check in to see that Zachary is eating well and cared for. As Toby and Cal visit out of curiosity, they develop a friendship that leads to taking Zachary to a drive-in movie and finally to his private baptism. Toby and Cal know that most of Zachary's stories deal with lies and dreams. But they also learn that all the people in town try to balance their own lies, perceptions, fears, and secret dreams, so if Zachary is a freak, he is not alone. At the end of the story, Myrtle Mae hangs her photographs in Ferris's restaurant to record the significant summer of Zachary Beaver.

Booktalk

Antler, Texas, has never seen anything like it. Zachary Beaver is the "fattest boy in the world." He doesn't go to school, and he doesn't have any friends. In fact, the town wonders if he can ever leave the trailer that brought him to town. Toby Wilson and Cal McKnight line up to pay their money like everyone else. They want to see the fat boy before the trailer moves to the next town. But Zachary's trailer doesn't move, and the town finds out that Zachary's 643 pounds doesn't set any fat records. Zachary might just be a big fat liar, but his lies aren't any fatter than anybody else's lies in Antler. Toby and Cal find a whole different world than the one they think they know *When Zachary Beaver Came to Town.*

Related Activities

1. Myrtie Mae records Antler's encounter with Zachary Beaver in a series of black-and-white photographs. Choose an event you feel shows the growth or journey of a group or individual. Organize a series of pictures that communicate the importance of that event. You might wish to ask your librarian to help you find photo essays that will provide examples.
2. Cal and Toby learn about friendship and loyalty during the Zachary Beaver summer. List the lessons you think they learned. Then compare and discuss that list with other members of the group.
3. The relationship between appearance and friendship is often confusing. Read *When Zachary Beaver Came to Town*, *Life in the Fat Lane* (Related Work 1), *Keeping the Moon* (Related Work 3), and *Staying Fat for Sarah Byrnes* (Related Work 2). Discuss the conclusions the books suggest about the relationship between appearance and friendship.
4. Read "Spade Scharnweber" on pages 24 and 25 of *Poetry After Lunch* (Related Work 6). Write another poem in which Spade expresses his feelings about his height.

5. In *Zachary Beaver Came to Town,* Wayne transforms an ordinary part of farming into a celebration and ultimately his own memorial service. In chapter 16 of *Touching Spirit Bear* (Related Work 4), Garvey makes eating a hot dog a celebration. Identify one ordinary part of your day that you think should be celebrated. Describe what that celebration might be like.

Related Works

1. Bennett, Cherie. **Life in the Fat Lane.** New York: Delacorte Press, 1998. 260p. $15.95. ISBN 0-385-32274-7. (See full booktalk in *Booktalks Plus,* 2001, pages 1 to 3.) Lara Ardeche learns to abandon her stereotypes about fat people when her weight balloons to over 200 pounds.
2. Crutcher, Chris. **Staying Fat for Sarah Byrnes.** New York: Laurel-Leaf Books, 1993. 216p. $4.50pa. ISBN 0-440-21906-X. A young man understands the terrible burden of his friend whose father disfigured her when she was a child.
3. Dessen, Sarah. **Keeping the Moon.** (See full booktalk in chapter 2.) A young girl spends the summer with her eccentric aunt and finds that appearance is not the most important part of a relationship.
4. Mikaelsen, Ben. **Touching Spirit Bear.** (See full booktalk in chapter 2.) In a supervised prison sentence on an Alaskan island, a young boy learns about celebrating life.
5. Nolan, Han. **A Face in Every Window.** (See full booktalk in chapter 1.) When James Patrick O'Brian's grandmother dies and his mother decides to discover who she is, James Patrick finds an entirely new world of people he thought he already knew.
6. Welch, Don. "Spade Scharnweber." In **Poetry After Lunch,** compiled by Joyce Armstrong Carroll and Edward E. Wilson. (See full booktalk in chapter 4.) **NF** In this coming-of-age poem, a young man's extreme height makes him popular with the other boys and gets him in trouble in the girls' locker room.

Efaw, Amy. **Battle Dress.**

New York: HarperCollins Publishers, 2000. 291p. $15.89. ISBN 0-06-028411-0.

Summary/Description

Andi Davis experiences the West Point Beast, the summer initiation program designed to weed out undisciplined candidates. She comes from a dysfunctional family. Her viciously critical mother and self-absorbed father create an environment she looks forward to leaving. No matter how tough the West Point hazing gets, Andi thinks it can't be worse than home. But it looks too much like home, and she believes her isolation and criticism will last forever. What she learns, however, is that the West Point battering is intended to make her stronger, not defeat her. As she comes up against one physical, mental, and emotional challenge after another, she discovers strengths she didn't realize, experiences more emotional bonding than she ever thought possible, and learns that tiny details can save or cost lives. At West Point, no matter how bizarre the request, there is a good reason. When Andi embraces rather than endures Beast hardships, she is not only a team member but also a leader.

An Author's Note explains the relationship between this fictional account and a real West Point experience. A map of The United States Military Academy clarifies the positions of the sites in the story. The Beast Chain of Command diagram illustrates the relationships among the officers and squad members. Quotations of cadences and inspiration key each chapter's tone and purpose.

Booktalk

Andi Davis has made it to West Point. Her brain is good, her body is sound, and because her family has been her emotional battering ram, she thinks nothing can get to her. Then she meets the Beast, the West Point initiation program that separates the real thing from the wanna-be. For an entire summer she will be hot, hungry, and exhausted. She won't do anything right, and if she expresses an opinion she is going to eat it.

If you are thinking about applying to one of the military academies, if you want a little different look at women's rights, if you just want to see what tough means, read *Battle Dress,* a world where "NEVER SURRENDER" is the motto and "NO EXCUSE, SIR" is the password.

Related Activities

1. Initially Andi Davis thinks the rules and hazing are a game she just has to get through. By the end of the novel, she sees the rules in a completely different light. Identify the events or characters in the novel that you feel change her mind. Describe her perception at the end of the novel.

2. *Born to Fly* (Related Work 2) describes a successful mission completed because of the skill and discipline of the crew and its leader. After reading *Born to Fly* and *Battle Dress,* discuss the similarities between the experiences of Shane Osborne and the fictional Andi Davis.

3. Read "To a Daughter Leaving Home" in *Poetry After Lunch* (Related Work 3). Discuss how the experience of learning to ride a bike applies to Andi even though her environment is much more hostile.
4. After reading *Battle Dress,* distinguish between working with and belonging to a group. Use examples from the novel and from your own life to explain the difference.
5. In the short story "The Transformations of Cindy R." from *Stay True* (Related Work 1), a young girl sends for a fairy godmother to improve her life but finds a much different truth. Compare Cindy's experience and Andi's experience. Discuss how each girl learns to rely on inner resources.
6. Research military academies on the Internet in the library. Ask your librarian for help if you need it. You might wish to research their traditions and histories as well as their requirements for admission and graduation.

Related Works

1. Mazer, Anne. "The Transformations of Cindy R." In **Stay True: Short Stories for Strong Girls,** edited by Marilyn Singer. New York: Scholastic Press, 1998. 204p. $16.95. ISBN 0-590-36031-0. A young girl sends for a fairy godmother to change her into a beautiful girl but then decides her own assertiveness will improve her life more. The story appears on pages 65 to 85.
2. Osborn, Shane with Malcolm McConnell. **Born to Fly: The Heroic Story of Downed U.S. Navy Pilot Lt. Shane Osborn.** (See full booktalk in chapter 1.) **NF** Osborne needs all the disciplined training he has received to land his plane safely and face Chinese officials after a hostile pilot confronts him, his plane, and the crew.
3. Pastan, Linda. "To a Daughter Leaving Home." In **Poetry After Lunch: Poems to Read Aloud** (See full booktalk in chapter 4.) Spring, TX: Absey & Co., 1997. 164p. $17.95. ISBN 1-888842-03-2. **NF** In this poem on page 31, a mother realizes her daughter began her path to independence when she learned to ride a bicycle.
4. Robinson, Sharon. **Jackie's Nine: Jackie Robinson's Values to Live By.** (See full booktalk in chapter 2.) **NF** Robinson explains the principles her father stood for. Andi Davis illustrates them.
5. Young, Karen Romano. **The Beetle and Me: A Love Story.** New York: Greenwillow Books, 1999. 181p. $15.00. ISBN 0-688-15922-2. Fifteen-year-old Daisy finds her independence from her dominating family in a nontraditional manner—by restoring a 1957 Love Bug that brought her parents together.

CℨC

Myers, Walter Dean. 145th Street: Short Stories.

New York: Delacorte Press, 2000. 151p. $15.95. ISBN 0-385-32137-6.

Summary/Description

In ten short stories about residents of Harlem's 145th Street, Myers portrays tragedy, frustration, achievement, and compassion. In the first and last stories, "Big Joe's Funeral" and "Block Party-145th Street Style," fifteen-year-old Peaches learns to accept Big Joe as her stepfather. "The Baddest Dog in Harlem," "Monkeyman," and "Kitty and Mack: A Love Story" demonstrate how Harlem's violence changes lives forever. "A Story in Three Parts" talks about drug addiction and a possible rebirth. "Fighter" shows a man's drive to support his family. "The Streak" and "Angela's Eyes" wander into the spiritual realm, and in "A Christmas Story," an old woman hopes to erase the world's fear of Harlem one person at a time. All having universal appeal, the stories describe the tightly knit family of 145th Street who conflict and cooperate to overcome the faults of some, encourage the accomplishments of others, and make Harlem a better place to live.

Booktalk

Big Joe, Monkeyman, Mother Fletcher, Peaches, Kitty, Mack, and Big Time all live in the hood—145th Street, Harlem. 145th Street laughs at death, faces down trouble, dresses up in its Sunday best, and believes love can save. Life on this street isn't "weird…but it's like intense." One man cashes in his insurance policy to stage his funeral while he's still alive. Another takes a part-time job that could kill him. Being friendly with the local police is a good idea, but one lady invites her local patrolman to Christmas dinner. Surrounded by guns, drugs, and poverty, the residents of 145th Street get *very* intense about life, death—and the afterlife. The street is a family, and the family—laughing, crying, fighting, and loving—is sticking together.

Related Activities

1. The stories are separate but framed by the neighborhood theme. How does Myers, in addition to using that frame, link the stories?
2. "A Story in Three Parts" is the only divided story in the volume. Read the entire story and then explain how those parts, which seem to talk about separate issues, build the story as a whole.

3. In both "Big Joe's Funeral" and "Block Party-145th Street Style," Peaches is a central character. How does she link the two stories? Discuss why Myers chose to place the stories first and last rather than back-to-back.
4. "Angela's Eyes" and "The Streak" both deal with the mysterious. Discuss how that element of the unknown or mystery affects the tone of each story.
5. The characters in "The Fighter" and "Monkeyman" both deal with violence, promise, and manhood but in much different ways. Compare the characters and the challenges they face.
6. "Kitty and Mack: A Love Story" and "A Christmas Story" focus on the virtue of patience. Explain the role patience plays in the life of each of the main characters.
7. Research the history of Harlem. You might wish to start by reading *Harlem* (Related Work 4). Although it is a poem, it suggests several aspects of Harlem that might be interesting to you. Also consult the more expansive Web site (Related Work 1). Share the information you find through an oral report or a visual display.

Related Works

1. East-Harlem History Page 1. Available: www.east-harlem.com /history.htm (Accessed August 2000). The Web site provides a full history of the development of East-Harlem.
2. Fleischman, Paul and Judy Pedersen (illus.). **Seedfolks**. (See full booktalk in chapter 4.) A young Vietnamese girl starts a garden in a vacant lot and inspires her neighbors to follow her example. The project creates neighborhood solidarity.
3. Myers, Walter Dean. **The Greatest: Muhammad Ali**. (See full booktalk in chapter 2.) **NF** This biography establishes Ali's importance to the African-American community.
4. Myers, Walter Dean (poem), and Christopher Myers (illus.). **Harlem**. New York: Scholastic Press, 1997. 30p. $16.95. ISBN 0-590-54340-7. (See full booktalk in Booktalks Plus, 2001, on pages 241 to 243.) **NF** This illustrated poem provides a backdrop for 145th Street: Short Stories.
5. Myers, Walter Dean. **Monster**. (See full booktalk in chapter 1.) A young man living in a tough neighborhood is accused of a murder and must decide if he is guilty or innocent.
6. Myers, Walter Dean. **Slam**. New York: Scholastic Press, 1996. 267p. $15.95. ISBN 0-590-48667-5. (See full booktalk in Booktalks Plus, 2001, on pages 110 to 112.) When Greg Harris transfers from his old

neighborhood school to a magnet school, he discovers that he must change the way he thinks and acts.

छ्‍ण

Packer, Alex J., Pamela Espeland, ed., and Jeff Tolbert (illus.). How Rude! The Teenagers' Guide to Good Manners, Proper Behavior, and Not Grossing People Out.

Minneapolis, MN: Free Spirit, 1997. 463p. $19.95.
ISBN 1-57542-024-4. **NF**

Summary/Description

How Rude! defines manners as tools to gain acceptance and cooperation in life rather than roadblocks to a happy life. Packer discusses the common situation of riding the bus as well as the uncommon situation of attending a black tie event. He focuses on school, the Internet, and dating as well as job applications, public events, and guests. He humorously makes the case for manners historically, socially, and emotionally. Acknowledging that rude adults often create awkward situations by asking questions such as "Aren't you a bit old to be in tenth grade?," Packer gives advice on how to deal with them.

How Rude! uses a reference format. The table of contents and index provide easy access to both general and specific topics. The List of Reproducible Pages includes the commandments and codes for family, bathroom, and divorce. Each chapter has a general introduction of the topic and questions from teenage readers. The "True Stories from the Manners Frontier" reveal Packer's own manners encounters. Charts and tables give examples, illustrations, and possible responses. A Chapter Quiz concluding each chapter accents the common sense of positive behavior.

Booktalk

Can you fit your entire social life on a wallet-size calendar? Do your teachers ask you to be absent? Have your parents tried to move without telling you?

If you would like to change your life, you can start today. Absolutely free! *How Rude!* tells you how to make friends, date, improve your grades, and get along with your family—at the same time. *How Rude!* even shows you how to deal with rude people, including adults, who make you want to be rude.

With a full alphabet of topics that include "abusive relationships," "cliques," "throwing up," "lip smacking," "mooching," "suck-ups," and "zits," *How Rude!* can make your life, and the lives of everybody around you, a little smoother.

Related Activities

1. In the inserts titled "True Stories from the Manners Frontier," Packer reports his own life experiences and what the experiences taught him. Each week, record one difficult life situation of your own. At the end of each incident, note what the incident taught you about handling people and situations.
2. Packer includes several lists. On page 368, he lists 40 Rude Things Teenagers Say to Parents. Try to rewrite each statement so it might be more acceptable. Use the Rude and Politely Assertive table on page 364 as a guideline.
3. On page 373, Packer lists statements that require an honest answer and statements that require a reassuring answer. Record questions or statements that fit those categories. Also record the answer given and the reaction in each exchange.
4. In "Beyond Rude: Abusive Relationships" on pages 259 to 260, Packer lists behavior that is always unacceptable from a boyfriend or girlfriend. Make a list of your own that describes positive behavior from a boyfriend or girlfriend.
5. Identify an area in your school, peer group, or home situation that constantly involves conflict. Make up a list of guidelines for the people in that situation to follow. You might want to discuss the list with the people involved. Then describe the reactions to and the practicality of the guidelines. You might wish to consult the List of Reproducible Pages on page xiii.
6. Keep a manners journal. You might want to start by including the results of activities 1 through 5, or you might wish to further research the manners of other cultures as well as your own. Note the "what" and "how" of each manner in your journal.

Related Works

1. Ferris, Jean. **Bad.** (See full booktalk in chapter 2.) This novel about a girl whose behavior puts her in a detention home raises good questions to discuss about manners and abuse.
2. Lubar, David. **Hidden Talents.** (See full booktalk in chapter 1.) Boys discover that the behaviors that have placed them in a last-chance alternative school can be focused into positive channels.

3. Strasser, Todd. **Give a Boy a Gun.** (See full booktalk in chapter 2.) Two boys closed out and treated rudely by high school cliques take their revenge in a Columbine-like attempt.
4. Williams, Terri. **Stay Strong: Simple Life Lessons for Teens.** New York: Scholastic Press, 2001. 240p. $15.95. ISBN 0-439-12971-0. **NF** This guide to interacting positively with the world makes a case for thoughtfulness and manners in chapter 6.
5. Young, Karen Romano. **Video.** New York: Greenwillow Books, 1999. 186p. $16.00. ISBN 0-688-16517-6. In an eighth-grade observation assignment, a girl begins to see the rude behavior that pushes people away from her.

Seeking Our Spirit

Galloway, Priscilla. **Snake Dreamer.**
New York: Delacorte Press, 1998. 231p. $14.95. ISBN 0-385-32264-X.

Summary/Description

Sixteen-year-old Dusa Thrashman almost kills her mother during a snake dream. When her doctor admits he cannot help her lose these horrifying visions, he suggests she watch a television interview of Dr. Teno Gordon and Dr. Yeli Gordon, two Greek physicians who treat snake dreamers. Dusa agrees to treatment on their Mediterranean island and enters the world of the mythical Gorgons. Under the guise of their clinic, the sisters are using the "patients" to find the head of Medusa, their sister. Through her dreams and trances, Dusa can lead the doctors to it. When they find the head and lock themselves in their laboratory to reattach it to their sister's body, Dusa finds Lucy, an emaciated patient who has contacted Dusa through a hidden tape and who is now dying of the snake dreamers' disease. As Dusa helps Lucy and tries to gain control of their situation, Dusa finds she can control her own snakes. When Dusa and Lucy finally locate Medusa, Lucy turns to stone, and Dusa learns that she is joined to Medusa and under her protection. Then, Dusa, with Medusa's and Perse's help, escapes the island. She shares the secret with her mother and finds evidence that Lucy existed and these events occurred. Her experience teaches her how to direct the frightening powers she possesses.

Booktalk

Ask how many people in the group have heard of Medusa. Show them her picture.

Snakes surrounded Medusa's head. Her face turned people to stone. But we know Medusa is only a mythological character—and there's nothing to fear. Right?

Well, sixteen-year-old Dusa is not so sure. When Dusa sleeps, slithering snakes surround her head also. They pull her into rage and desperation because Dusa is a *Snake Dreamer.* No one can drive away the snakes' fury. Then two doctors magically appear and promise to cure her. But will these talented and disturbing women save Dusa or drive her deeper into the hissing, angry world of the menacing, mythical Medusa?

Related Activities

1. Research the story of Medusa and her sisters. Identify details from the myth that Priscilla Galloway uses in her novel. Explain how these details add to the story's effectiveness.

2. Find the meanings of the following words. Explain how they add meaning and tone to the text. Write a new sentence for each word, using a context clue to reveal the word's meaning.

spurious, page 1	incredulous, page 26
euphoria, page 2	lassitude, page 160
charlatans, page 7	translucent, page 197
deprecating, page 9	lambent, page 209

3. On pages 98 and 99, Dusa, Teno, and Yali talk about the history of peoples' attitudes toward snakes. Research the role of snakes in the healing and spiritual worlds. Share your information with the group.

4. On pages 184 and 185, Lucy Atherton claims the power to see auras. Other sources Dusa has read have labeled this power hysteria. Further research both points of view. Share your findings and feelings with the group.

5. On pages 202 to 211, Medusa speaks to and bonds with Dusa. Based on this conversation and the events that follow it, describe Medusa's character.

6. The novel accents the snake's power for both good and evil. Discuss why the author created a character who learned to cooperate with the snakes rather than one who developed the power to eliminate them. How might these snakes be considered metaphorical?

7. *Snake Dreamer, Signs and Wonders* (Related Work 1), *The Spring Tone* (Related Work 5), and "becoming" from *half-human* (Related Work 4) deal with young women emerging into womanhood. Each girl must learn to control her newly discovered powers. Compare the what, how, and why of each girl's journey.

Related Works

1. Collins, Pat Lowery. **Signs and Wonders.** New York: Houghton Mifflin Company, 1999. 176p. $15.00. ISBN 0-395-97119-5. Fifteen-year-old Taswell's false pregnancy is a symptom of her emotional turmoil. Finally her stepmother's attempts to include her in the family help her to develop healthy relationships with real people.
2. Fleischman, Paul. **Mind's Eye.** (See full booktalk in chapter 3.) A sixteen-year-old girl, paralyzed in a riding accident, wishes for Medusa's power to turn people to stone.
3. Lubar, David. **Hidden Talents.** (See full booktalk in chapter 1.) Young men in an alternative school learn to direct their unusual talents in a positive direction.
4. Springer, Nancy. "becoming." In **half-human,** edited by Bruce Coville. (See full booktalk in chapter 2.) Dusie Gorgon discovers she is part of the Gorgon family with the ability to turn people to stone.
5. Yumoto, Kazumi. **The Spring Tone.** Translated by Cathy Hirano. New York: Farrar Straus Giroux, 1999. 165p. $16.00. ISBN 0-374-37153-9. A young girl emerging into womanhood sees herself as a monster she cannot control.

🐍🐍

McDonald, Joyce. Swallowing Stones.
New York: Laurel-Leaf Books, 1997. 245p. $4.50. ISBN 0-440-22672-4.

Summary/Description

Michael MacKenzie fires his rifle, a gift for his seventeenth birthday, and kills a man he has never met, Jenna Ward's father. When he and his friend, Joe Sadowski, hear the radio broadcast telling about the mysterious death and realize their joyful shot in the air might have killed the man, Michael buries the gun in his backyard. But eventually the investigation leads to his house. Michael says Joe borrowed the gun. Joe will not betray Michael by exposing the lie, but vents his anger on Amy Ruggerio, already a social outcast, whom Michael first takes advantage of and then learns to trust and respect as a friend. In his relationships with Joe and Amy, Michael learns the difference between respecting people and using them. Finally, Michael decides to take responsibility for his actions and confess.

As Michael deals with his guilt and Jenna deals with her grief, both are drawn to The Ghost Tree, a Native American sacred place where one talks with ancestors. Through visits and dreams, they focus on each other and the accident. The book ends with Michael driving to Jenna's house in the early morning to confess. He finds Jenna sleeping in The Ghost Tree.

Booktalk

Dealing with life sometimes means *Swallowing Stones*, hard and cutting experiences that can tear a person to pieces. Michael MacKenzie's stone is an accidental murder. When he fires his new rifle in the air, the bullet travels over a mile and kills a man unlucky enough to be repairing his roof. It's just an accident, but how can Michael tell that to the police, the man's wife and daughter, his friends, his family, and himself? Before that single shot, Michael is a boy with an almost fairy-tale future. After that shot, he must decide if he's a man brave enough to face reality.

Related Activities

1. The Ghost Tree is central to the novel. Discuss how the author uses it to carry out his purpose.
2. Amy Ruggerio is a minor but important character. Discuss what her character reveals about both Joe and Michael.
3. Both *Swallowing Stones* and *Speak* (Related Work 1) deal with a hidden crime committed at a teenage party. Compare the situations and the crimes' results.
4. After reading *Kids and Guns* (Related Work 4), discuss how Michael's attitude toward guns contributed to the accident. Continue to research accidents that have occurred through misuse of guns. Share the information with the group.
5. Compare the accidents in *Swallowing Stones* and *Nobody Else Needs to Know* (Related Work 5). Discuss how the accident in each case contributes to the character's growth. Then write an epilogue for one of the two novels that describes that character and his situation ten years after the accident.

Related Works

1. Anderson, Laurie Halse. **Speak.** (See full booktalk in chapter 2.) Because Melinda Sordino's reported rape causes a raid on an in-group party, she is shunned for the rest of the school year.
2. Fraustino, Lisa Rowe. **Dirty Laundry: Stories About Family Secrets.** New York: Viking Press, 1998. 181p. $16.99. ISBN 0-670-

87911-8. The revelation in each story helps or hurts the main character, but in every case, the secret needs to be revealed.

3. Kay, Philip, Andria Estepa, and Al Desetta. **Things Get Hectic: Teens Write About the Violence That Surrounds Them.** New York: Touchstone Books, 1998. 282p. $13.00. ISBN 0-684-83754-4. **NF** Two essays—"Why I Carry a Gun" on pages 119 to 121 and "Why I Don't Have a Gun" on pages 122 to 124—are both by anonymous authors. The one author carries the weapon for self-defense. The other maintains that carrying the gun will guarantee trouble rather than prevent it.

4. Schwarz, Ted. **Kids and Guns.** New York: Franklin Watts, 1999. 128p. $24.00. ISBN 0-531-11723-5. **NF** Schwarz stresses the importance of gun education in every community.

5. Tomey, Ingrid. **Nobody Else Needs to Know.** New York: Delacorte Press, 1999. 229p. $15.95. ISBN 0-385-32624-6. After seriously injuring a little girl in a car accident, Webber Freegy, an underage driver, must decide if he will take responsibility for his actions or let his grandfather take the blame for him.

Almond, David. **Skellig.**

New York: Delacorte Press, 1999. 182p. $15.95. ISBN 0-385-32653-X.

Summary/Description

Michael's family moves into a new home badly in need of repair. Dr. Dan, whom Michael refers to as Dr. Death, frequently visits the house to check on Michael's premature little sister. Upset by the move, the disrepair of the house, and his sister's health, young Michael explores a dilapidated storage shed and discovers Skellig, an old man covered with cobwebs and living on bugs and mice. He also meets Mina, his next-door neighbor, who is home schooled by her mother. Mina sees Skellig, too, and together they secretly feed and care for him, hoping they can make him strong. Michael's encounters with Skellig parallel his anxiety over the baby's illness. When Skellig disappears, Michael assumes the baby has died; but he learns that Skellig went to the hospital to save her and that his mother had a reassuring vision of a Skellig-like creature the night before the baby's successful surgery. After Michael's sister recovers, Skellig confirms that Michael, Mina, and the baby are special people who share his spiritual strength and explains that he is going someplace else to help.

Booktalk

Michael's parents moved away from Michael's friends and bought a broken-down house once owned by a dead man. Now they have a broken baby, too, who probably won't live very long and who takes all the family's time. With nothing to do, Michael decides to poke around one of their new dilapidated buildings. He finds spiders, mice, and *Skellig*, an old, grumpy, and sick creature that likes aspirin and Chinese food. Then Michael meets Mina, his very different next-door neighbor. She has a blackbird, knows all about owls and dinosaurs, and sees Skellig too. Are they having bad dreams or mental breakdowns, or are they about to live a miracle? Believing what they see but hiding their secrets from the rest of the world, Michael and Mina learn about faith, their spirit, and the power of tiny things.

Related Activities

1. Discuss whether Skellig is "real."
2. *Dancing on the Edge* (Related Work 4), *Kit's Wilderness* (Related Work 1), and *Skellig* all deal with the spiritual world. Discuss the role the spiritual world plays in each of the stories.
3. *Skellig* and *Pobby and Dingam* (Related Work 5) include "imaginary" figures that have a relationship to death. Compare and contrast the techniques and purpose of the two novels as well as their levels of optimism or hope.
4. "The Feather" in *Orange Candy Slices and Other Secret Tales* (Related Work 2) presents another angel figure that has strange eating habits and communicates with and saves children. Analyze the characteristics of this figure and of Skellig. Then make up your own spiritual figure that might assist people in sickness and grief. Write or draw a portrait. Explain the reason for the characteristics you give the figure.
5. Further research the concept of angels and the roles they play in healing. Relate your information to Skellig, and share your information and parallels with the group.

Related Works

1. Almond, David. **Kit's Wilderness.** (See full booktalk in chapter 4.) Three young friends use their talent and the legends and history surrounding them to build strong friendships and positive lives.
2. Canales, Viola. "The Feather." In **Orange Candy Slices and Other Secret Tales.** Houston, TX: Piñata Books, 2001. 121p. $9.95pa. ISBN 1-55885-332-4. A young girl dreams about an angel who loves to eat cake and save children.

3. Erdman, David V. **The Illuminated Blake: William Blake's Complete Illuminated Works with a Plate-by-Plate Commentary.** Minola, NY: Dover Publications, 1992. 416p. $26.95. ISBN 0486272346. **NF** This book contains Blake's drawings that influenced Almond in his creation of the character Skellig.
4. Nolan, Han. **Dancing on the Edge.** (See full booktalk in chapter 1.) Lies and loneliness push a young girl into an unhealthy fantasy world.
5. Rice, Ben. **Pobby and Dingam.** New York: Alfred A. Knopf, 2000. 94p. $16.00. ISBN 0-375-41127-5. A young girl's imaginary friends become a real part of a dysfunctional family and their community.

෴

Coville, Bruce (comp. and ed.) and Marc Tauss (photo illus.). half-human.
New York: Scholastic Press, 2001. 224p. $15.95. ISBN 0-590-95944-1.

Summary/Description

E ach story in this fantasy collection describes a person "like us, but not quite" who must decide how that difference will affect his or her relationship to the human world. Bruce Coville, Jane Yolen, Tamora Pierce, D.J. Malcolm, Jude Mandell, Janni Lee Simner, Nancy Springer, Tim Waggoner, and Gregory Maguire tell about selkies, a half-human tree, a gorgon, a dragon, a mermaid, scarecrows, a centaur, and a bird-man who must decide how to combine the strengths and challenges of two worlds. Coville's introduction suggests booktalks and classroom applications as he points out that each unusual character shares with the reader the universal journey of identity. Lawrence Schimel's poem "how to make a human," appropriately placed in the center of the collection, will promote a lively discussion about what it means to be human. Author information at the end includes suggestions for more good reading.

Booktalk

Ask how many people like surprises. Ask them to describe some of the surprises that have been pleasant and some that have not.

The book *half-human* is full of surprises. Dusie Gorgon wakes up one morning and discovers that her head is full of snakes—the ultimate bad hair day. Suddenly, a tree finds itself dying and being reborn as a man. That colt everyone in Arianne's family waits for turns out to be a centaur, the kind of surprise people read about in those grocery store newspapers. And there are even more surprises for and from scarecrows, princesses, and mermaids. But the real news is what these characters do. They could cry, get angry, or hide in the basement, but they don't. Instead, they figure out that being *half-human* might give them an edge that everybody else can just wish for. Then they give back a few surprises of their own.

Related Activities

1. Read Coville's introduction. Discuss his interpretation of half-human and how that interpretation applies to the study of literature and our own lives.
2. Coville comments in his introduction that the half-human stories he received were much different than he expected. Ask your librarian to help you research half-human creatures in fairy tales, folk tales, and mythologies. Share your findings with the group. Ask each person to choose one of the creatures and build a story around it or draw a picture of it.
3. In "water's edge," "linnea," and "the hardest, kindest gift," water is a central factor. Explain the significance of the setting in each story.
4. In "becoming," "water's edge," "linnea," "princess dragonblood," "soaring," and "the hardest, kindest gift," the main character's difference or situation is a product of his family. Discuss the result of the interaction between the family influence and the character's reaction to it.
5. Choose one story from the collection and change the character's reaction to the difference. Discuss how that change would alter the story. Then discuss how reaction to the difference applies to real life.

Related Works

1. Cart, Michael. **Tomorrowland: 10 Stories About the Future.** (See full booktalk in chapter 4.) The story "Homo…Sapiens?" on pages 1 to 5 questions the wisdom of the human race. "The Other Half of Me," on pages 145 to 156, talks about a new difference some children realize: being born from a single mother and a donated sperm.
2. Haddix, Margaret Peterson. **Turnabout.** New York: Simon & Schuster, 2000. 223p. $17.00. ISBN 0-689-82187-5. After living two lifetimes, two women decide to tell the world about the challenges of living forever. The theme of mortality is related to "the hardest, kindest gift."
3. Skurzynski, Gloria. "Nethergrave." In **On the Edge: Stories at the Brink,** edited by Lois Duncan. New York: Simon & Schuster Books for Young Readers, 2000. 211p. $17.00. ISBN 0-689-82251-0. Overwhelmed by the peer pressure of his boarding school, an eighth grader leaves this world and takes on an identity in the computer world. The story appears on pages 25 to 39.

4. Vande Velde, Vivian. **The Rumpelstiltskin Problem.** (See full booktalk in chapter 4.) Like Gregory Maguire in "scarecrow" from *half-human*, Vivian Vande Velde takes a fairy tale and uses it to imply darker and more mature themes.

5. Wilde, Oscar. **Complete Fairy Tales of Oscar Wilde.** New York: Penguin Books, 1990. 221p. $5.95pa. (Signet Classics). ISBN 0-451-52435-7. In "The Fisherman and his Soul," Wilde raises the question of the power of love over the human soul. Is that power good or evil, and which defines a human being?

6. Yolen, Jane, Shulamith Oppenheim, and Paul Hoffman (illus.). **The Fish Prince and Other Stories: Mermen Folk Tales.** New York: Interlink, 2001. 160p. $29.95. ISBN 1-56656-389-5. Chapter 3 deals extensively with the seal people, the focus of "water's edge" by Janni Lee Simner. The book describes folk tales and their connections and origins.

ርৡৡ

Philip, Neil. **The Great Mystery: Myths of Native America.**

New York: Clarion Books, 2001. 145p. $25.00. ISBN 0-395-98405-X. **NF**

Summary/Description

In the first chapter, "Trail of Beauty," Philip defines myth, explains its evolution, describes the purpose of related rituals, and identifies the common themes and motifs of Native American belief. Subsequent chapters focus on the specific myths for each region of North America from the Southwest to the Arctic. Each chapter emphasizes Native American people's relationship with nature and how that relationship influences human interaction and attitudes toward ownership. The pictures and extensive captions act as a book within a book. Looking at the pictures and reading the captions before reading the main text will provide a useful context. An extensive bibliography provides additional sources for each chapter. A name and topic index gives easy access to information.

Booktalk

Show several of the pictures. Discuss the similarities the audience might see in the pictures you choose. All these pictures deal with people involved in their religious beliefs. Discuss what the pictures suggest about the values of the believers.

Native Americans never built great churches or passed out holy books. For these cultures, the earth and sky are sacred places—not hostile elements blocked out by stuffy buildings that people say are sacred. The stories, songs, and ceremonies change because inspiration comes differently to each teller. But all agree in *The Great Mystery* of existence that earth and sky are the sacred places, that the spirits have a sense of humor, that a special spirit teaches us how to live, and that destruction renews as well as destroys.

Related Activities

1. Choose one chapter in *The Great Mystery.* Referring to the sources listed for the chapter, find additional information about Native American customs. Ask your librarian to help you find additional sources in the library or on the Internet.
2. The title of chapter 1 alludes to the poem "In Beauty May I Walk" from *In a Sacred Manner I Live* (Related Work 4). Read the poem aloud. Then discuss why Philip might have chosen this allusion to introduce *The Great Mystery.*
3. In *Touching Spirit Bear* (Related Work 3), Cole Mathews is sentenced to an Alaskan island for one year. His experience is governed by Native American beliefs. Read chapters 8 and 9. Then discuss the Native American beliefs and symbols you feel clarify Cole's transformation.
4. Divide a map of North America according to the chapters in *The Great Mystery.* List the names of the tribes in each area.
5. In *The Golden Compass* (Related Work 6), *The Subtle Knife* (Related Work 7), and *The Amber Spyglass* (Related Work 5) of His Dark Materials Trilogy, Philip Pullman combines myths from several cultures. After reading the trilogy and *The Great Mystery*, identify elements of the stories that might be based on Native American myths or beliefs. Explain your choices.

Related Works

1. Bruchac, Joseph. **The Journal of Jesse Smoke.** New York: Scholastic Incorporated, 2001. 203p. (My Name is America). $10.95. ISBN 0-439-12197-3. A sixteen-year-old Cherokee who has successfully assimilated into the white man's culture is driven from the land. His journal tells Cherokee spiritual and political stories as well as his personal story.
2. Matcheck, Diane. **The Sacrifice.** New York: Farrar Straus Giroux, 1998. 198p. $16.00. ISBN 0-374-36378-1. (See full booktalk in *Booktalks Plus*, 2001, on pages 89 to 91.) A fifteen-year-old girl seeks her destiny as the Great One and discovers that the signs of the gods are extremely difficult to follow.

3. Mikaelsen, Ben. **Touching Spirit Bear.** (See full booktalk in chapter 2.) Sentenced to a remote Alaskan island for one year, Cole Mathews learns respect for nature, joy in living, and personal responsibility in the Tlingit tradition. On page 120 of *The Great Mystery* is a picture of a Tlingit woman dressed for potlatch dancing.

4. Philip, Neil, ed. **In a Sacred Manner I Live: Native American Wisdom.** (See full booktalk in chapter 1.) **NF** "In Beauty I Walk" appears on page 19. In this collection of prayers, speeches, and reflections, Native Americans express their spiritual beliefs and visions.

5. Pullman, Philip. **The Amber Spyglass.** (See full booktalk in chapter 3.) In this third book of His Dark Materials trilogy, Mary Malone, a physicist, discovers that if inhabitants of one world travel to another, they will destroy the entire universe.

6. Pullman, Philip. **The Golden Compass.** (See full booktalk in chapter 3.) In this first book of His Dark Materials trilogy, Lyra discovers her parentage and finds herself working with a renegade bear to rescue stolen children.

7. Pullman, Philip. **The Subtle Knife.** (See full booktalk in chapter 3.) In this second book of His Dark Materials trilogy, Will Parry searches for the father who deserted him and his mother. He allies himself with Lyra in a world where each person has a daemon, an animal representation of the spirit within.

8. Quinn, David Beers. **Set Fair for Roanoke: Voyages and Colonies, 1584–1606.** Chapel Hill, NC: University of North Carolina Press, 1985. **NF** On pages 220–228, Quinn describes Thomas Harriot's perception of Indian beliefs that might have already been corrupted by explorers and Harriot's desire to convert them to Christianity.

☙❧

Second Sight: Stories for a New Millennium.
New York: Philomel Books, 1999. 122p. $14.99. ISBN 0-399-23458-6.

Summary/Description

This collection focuses on significant changes in people's lives and the people's perceptions of those changes in relation to superstition, family, and hope. In spite of the millennium topic, the stories have universal application. Settings include the world of the Vikings, modern Mexico influenced by ancient Mexico, small-town America, a radio station, and a rest home. Authors are Avi, Janet Taylor Lisle, Rita Williams-Garcia, Nancy Springer, Michael Cadnum, Natalie Babbitt, and Richard

Peck. An About the Authors section at the end of the novel gives a brief explanation about each writer.

Booktalk

What do an orphan slave, an explorer in a hot air balloon, and a lady who has lived in three centuries share? A fascination with and a fear of what will happen tomorrow. Whether the story is about superstitions, divorce, religion, family, old age, or faith, the characters in these eight stories, like us, worry about what will come next. But—ready or not—tomorrow will come. And reading these *Stories for a New Millennium* can give us a *Second Sight* to help us welcome the day.

Related Activities

1. Note how time in each story relates to that story's purpose. Discuss with others in the group your perceptions of the way the story uses time.
2. Both "Oswin's Millennium" from *Second Sight* and "Night of the Plague" from *Tomorrowland* (Related Work 1) are set in monasteries at a millennium and a time of possible disaster. After reading the two stories, compare how the authors use these settings and the element of faith the settings imply to accomplish their purposes.
3. Compare the definition and interpretation of "second sight" Richard Peck employs in his short story "The Three-Century Woman" and his novel *Ghosts I Have Been* (Related Work 4).
4. Each title in this collection applies to its story in different ways. Discuss the different applications you find with others who have also read the stories.
5. After reading all the stories, discuss which stories have universal application and which stories are limited by the millennium theme. Further research the perceptions and history of the millennium concept. Share them with the group and relate them to universal human concerns.

Related Works

1. Gibbs, James Cross. "Night of the Plague." In **Tomorrowland: 10 Stories About the Future.** (See full booktalk in chapter 4.) A sixteen-year-old monk tries to leave the monastery that is treating plague victims until he is assured that the disease does not mean the world is ending. The story appears on pages 159 to 170.
2. Haddix, Margaret Peterson. **Turnabout.** New York: Simon & Schuster, 2000. 223p. $17.00. ISBN 0-689-82187-5. Amelia Lenore Hazelwood, at one hundred and one in the year 2000, participates in

an experiment that reverses her age. It is a great what-if companion to "The Three-Century Woman" by Richard Peck.

3. Newth, Mette. **The Transformation.** (See full booktalk in chapter 4.) The spiritual and earthly worlds combine when a Greenland native and a brother sent to convert her people blend their lives and spirits.

4. Peck, Richard. **Ghosts I Have Been.** New York: Viking Press, 1977. 214p. $20.00. ISBN 0-670-33813-3. Blossom Culp's extrasensory perception allows her to see tragic events on the Titanic.

5. Fleischman, Paul. **Mind's Eye.** (See full booktalk in chapter 3.) An eighty-eight-year-old resident of a convalescent home teaches sixteen-year-old Courtney how imagination and a second sight can release her from the confining world of her bed.

乙沙

Napoli, Donna Jo. Crazy Jack.

New York: Delacorte Press, 1999. 134p. $15.95. ISBN 0-385-32627-0.

Summary/Description

This retelling of "Jack and the Beanstalk" portrays Jack as a visionary who learns the wisdom of his father's advice—advice his father forgot. The important parts of life are "to have food on the table and a roof over our heads, but most of all, to have each other." When Jack is nine, his father loses the family fields in a wager, runs to the cliff, and apparently commits suicide. Each year, Jack throws himself at the side of that cliff but can never climb it. In the seventh year, Jack encounters a sprite dressed in his father's clothes who trades him rainbow beans for their last cow. Convinced Jack is mad, Jack's mother decides to support them alone. Flora, Jack's love, fears marrying *Crazy Jack* and decides she will marry William, who can give her everything. But as the beanstalk grows, Flora helps gather the beans. Jack climbs it twice. He steals the chicken that lays the golden egg and the giant's pot of gold. The beanstalk provides a cash crop of regular-size beans. The hen produces endless normal eggs and eventually a chicken flock. The pot of gold becomes a bottomless pot of stones that Jack uses to build a house for himself, his mother, and Flora. On Jack's last trip to the giant's kingdom, he discovers that the giant ate Jack's father. Jack tries to save the giant's abused mistress, who has helped him and his father, but she is too attached to the treasures she has accumulated. They steal the lyre while the giant sleeps, but the giant wakes up, kills her, and chases Jack down the beanstalk. When Jack returns to earth, he produces beautiful music, the song of Flora, and decides to make his house Flora's wedding gift. The night before her wedding, Flora ponders the beauty and happiness Jack brings her and marries him. Realizing what is important, Jack and Flora have everything.

Booktalk

"Jack and the Beanstalk"—you all know the story. A boy (who people think isn't too bright) trades the last family cow for a handful of beans, climbs the beanstalk, outwits a giant, and lives happily ever after. But that's just a small part of the bigger picture. Magic in Jack's world didn't solve all problems; it just gave desperate people a few more choices. *Crazy Jack* adds the adult details—suicide, love, greed, prejudice, and seduction. At sixteen, Jack, starving and discouraged, must face them all. He decides to take a risk, a risk that brings him face to face with the man-eating, woman-hating, money-loving giant. Should Jack fight him, try to escape, or become like the giant—rich, powerful, and successful?

Related Activities

1. Choose another children's story. Rewrite it for a young-adult audience.
2. Many times in the story Napoli shifts back and forth from magic to reality. Discuss how these shifts help her accomplish her purpose.
3. *Crazy Jack* is a life parable. Explain what you think each character, event, and object represents. In one sentence, write the parable's lesson.
4. The giant's world is black and white except for the gold. Discuss why Napoli makes that choice.
5. Napoli includes the issues of vegetarianism and prejudice into her story. Discuss how these issues relate or fail to relate to the story's overall purpose.
6. Read several versions of "Jack and the Beanstalk" (Related Works 2 and 3). Ask your librarian to help you use the library's resources and the Internet to research the story's origin and use. State the purpose of the story. Compare that purpose with Napoli's purpose in *Crazy Jack*.

Related Works

1. **Collins Complete Works of Oscar Wilde: Centenary Edition.** New York: HarperCollins Publishers, 1999. 1268p. $32.46. ISBN 0-00-472372-4. In "The Fisherman and His Soul," a young fisherman falls in love with a mermaid and discovers love is more important than wisdom, riches, or lust. The story appears on pages 236 to 259.
2. Garner, James Finn. **Politically Correct Bedtime Stories.** New York: Macmillan Publishing Company, 1994. 79p. $8.95. ISBN 0-02-542730-X. This version of "Jack and the Beanstalk" centers on envi-

ronmental issues and the possibility of a better life away from man's world.

3. *Jack and the Beanstalk/Jack the Giant Killer: Text and Images.* Available: www-dept.usm.edu/~engdept/jack/inventt.htm (Accessed June 2002). In this version, Jack's father gave his money away to help others. Jack eventually learns to do the same.

4. Maguire, Gregory. "scarecrow." In **half-human,** edited by Bruce Coville. (See full booktalk in chapter 2.) Maguire conjectures why the Scarecrow from the Wizard of Oz thought he needed a brain.

5. Napoli, Donna Jo. **Zel.** New York: Dutton Children's Books, 1996. 227p. $15.99. ISBN 0-525-45612-0. In this converted Rapunzel tale, Napoli again emphasizes the importance of true love over wealth and safety. Zel rebels against her overprotective mother, and Konrad rebels against his father and station to find and marry her.

6. Vande Velde, Vivian. **The Rumpelstiltskin Problem.** (See full booktalk in chapter 4.) Vande Velde questions the logic of the story and then rewrites it six different ways.

Beagle, Peter S. A Dance for Emilia.

New York: ROC/New American Library, 2000. 87p. $14.95. ISBN 0-451-45800-1.

Summary/Description

In this charming story about love and grief, two adult friends of a deceased man named Sam miss him so much that his spirit comes back to live in his cat, Millamant. Sam dreamed of being a famous dancer but never had the talent. Both Jacob, his childhood friend, and Emily, a young abused woman he comforted, understood his frustration. When the cat begins dancing—even mimicking Gene Kelly in *Singing in the Rain*—both Jacob and Emily recognize Sam's spirit. Then Sam speaks to them and insists he will always remember Jacob and Emily, whom he romantically renamed Emilia, and that they should let him go. Accepting his death, Emily marries, moves away, and has a baby. When Jacob visits her, he discovers that the little girl who loves to play with the baby has many of Sam's characteristics. This book, for both young adults and adults, will generate a great deal of discussion about the power of spirits.

Booktalk

Sam always wanted to be a great dancer, but he never had the right body. Now he has one that's more pliable than he ever dreamed. Unfortunately, he has to share it with his cat. Why?

Sam died, but his friends didn't want him to. They miss him so much that they wish his spirit back. Neither Jacob, Sam's childhood friend, nor Emily, the last woman Sam loved, know they can do such a thing—until they see Sam's cat, the one Emily inherited, start to dance. They know that only Sam would ever want to move like that. Then the cat starts talking. It's definitely Sam, a man in a cat stuck between two worlds. How they sort their feelings and solve their problems turns into a beautiful dance—*A Dance for Emilia.*

Related Activities

1. In the first few pages of the novel, Beagle establishes Sam's character. Discuss how Jacob's memories and musings about Sam prepare the reader for the end of the story.
2. Dancing ferociously, Sam captivates his audiences but knows he will never be a dancer. Read his analysis on page 17 that begins "I was *never* the best!" and ends with the paragraph. Discuss what this paragraph reveals about him. Now describe yourself by completing the sentence "I was *never…*" and write a paragraph that explains your statement.
3. On page 24, Jacob criticizes Sam for quitting the dance. The paragraph begins "I still dance." Discuss what that paragraph reveals about Sam and his perspective on life.
4. Both Jacob and Sam feel they have had enough negative romances to open the Museum of Truly Weird Relationships. Sam, however, does not feel Emily will ever be part of that museum. Discuss his feelings in light of the rest of the novel.
5. Sam compares being dead and not being involved to "snow on a TV set." How might that comparison apply to someone living?
6. Following Sam's character in life and his appearance in Millamant and Luz, write an extended definition of life through Sam's perspective.
7. Continue to research the stories involving the dead returning to life. Classify them according to how this supernatural element is used. Three classifications might be humor, horror, or insight. Then present a booklist or series of supernatural booktalks to the group.

Related Works

1. Alcock, Vivien. "QWERTYUIOP." In **Help Wanted: Short Stories About Young People Working,** compiled by Anita Silvey. New York: Little, Brown, 1997. 174p. $15.95. ISBN 0-316-79148-2. To keep her job, a secretary must convince the former secretary, now deceased, to stop haunting her typewriter. The story appears on pages 15 to 28.

2. Beagle, Peter. **Tamsin.** (See full booktalk in chapter 1.) Beagle blends the lives of living and dead to illustrate the meaning of love and purpose.

3. Coville, Bruce. **Odder Than Ever.** New York: Harcourt Brace and Company, 1999. 146p. $16.00. ISBN 0-15-201747-X. In Coville's short story "Biscuits of Glory," on pages 17 to 24, a ghostly baker must make biscuits every Saturday night. They are so light that the narrator who eats them floats even when he thinks about them.

4. Griffin, Adele. **The Other Shepards.** (See full booktalk in chapter 1.) A girl killed in a car accident returns to help her younger sisters move on with their lives.

5. Rylant, Cynthia. **The Heavenly Village.** New York: The Blue Sky Press, 1999. 95p. $15.95. ISBN 0-439-04096-5. (See full booktalk in *Booktalks Plus*, 2001, pages 52 and 53.) This series of short stories tells about a village between heaven and Earth for homebodies who still have business in the world.

CRED

Voigt, Cynthia. Elske.
New York: Atheneum Books for Young Readers/Anne Schwartz, 1999. 245p. $18.00. ISBN 0-689-82472-6.

Summary/Description

Elske, the granddaughter of a Wolfer captive, is designated The Death Maiden to the Volkking (king). When he dies, she will strip, enter the Death House, suffer gang rape by the chieftains, and then burn with the king's body. Elske's fate is the tribe's revenge on the grandmother, the captive who has a powerful influence in the community. The grandmother takes Elske's place in the Death House and burns it and the chieftains. Elske escapes and meets friendly travelers who take her to Trastad. She becomes the valuable servant of Var Jerrol, "the eyes and ears of the Council" and a wealthy trader. Because she can speak both the Northern and Southern languages, she spies and translates for him but also learns the secrets of black powder and how to negotiate for herself. When she refuses to marry the man chosen for her, she is assigned to the rebellious princess Beriel, who has been sent to find a husband. Elske discovers that the princess wishes to return to her country to claim her title of queen, but as the victim of a gang rape planned by her brother, could die for the disgraceful birth. Elske helps Beriel hide her pregnancy and gives the baby to a childless couple. Free of disgrace, Beriel returns with Elske to her country, organizes an army, and defeats her brother.

Elske helps thwart a Wolfer invasion. Both women become national heroes and marry the men who supported them. The Epilogue tells about their successful lives and their strong descendants. A map at the beginning of the novel depicts the fantasy kingdom.

Booktalk

Elske is the Death Maiden. Her future is set. When the Wolfer king dies, she will burn with him and join him in the next life. But Elske's grandmother helps her escape this "fate," and in her flight, Elske must think and fight better than the savage warriors and shrewd traders who want to control her. Then she meets another woman who defies the power and abuse of men. Beriel is a dispossessed queen determined to regain her kingdom. Joining Beriel, Elske continues her journey, but will their strength bring them love and power or destruction, loneliness, and defeat?

Related Activities

1. Although Elske's world is fantasy, many of the issues that confront her are real and modern. List the conflicts or challenges she encounters. Then explain how that same conflict or challenge might appear in the modern world.
2. Gradually Elske changes her identity or vision of herself. Explain how she finally perceives herself and what events led her to that perception.
3. Elske becomes a significant force in war. Identify the qualities that help her become successful.
4. Obedience and freedom are significant issues in *Elske, The Fated Sky* (Related Work 1), *The Transformation* (Related Work 2), *The One-Armed Queen* (Related Work 5), and *His Dark Materials Trilogy* (Related Work 3). After reading each of the works, discuss the role obedience and freedom play in each work. Then write an essay in which you express your own opinion about obedience and freedom. Compare your conclusions with the opinions of other members of the group.
5. *Elske* presents women as rulers, fighters, spies, and intellectuals. With the help of your librarian, research the life of one woman who fits into one of these three groups. Prepare a display of her life and accomplishments.

Related Works

1. Branford, Henrietta. **The Fated Sky.** Cambridge, MA: Candlewick Press, 1999. 156p. $16.99. ISBN 0-7636-0775-4. (See full booktalk in

Booktalks Plus, 2001, pages 48 to 50.) In this Viking tale, sixteen-year-old Ran flees the harsh, magical world of the Vikings to build her own life.

2. Newth, Mette. **The Transformation.** (See full booktalk in chapter 4.) Navrana takes on the responsibility of her family and joins with Brendan, the survivor of an Augustine monastery to seek their common destiny.

3. Pullman, Philip. **His Dark Materials Trilogy**. (See full booktalk in chapter 3.) Pullman combines gender roles and issues of good and evil in his trilogy: **The Golden Compass**, **The Subtle Knife**, and **The Amber Spyglass**. Lyra is a central figure in the war between good and evil translated as complete obedience versus freedom.

4. Sprague, Marsha M. and Lori Risher. "Using Fantasy Literature to Explore Gender Issues." *The ALAN Review.* (Winter 2002) 39–42. **NF** Although the article describes specific techniques used in a seventh grade setting, the methods could be used in classes involving older students and more sophisticated fantasy literature.

5. Yolen, Jane. **The One-Armed Queen.** New York: Tor Books, 1998. 329p. $23.95. ISBN 0-312-85243-6. Thirteen-year-old Scillia fights her foster brothers to take over the kingdom as her foster parents wish.

Testing Our Physical Limits

෴෴

Bachrach, Susan D. The Nazi Olympics: Berlin 1936.

Boston: Little, Brown, 2000. 136p. $21.95. ISBN 0-316-07086-6. **NF**

Summary/Description

Part One describes the historical backdrop for the 1936 Olympics. Hitler grows more powerful, and minority groups—the largest being Jews—are undesirables. Part Two describes the Nazi obsession with physical superiority, the Nazi takeover of the Olympics, and the persecution of "undesirables." Part Three explains the boycott debate, especially in the United States. When the United States agrees to send teams to Germany, African-American and Jewish athletes are pressured not to participate. Because both groups are discriminated against in the United States, many African-American and some Jewish athletes decide to compete. Jewish athletes from other countries who refuse to participate are punished. Part Four shows that despite the strong performance of non-

Aryan athletes such as Jesse Owens, the Nazi Olympics proves to be a powerful propaganda showcase for Germany, with one of Hitler's goals in world conquest being to dominate the Olympics forever. A Timeline shows the interaction between political and Olympic events. The authors give extensive suggestions for further reading, and pictures, both color and black-and-white, show how prejudice rather than ability dominated this infamous Olympic event.

Booktalk

Go for the gold! That's what we often think when we hear the word Olympics. Even though we talk about how the events symbolize world co-operation and encourage peace, we really want *our* country to win. In 1936, when Berlin hosted the Olympics, Hitler wanted Germany to win much more than the athletic contests. For Hitler, the games were a weapon, a propaganda tool proving that the world should submit to Hitler's Aryan ideal. Non-Aryan's proved him wrong, but not everyone could see the truth behind the glittering German show. Even as the world moved toward war, many thought Germany would be the perfect perma-nent site for the Olympic Games. The world argued, watched, boycotted, and competed as games of physical strength and honor became games of politics and discrimination. *The Nazi Olympics* tells how a golden event, tarnished with lies and injustice, aided the final solution and forced us to examine our dreams, ideals, and games a little more carefully.

Related Activities

1. Research the United States participation in the Olympic Games on the Internet and in the library. List any gold, silver, and bronze win-ners from the United States.

2. In the Nazi Olympics, Hitler wished to showcase the German ideal of manhood. This ideal is discussed in the fiction *Soldier Boys* (Re-lated Work 3) and *Brothers in Valor* (Related Work 8). Explain how this ideal supported or conflicted with the Olympic ideals.

3. In *The Olympic Games* (Related Work 2), Currie illustrates how dis-agreement has shaped the Olympics. One of those disagreements centers on politics. After reading about the Nazi Olympics and other political boycotts, discuss whether athletes should be treated as indi-viduals or as citizens of nations.

4. Currie, in *The Olympic Games* (Related Work 2), includes Sugges-tions for Further Reading, Works Consulted, and Web Resources. Choose one of the sources listed, read it, and share the information you find with the group. Ask your librarian to help you find addi-tional or substitute sources.

5. Choose one American athlete who competed in the Olympics. Find as much information about the person as you can. Explain how that individual contributed or failed to contribute to the Olympic ideal.

Related Works

1. Corbett, Sara. **Venus to the Hoop.** New York: Anchor Books, 1997. 341p. $12.95pa. ISBN 0-385-49352-5. (See full booktalk in *Booktalks Plus,* 2001, pages 99 to 101.) **NF** This story of the 1996 women's U.S. Olympic basketball team shows how the drive of fourteen women finally gained respect for women's basketball, even in comparison with the men's Dream Team.

2. Currie, Stephen. **The Olympic Games.** San Diego, CA: Lucent Books, 1999. 111p. (Overview Series). $27.45. ISBN 1-56006-395-5. **NF** Currie reviews the issues of professional and amateur status, politics, commercialism, equitable participation, and drugs that have shaped the Olympics.

3. Hughes, Dean. **Soldier Boys.** (See full booktalk in chapter 1.) A teenage German and a teenage American soldier cross paths at The Battle of the Bulge. The German soldier comes to the battle with the ideals of physical superiority.

4. **Jackie Robinson.** Produced by A&E and CEL Communications, 1991. 44 min. Videocassette. Color. (Biography). $14.95. AAE-10415. The documentary includes Robinson's remarks about how little his brother's silver medal, won in the 1936 Olympics, meant to the American public.

5. Myers, Walter Dean. **The Greatest: Muhammad Ali.** (See full booktalk in chapter 2.) **NF** An Olympic Gold winner in 1960, Ali brought an entirely new attitude to the Olympics and the ring.

6. Oxlade, Chris and David Ballheimer. **Olympic Games.** New York: Alfred A Knopf/Dorling Kindersley Publishing, 1999. 60p. (Eyewitness Books). $19.00. ISBN 0-7894-6489-6. **NF** Oxlade and Ballheimer include the 1936 Olympics in several aspects of their description but highlight it in "Spoilsports," the chapter that details every Olympics marred by conflict.

7. Park, Linda Sue. **When My Name Was Keoko: A Novel of Korea in World War II.** New York: Clarion Books, 2002. 199p. $16.00. In chapter 2, one of the narrators remembers the 1936 Olympics, in which the Japanese, who occupied Korea, gave a Korean runner a Japanese name and required him to run under the Japanese flag.

8. Tunnell, Michael O. **Brothers in Valor: A Story of Resistance.** New York: Holiday House, 2001. 260p. $16.95. ISBN 0-8234-1541-4.

Rudy Ollenik tells about his participation in the Helmuth Hubener Group that resisted Hitler during World War II.

ᘓᘔ

Strasser, Todd. **Give a Boy a Gun.**

New York: Simon & Schuster, 2000. 146p. $16.00. ISBN 0-689-81112-8.

Summary/Description

Denise Shipley, a college journalism student and stepsister of one of the perpetrators, gathers interview information from the victims, parents, teachers, and neighbors involved in a terrorist act carried out in the Middletown High School gymnasium. Statements and e-mail conversations she organizes in her story reveal how two boys, bullied and teased by the school's jocks, build their hate and how they plan their rebellion by holding an entire school dance at gunpoint in a booby-trapped gym. The two boys shoot a faculty member and maim the football star who has harassed them the most. When they realize that one of their friends is in the group and that the friend is willing to defy them to save the football star's life, their plan unravels. Gary, Denise's stepbrother, commits suicide, and Brendan, his friend, is almost beaten to death by the athletes he has held at gunpoint. The interviews and conversations suggest that guns, intolerance, video games, media violence, and adult irresponsibility all contributed to the tragedy. At the bottom of almost every page, Strasser includes a fact about child and young-adult violence. Incidents of violence and news items about gun control are listed under "While This Book Was Being Written." A Partial List of School Shootings provides the titles of news articles in several publications such as the *Wall Street Journal*, *The New York Times*, *Rolling Stone*, the *Windsor Star* of Canada, *Time* magazine, and the *Rocky Mountain News*. In "Final Thoughts," Strasser lists books, magazine articles, printed material, and a list of Web sites for more information.

Booktalk

Bring in headlines of school violence or read from the list of school shootings on pages 137 to 142.

In 1999 you were more likely to be killed while attending an American school than while flying on an American airplane. Why? Because you probably were attending school with students like Gary and Brendan. They are a little different, and nobody at Middletown High School likes people who are different. So the Middletown in-crowd makes fun of them, pushes them in the halls, and even swirls their heads in the school toilets. Gary and Brendan aren't strong enough to fight back with their fists. They build bombs and buy guns. Then they come to the school dance. Could this happen at your school? Reading *Give a Boy a Gun* could help you to keep your own school and family out of the headlines.

Activities

1. Final Thoughts lists further sources of information about violence. Choose one of the sources and share information from that source with the group. Research or ask your librarian to help you find additional sources.
2. Read the excerpt from Strasser's speech "Million Mom March" in *VOYA* magazine (Related Work 5). List Strasser's major ideas. Agree and/or disagree with them. Use specifics that support the opinions you express.
3. After reading *Kids and Guns* (Related Work 4) by Ted Schwarz, discuss what reports, inferences, and opinions in his nonfiction analysis apply to the characters in *Give a Boy a Gun.* Note particularly chapters 1, 2, 3, 6, and 8 of *Kids and Guns.*
4. In *Give a Boy a Gun,* Brendan and Gary feel threatened and angry with the social cliques and the school hierarchy that give the jocks so much power. In the short story "The Truth in the Case of Eliza Mary Muller, by Herself" (Related Work 1), a young girl shoots the brother-in-law who attacks her but does not feel justified. Discuss the thinking presented in these two works. Then write a paragraph in which you state your own opinion about each character's point of view.
5. *Give a Boy a Gun, Swallowing Stones* (Related Work 2), and *Making Up Megaboy* (Related Work 7) use fictional characters to communicate ideas about young people and guns. List each author's ideas.
6. After viewing *Vigilantes* (Related Work 6), discuss whether school shooters such as those depicted in *Give a Boy a Gun* might be considered this country's new version of vigilantes.

Related Works

1. Griffin, Pim R. "The Truth in the Case of Eliza Mary Muller, by Herself." In **Stay True: Short Stories for Strong Girls,** edited by Marilyn Singer. New York: Scholastic Press, 1998. 204p. $16.95. ISBN 0-590-36031-0. A young girl shoots her brother-in-law who beats up her sister and threatens to attack her. Afterward she feels she could have sought another way to handle the problem. The story appears on pages 109 to 126.

2. McDonald, Joyce. **Swallowing Stones.** (See full booktalk in chapter 2.) Shooting a rifle into the air, the main character accidentally kills a man. He tries to cover up the incident but finally takes responsibility for his actions.

3. Myers, Walter Dean. **145th Street: Short Stories.** (See full booktalk in chapter 2.) In the short story "The Baddest Dog in Harlem" on pages 15 to 25, a young boy is killed by police fire as he looks out the window. In "Kitty and Mack: A Love Story," on pages 87 to 103, a high school athlete loses his foot because he is caught in a drive-by shooting.

4. Schwarz, Ted. **Kids and Guns.** New York: Franklin Watts, 1999. 128p. $24.00. ISBN 0-531-11723-5. **NF** In chapter 1, Schwarz reviews recent shootings and the unlikely perpetrators. In the chapters that follow, he considers those actions in the framework of Americans' attitudes toward guns.

5. Shoemaker, Joel. "Todd Strasser Takes Aim at School Shootings: An Interview." *VOYA* (June 2001) 100–103. **NF** Strasser discusses how he developed his idea for *Give a Boy a Gun.* The second half of the article is an excerpt from Strasser's speech for the Million Mom March in which he compares the gun crisis to other problems such as disease and faulty tires to which the national response has been much stronger.

6. **Vigilantes.** Produced by A&E Television Networks, 1999. 50 min. Videocassette. Color. (History's Mysteries). $19.95. AAE-42602. The documentary divides the history of vigilantes into the Western groups that punished lawbreakers and the Southern groups that repressed people.

7. Walker, Virginia (text) and Katrina Roechelein (graphics). **Making Up Megaboy.** New York: DK Publishing/Richard Jackson, 1998. 63p. $16.95. ISBN 0-7894-2488-6. (See full booktalk in *Booktalks Plus*, 2001, pages 82 to 84.) Robbie Jones, on his thirteenth birthday, shoots the elderly owner of a liquor store. The story is built with the perceptions of witnesses, friends, acquaintances, police, and family.

⚜⚜

Cormier, Robert. **Heroes.**

New York: Delacorte Press, 1998. 135p. $15.95. ISBN 0-385-32590-8.

Summary/Description

Francis Joseph Cassavant tells his story. The novel opens at the end of World War II. Francis returns to Frenchtown in Monument without a face. He won the Silver Star for saving his company by falling on a grenade. Actually, he tried to kill himself. Now he's come back to kill the man who caused him to go to war, Larry LaSalle.

Larry LaSalle, before the war, headed the "Wreck Center," a teen gathering place. Popular, talented, and manipulative, he takes a special interest in Francis and Nicole Renard, Francis's girlfriend. When World War II begins, LaSalle enlists. When he wins the Silver Star, he returns to a hero's welcome. For a special evening, he reopens the Wreck Center and celebrates with his teenage followers. At the end of the evening, he persuades Francis to go home because LaSalle wants to have one dance alone with Nicole, even though Nicole asks Francis not to leave. Waiting outside, Francis knows Nicole is being raped but does not help her. Her resulting pain and disgust drive Francis to lie about his age, enlist, and try to kill himself.

Larry LaSalle returns to the town also. When Francis confronts him, he discovers that Larry LaSalle has lost both his legs and that all his good works were intended to make up for his weakness—molesting and attacking young girls. LaSalle persuades Francis not to ruin his own life with murder and confesses that he has contemplated suicide. As Francis leaves, he hears the shot that kills LaSalle. Then he seeks out Nicole Renard, who has moved to another town. He finds that she no longer blames Francis, but hardened by the experience, wishes to seek her own identity. When Francis leaves her, his decision is unclear. Will he rebuild his face and life or kill himself?

Booktalk

Display a picture of the Silver Star or the medal itself. Ask students if they know what a Silver Star is.

Heroes tells the stories of two Silver Star winners. World War II is over, and the heroes come home. Joseph Cassavant won his Silver Star but lost his face in the process. Now he wants to kill another Silver Star winner, the one who took away his happiness. The battles off the field seem harder than military combat. Can Francis kill a man he grew up admiring? Can he win back the love he betrayed? Can he live with what is left of Francis Joseph Cassavant? The medal can tell Francis he's a hero, but it can't tell him—or the man he wants to kill—how *Heroes* are supposed to live.

Related Activities

1. Begin to read on page 1 and continue to the division on page 3. Francis Joseph Cassavant is eighteen years old and he's a hero. Discuss what these opening pages tell us about Cormier's view of heroism?

This activity might also be a strong booktalk if you wish to share the opening with the group.

2. Read pages 108 to 118. In this chapter, the two Silver Star winners confront each other. Discuss the following questions. What does the confrontation reveal about each of them? What does it suggest about heroism?

3. Read from "I remember…" to the end of the novel (pages 134 to 135). Discuss the tone of the passage and then all the possible endings. Write a final chapter that takes place ten years after the story ends.

4. Francis comes home from the war without a face. Larry LaSalle comes home without legs. Discuss how these injuries might be used figuratively.

5. Read the final paragraph of *Bowie* (Related Work 4). Discuss what that paragraph suggests about all heroes and the concept of heroism. Ask your librarian to help you research the concept of heroism in war or conflict. You might compare definitions of heroism from two different cultures.

Related Works

1. Anderson, Laurie Halse. **Speak.** (See full booktalk in chapter 2.) Before entering ninth grade, Melinda Sordino is raped by a handsome, charismatic star athlete. Her guilt and fear drive her to a self-destructive silence.

2. Bode, Janet. **Voices of Rape.** New York: Franklin Watts, 1998 rev. ed. 160p. $25.00. ISBN 0-531-11518-6. **NF** The book explains how the entire community is involved in the problem of rape.

3. "A Bouquet for Bob." *VOYA.* (February 2001) 390–393. **NF** This article is a series of tributes to Cormier, all of which indicate that he himself is a hero.

4. Eickhoff, Randy Lee and Leonard C. Lewis. **Bowie.** New York: Forge, 1998. 304p. $23.95. ISBN 0-312-86619-4. Giving many perceptions of Jim Bowie, one of the fallen heroes of the Alamo, the novel suggests that no man can match the hero legends that surround him.

5. Hughes, Dean. **Soldier Boys.** (See full booktalk in chapter 1.) Two teenagers who go to war for personal glory discover the importance of a different kind of heroism.

6. Sparks, Beatrice, ed. **Annie's Baby: The Diary of Anonymous, A Pregnant Teenager.** New York: Avon Books, 1998. 245p. $4.50pa. ISBN 0-380-79141-2. Annie, wanting to be part of the popular group, enters into an abusive relationship that involves rape, humiliation, and an unexpected pregnancy.

CgꙄ

Deuker, Carl. **Painting the Black.**

Boston, MA: Houghton Mifflin Company, 1997. 248p. $14.95. ISBN 0-395-82848-1.

Summary/Description

Ryan Ward, seriously hurt in a fall from a tree, loses all hope of excelling in sports. Josh Daniels moves in across the street just before their senior year and inspires Ryan to hone his catching skills so he can catch for Josh. Josh's best pitch is a slider. Because Ryan is the only catcher on the team who can handle the pitch, he is on the team.

Josh uses athletic skill and fame to break school rules. He forms a male-athlete cafeteria table that dominates the school and harasses girls. The harassment escalates to two serious incidents. He pulls one girl's blouse off in the cafeteria, and he and another boy attack a girl by whom he feels threatened. Ryan interrupts the attack. Josh assumes Ryan will cover for him so Josh can help the team win the baseball championship, but Ryan chooses personal integrity over winning. After Ryan reveals that Josh was involved in the attack, Josh is shunned.

Painting the Black does not characterize athletics or athletes as either all good or all bad. Having worked hard in athletics, Ryan knows he can achieve other difficult goals. Ryan's telling on Josh helps the girl who has been attacked but does not harm Josh, who wins a million-dollar major-league contract. Selfish and self-centered Josh lives as he pitches, on the edge or *Painting the Black*, and the story illustrates that society's attitude toward athletes allows Josh to push the rules to the limit.

Booktalk

Ask how many people know what Painting the Black means. If no one can explain that phrase, read the first paragraph of the book aloud.

Josh Daniels moves to town in his senior year. That could be difficult for anyone, but Josh also has some very high goals. He wants to be the school's star quarterback and star pitcher. Then he can make the headlines, get into some good schools, and maybe get a big fat contract with a major league organization. But Josh needs some help. He needs someone to get him in, show him the ropes, and help him be a star. That person will be his catcher—Ryan Ward.

Ryan didn't think he could ever play baseball again, but suddenly, with Josh's help, he's getting in shape and learning all the right moves. When the moves get meaner and a lot more dangerous, Ryan discovers that Josh is *Painting the Black* on and off the field. Then Ryan has to make some calls that are more important and unpopular than slider or fastball.

Related Activities

1. In his novel, Carl Deuker uses the phrase "painting the black" to describe how Josh lives his life. In the poem "The Pitcher" (Related Work 3), Robert Francis also uses baseball figuratively. The pitcher represents more than a person standing on the mound. He also represents anyone communicating with another or making a "pitch." Read "The Pitcher." Discuss what the speaker is saying, and identify people or groups of people the speaker might be describing. Then discuss how the poem might apply to both Josh and Ryan in *Painting the Black.*

2. In both *Painting the Black* and *Safe at Second* (Related Work 4), the main characters worship high school baseball stars. Compare the two novels. Discuss how the main character in each novel comes to realize his self-worth.

3. In both *Painting the Black* and *Heroes* (Related Work 2), a young man realizes his personal hero has attacked a young girl. Both young men have the opportunity to act during and after the attack. Ryan, of *Painting the Black,* interrupts the attack. Francis, of *Heroes,* allows his hero to complete a rape. Compare the two characters, the decisions they make, and the results of those decisions.

4. In both *Painting the Black* and *Bull Catcher* (Related Work 1), the main characters conclude that their academic chances are better than their athletic ones. Compare the two characters and the factors that influenced their decisions.

5. Research the percentage of high school athletes who make it to the major leagues and high salaries. Share your findings with the group.

6. *Jackie's Nine* (Related Work 5) explains and illustrates the values Jackie Robinson practiced on and off the field. List the values of Josh Daniels in *Painting the Black.* Illustrate how his actions demonstrate each value.

Related Works

1. Carter, Alden R. **Bull Catcher.** New York: Scholastic Press, 1997. 279p. $15.95. ISBN 0-590-50958-6. (See full booktalk in *Booktalks Plus,* 2001, pages 96 to 98.) Neil Larsen decides academics will give him more rewards than the athletics his friends encourage him to pursue.

2. Cormier, Robert. **Heroes.** (See full booktalk in chapter 2.) A young man allows the man he idolizes to rape a young girl. Then he must live with the consequences of his decision.

3. Francis, Robert. "The Pitcher." In **Teaching Poetry in High School,** by Albert B. Somers. Urbana, IL: National Council of Teachers of English (NCTE), 1999. 219p. $19.95. ISBN 0-8141-

5289-9. **NF** The poem, paired with "The Base Stealer," also by Francis, illustrates Somers's point that short poems with appealing content can communicate important themes without preaching. The pitcher portrayed in the poem "The Pitcher" can symbolize anyone communicating with the purpose of fooling the receiver.

4. Johnson, Scott. **Safe at Second.** New York: Philomel Books, 1999. 254p. $17.99. ISBN 0-399-23365-2. (See full booktalk in *Booktalks Plus*, 2001, pages 101 to 103.) Paulie worships Todd Bannister, the star high school pitcher, but must develop his own strengths when a line drive destroys Todd's eye and his chances for a major league career.

5. Robinson, Sharon. **Jackie's Nine: Jackie Robinson's Values to Live By.** (See full booktalk in chapter 2.) **NF** Jackie Robinson's values to live by include courage, determination, teamwork, persistence, integrity, citizenship, justice, commitment, and excellence.

Robinson, Sharon. Jackie's Nine: Jackie Robinson's Values to Live By.

New York: Scholastic Incorporated, 2001. 192p. $15.95. ISBN 0-439-23764-5. **NF**

Summary/Description

Sharon Robinson's articles illustrate the nine principles she feels guided her father's life—courage, determination, teamwork, persistence, integrity, citizenship, justice, commitment, and excellence. An essay by Sharon Robinson introduces each principle, and a short commentary preceding each article explains how the article fits into the section. In addition to essays by Jackie Robinson and his family, Robinson includes essays by authors such as Dr. Martin Luther King, Reverend Jesse L. Jackson, Jules Tygiel, Christopher Reeves, and David Remnick. She also profiles others who have lived by these principles—Elizabeth Eckford, Roberto Clemente, Muhammad Ali, Michael Jordon, Christopher Reeves, and Oprah Winfrey. The selections, short enough to be read aloud, illustrate the importance of personal choices based on strong positive values. The many pictures illustrate the life and times of the people discussed.

Booktalk

Ask how many people in the group know the name Jackie Robinson.

In 1945, Jackie Robinson broke baseball's color barrier by entering the National Baseball League. Like many other African-American players in the Negro leagues, he could play as well or better than any white player.

But like other African-American players, he was judged by his skin color instead of his talent. The man who would cross that color line had to do more than run bases and bat a ball. He had to change millions of minds and hearts. Now his daughter tells about the qualities and beliefs that helped him persuade a nation: courage, determination, teamwork, persistence, integrity, citizenship, justice, commitment, and excellence. Jackie Robinson brought these values with him to baseball, and he continued to live by them when he retired. They led him to march with Dr. Martin Luther King and win the praise of Presidents. The same values have helped Christopher Reeves, Michael Jordan, Roberto Clemente, and Oprah Winfrey. Find out what *Jackie's Nine* can do for you.

Related Activities

1. Each day, read one essay aloud. React to it either in journal writing or in discussion.
2. After reading all the essays in a section, list the specifics in each essay that illustrate that value. Then find two or three other specific articles or books that illustrate that value. Share those specifics and the reasons for your choices with the group.
3. Listen to and discuss the examples from activity 2 that are chosen by each person. Group them and then explain each grouping. For example, courage examples might be divided into physical courage, emotional courage, and mental courage. Explain each group and write a sentence that anticipates or acts as a topic sentence for the specific examples.
4. Arrange the sentences from activity 3 in the order you feel they should be discussed. Write a sentence that anticipates or acts as a topic sentence for the sentences developed in activity 3.
5. Arranging all the sentences written in activity 3 in an outline and then drawing from the examples to illustrate each value, write a composition or speech that describes or defines one of the nine values illustrated in *Jackie's Nine*. Be sure to include why the value is important to explain, and illustrate the value with an example.
6. Research the color line in baseball. You might wish to start by reading *The Negro Leagues* (Related Work 7). Share your information with the group.

Related Works

1. Brokaw, Tom. **The Greatest Generation.** New York: Random House, 1998. 412p. $24.95. ISBN 0-375-50202-5. **NF** On pages 193 to 202, Johnnie Holmes relates the honorable behavior of Jackie Robinson.

2. Copley, Robert E. **The Tall Mexican: The Life of Hank Aguirre All-Star Pitcher, Businessman, Humanitarian.** Houston, TX: Piñata Books, 2000. 159p. $9.95pa. ISBN 1-55885-294-8. **NF** Aguirre, winner of the Roberto Clemente Award for Excellence, completed a successful baseball career and then committed himself to the "advancement of Hispanic Americans." This straightforward biography tells about his successes and failures in his athletic and business careers.

3. **Jackie Robinson.** Produced by A&E and CEL Communications, 1991. 44 min. Videocassette. Color. (Biography) $14.95. AAE-20102. This documentary portrays Jackie Robinson as a determined man in politics and social action as well as athletics.

4. Lynch, Chris. **Gold Dust.** New York: HarperCollins Publishers, 2000. 196p. $15.95. ISBN 0-06-028174-X. Set in the 1970s, this story centers on the fantasy a young baseball player has about the Boston Red Sox rookies, the Gold Dust twins, and how that fantasy forces him to face some cruel facts about prejudice.

5. Myers, Walter Dean. **The Greatest: Muhammad Ali.** (See full booktalk in chapter 2.) **NF** Like Jackie Robinson, Ali used his athletic ability to break color barriers, but his attitude and activism were much more militant than Robinson's.

6. Myers, Walter Dean. **The Journal of Biddy Owens: The Negro Leagues.** New York: Scholastic Incorporated, 2001. 144p. (My Name is America). $10.95. ISBN 0-439-09503-4. Seventeen-year-old Biddy Owens travels with the Birmingham Black Barons in the 1948 season, the last big season of the Negro Leagues.

7. Riley, James A. **The Negro Leagues.** Philadelphia, PA: Chelsea House Publishers, 1997. 102p. $9.95. ISBN 0-7910-2591-8. Riley emphasizes the talent of the players who were born too soon to benefit from the integration of baseball, but also points out that Moses Fleetwood Walker was the first African-American to play major-league baseball.

൚൚

Myers, Walter Dean. The Greatest: Muhammad Ali.

New York: Scholastic Press, 2000. 192p. $16.95. ISBN 0-590-54342-3. **NF**

Summary/Description

The Greatest opens with a blow-by-blow account of the Liston-Clay fight that made Cassius Marcellus Clay the world heavyweight champion. The rest of the biography answers the question many asked after the fight, "Who is this guy?" In Part I, Myers relates how boxing offered Ali and other boys his age a way to stay straight and off the streets. Cassius Clay's talent and dedication led to the Olympic Gold in 1960 and the heavyweight title in 1964. His mouth outside the ring and his "dance" in the ring made him charismatic and controversial.

In Part II, Myers explains the spiritual journey that led Clay to the nation of Islam, a new name (Muhammad Ali), and political protest. His religious affiliation and refusal to go to Vietnam threatened powerful establishments, who tried to defeat Ali by taking his title and barring him from the ring. Ali withstood both political and physical blows. He used a hostile media to increase the audience's interest and fighters' revenue.

Myers emphasizes that repeated physical punishment is any fighter's greatest opponent. Part III describes Ali's most publicized fights: the "Rumble in the Jungle," the "Thrilla in Manila," and Ali's battle against Parkinson's disease. Myers suggests that Ali, like many great fighters before him, has become a victim of the brutal sport that continues to be a way out of dead-end lives.

Booktalk

Some called him Cassius Clay. Some called him the Louisville Lip. But he called himself *The Greatest,* and he named himself Muhammad Ali. Determined to "float like a butterfly, sting like a bee," he changed the boxing ring into a dance floor and used his mind as well as his fists to battle boxers, politicians, and the media. He showed the world that a black man can choose his spiritual path and carve his own destiny, even when that destiny includes a crippling illness. *The Greatest: Muhammad Ali* tells the story of a without-a-doubt champion in a brutal sport and a brutal world.

Related Activities

1. Both *Boxing in Black and White* (Related Work 1) and *The Greatest: Muhammad Ali* compare Jack Johnson and Ali in their fighting styles and their impact on the public. Research the lives, styles, and times of both fighters. Share your information with the group.

2. Myers refers to Ali's pride as a black man and his participation in Islam. Research the 1960s and the conflicts within the African-American community as well as the conflicts between the Anglo and African-American communities over the issue of civil rights. You might wish to start with *The Assassination of Malcolm X* (Related Work 3) and *The Assassination of Martin Luther King Jr.* (Related Work 2).

3. In *Fighting Ruben Wolfe* (Related Work 6), two brothers in a very different culture discover that the fighting that gives them fame and fortune is defining them and their relationship. After reading the novel and the Myers biography of Muhammad Ali, discuss the challenges depicted in these fiction and nonfiction accounts. Consider which challenges seem restricted to the sport and which challenges are universal.

4. In *Jackie's Nine* (Related Work 5), Robinson lists the qualities that defined Robinson. Ali is included in that book as an example of integrity. List other qualities you feel define Ali. Explain your reasons with examples from his life.

5. Read the closing quotation on page 155. In your own words, explain what the statement means. Then agree and/or disagree with it. Use specific examples to support your opinion.

Related Works

1. Bacho, Peter. **Boxing in Black and White.** New York: Henry Holt and Company, 1999. 122p. $18.95. ISBN 0-8050-5779-X. **NF** This analysis of boxing and the racial problems its participants symbolize includes two full chapters ("Muhammad Ali' and "The End of Exile—'The Greatest' Returns") about Ali and his times.

2. Ching, Jacqueline. **The Assassination of Martin Luther King Jr.** New York: Rosen Publishing Group, 2002. 64p. (The Library of Political Assassinations). $19.95. ISBN 0-8239-3543-4. **NF** Like the other books in the series, the Martin Luther King volume opens with a description of the assassination and then explains King's life and beliefs. Two timelines—one tracing his life and one tracing his times—are included, as are addresses, Web sites, videos, and a bibliography of additional sources.

3. Draper, Allison Stark. **The Assassination of Malcolm X.** New York: Rosen Publishing Group, 2002. 64p. (The Library of Political Assassinations). $19.95. ISBN 0-8239-3542-6. **NF** This volume portrays Malcolm X as one of the most aggressive and controversial African-American leaders. See the Martin Luther King Jr. entry (Related Works 3) for a description of the book's format.

4. Myers, Walter Dean. **145th Street: Short Stories.** (See full book-talk in chapter 2.) The dialog that opens "The Baddest Dog in Harlem" on pages 15 to 25 shows how important Ali is to a Harlem neighborhood. The short story "Fighter" on pages 27 to 38 emphasizes Myers's message in *The Greatest*. The main character is dying because he trusts his fists rather than his brain to earn money for his family.

5. Remnik, David. "Old Man by the Fire." In **Jackie's Nine,** by Sharon Robinson. (See full booktalk in chapter 2.) **NF** The article in the Integrity section discusses Ali's refusal of the draft.
6. Zusak, Markus. **Fighting Ruben Wolfe.** New York: Arthur A. Levine Books, 2000. 224p. $15.95. ISBN 0-439-24188-X. Two brothers discover fighting as a lucrative escape from their family problems, but like Ali, they soon find the sport defining them.

Karr, Kathleen. The Boxer.

New York: Farrar Straus Giroux, 2000. 169p. $16.00. ISBN 0-374-30921-3.

Summary/Description

Fifteen-year-old John Aloysius Xavier Woods works in a sweatshop in New York's Lower East Side during the late nineteenth century. The oldest of six children, he helps his mother support the family his father deserted two years before. He takes a saloon's offer of a five-dollar purse for a boxing match. The police raid the saloon. In jail John meets Michael O'Shaunnessey, a renowned boxer, who changes John into the winning Johnny "the Chopper" Woods.

Released from prison, Johnny discovers that boxing in private clubs is legal. He boxes, supports his family, attends a vocational high school, and saves for a small house in Brooklyn. Offered a bribe to throw a fight, Johnny decides to abandon boxing, but finds his savings eaten up by a whooping cough epidemic.

Michael O'Shaunnessey reappears. Working at the New York Athletic Club, he hires Johnny. O'Shaunnessey trains Johnny for bigger professional fights, and when Johnny wins a thousand-dollar purse, he moves the family to Brooklyn where, by furthering their education, they can use their minds instead of their fists to succeed.

Booktalk

Fifteen-year-old John Aloysius Xavier Woods works in a sweatshop all day. He gives his pay to his mother for his five brothers and sisters, keeping a dime for himself. On his way home from work one day, he sees a sign on Brodie's saloon. *Read the boxed announcement in bold print on page 6.* Five dollars is more than John makes in two weeks.

In 1895, boxing in New York is illegal. John knows that. The house fighter is breaking the bones of everyone who comes up against him. John knows that, too. But John, smaller and younger than all the other fighters, decides to go for the gold. He gets six months in prison instead of the purse, discovers the best boxers are behind bars, and becomes Johnny "the Chopper" Woods. His fists give him money and fame, but how long can his body and brain survive the life of *The Boxer?*

Related Activities

1. John, the main character, helps his family but recognizes the need for all the family members to help themselves. Discuss how he shows his willingness to help and his reluctance to be anyone's sole means of support.
2. After reading *97 Orchard Street, New York: Stories of Immigrant Life* (Related Work 3), draw or paint an illustration of the room or apartment the Woods family might have rented.
3. After reading "Fighter" in *145th Street: Short Stories* (Related Work 4), compare the main character in "Fighter" with John Woods in *The Boxer.*
4. John Woods begins to fight because he sees it as an opportunity to earn more money than he can earn in a sweatshop. Beginning with *Kids on Strike* (Related Work 2), research the conditions of labor during the late nineteenth and early twentieth centuries. Your librarian can guide you to additional sources.
5. John's story raises many questions about right and wrong in work, lawmaking, and family life. Identify those issues and how you feel about Karr's portrayal of them.

Related Works

1. Bacho, Peter. **Boxing in Black and White.** New York: Henry Holt and Company, 1999. 122p. $18.95. ISBN 0-8050-5779-X. **NF** Bacho discusses how the sport of boxing, a means for the poor to earn money, became a metaphor for black/white relations in the United States.
2. Bartoletti, Susan Campbell. **Kids On Strike.** Boston, MA: Houghton Mifflin Company, 1999. 208p. $20.00. ISBN 0-395-88892-1. **NF** This nonfiction account, filled with pictures and stories of hardship and self-improvement, describes over one hundred years of child labor.
3. Granfield, Linda (text) and Arlene Alda (photographs). **97 Orchard Street, New York: Stories of Immigrant Life.** New York: Tundra Books of Northern New York, 2001. 57p. $15.00. ISBN 0-88776-580-7. **NF** Based on the research and restoration of the Lower East Side Tenement Museum, this slim volume of pictures, sketches, and text vividly depicts life for the immigrant families of the period. The nonfiction strongly supports Karr's fictional presentation.

4.   Myers, Walter Dean. **145th Street: Short Stories.** (See full book-talk in chapter 2.) Unlike John in *The Boxer,* the main character of "Fighter" on pages 27 to 38 sees using his fists as his only option for earning money for his family.

5.   Overstreet, Deborah Wilson. "Organize! A Look at Labor History in Young Adult Books." *The ALAN Review* (Fall 2001) 60–66. **NF** Overstreet summarizes, criticizes, and recommends fiction and nonfiction books that give insight into the fight for labor rights. She provides a bibliography of Works Cited and recommended young-adult nonfiction. Her discussion includes the child abuse and blatant racism against the Irish during the time period.

Cross, Gillian. **Tightrope.**

New York: Holiday House, 1999. 216p. $16.95. ISBN 0-8234-1512-0.

Summary/Description

Fourteen-year-old Ashley Putnam takes care of her invalid mother. At night she "tags" buildings by painting "Cindy" across a blank wall. Tagging the wall on Fat Annie's store, she attracts the attention of Eddie Beale, a local gang leader. Eddie begins to help Ashley and her mother, but Eddie helps only those who perform for him, such as Joe, an abused boy who does imitations, and Sam, Eddie's girlfriend, who swallows fire.

Ashley begins receiving messages from a stalker. Eddie blames Fat Annie's son, Geoffrey Galt, a quiet, middle-aged guy nicknamed Hyena. Ashley confronts Galt, realizes that he has been set up, discovers that he thinks she is a good girl unaffected by gang intimidation, and learns that the Galts refuse to pay Eddie protection money. Ashley confronts Eddie. He threatens her and her mother. To prove his power, he humiliates Sam in front of Sam's mother and Joe, Eddie's eyes and ears on the street. Deciding to clear the Hyena's name, Ashley paints an announcement of a street meeting on Fat Annie's store. Eddie shows up with his supporters and a loudspeaker to distract the crowd, but wheelchair user Tony Cavalieri, whom Eddie's men beat up, focuses the crowd on Ashley. Ashley begins a dangerous acrobatic act, but Eddie's acts are better. Then Sam and Joe use their imitations and fire act against Eddie. Tony alerts the crowd that Eddie's men are about to attack Ashley. Startled, Ashley falls, and Galt runs forward to catch her. Horrified by the terrible accident and two broken bodies, the crowd drives Eddie away. Ashley and Galt recover. Ashley now has a support group in a gang-dominated culture.

At the end of each chapter, one of the characters describes how he or she perceives the events or people in the chapter.

Booktalk

Fourteen-year-old Ashley Putnam is walking a *Tightrope*. She wants to do well in school, care for her sick mother, and help her seven-year-old twin sisters. But she also wants to have friends, fun, and even some thrills. She decides to become the mysterious "Cindy," so she sneaks out of her room at night and paints her mystery name on city walls. Ashley gets more thrills and attention than she bargained for. The local gang boss wants to see her. The neighbors drop in to visit her mother, and party friends appear. Then a stalker sends her disturbing notes and bloody symbols. Can she still keep her balance, or are Ashley and her mysterious Cindy due for a deadly fall?

Related Activities

1. In *Bowie* (Related Work 2), the author tells the same event from several points of view. At the end of each *Tightrope* chapter, one of the characters reveals how he or she has perceived an event. Read the various perceptions in both works. Discuss what the inferences and judgments reveal about each speaker.
2. Choose an event or a conversation you have observed during the day. Then write either two versions of it or a description of the event from your point of view and another person's point of view.
3. Ashley's inferences or guesses lead her to some bad judgments. How does Eddie Beale manipulate her perceptions? How is she able to finally clarify her thinking?
4. Ashley gets thrills and attention from graffiti and using the name Cindy. Discuss Ashley's choices and reactions. Then discuss the messages you would write and the name you would use if you were a graffiti artist.
5. In *Facing the Dark* (Related Work 3) and *Tightrope*, the authors use different perceptions of the same event, surprise characters, and gangs to build their mysteries. After reading the two novels, compare how each technique helps the writer build excitement and suspense.
6. Continue to research how gangs form and how they affect the people living in their territories. You might wish to start by reading *Gangs: Opposing Viewpoints* (Related Work 1).

Related Works

1. Egendorf, Laura. **Gangs: Opposing Viewpoints.** San Diego, CA: Greenhaven Press, 2001. 170p. (Opposing Viewpoints Series). $23.00.

ISBN 0-7377-0510-8. **NF** The articles emphasize that gangs thrive in homes where teenagers crave attention.

2.   Eickhoff, Randy Lee and Leonard C. Lewis. **Bowie.** New York: Forge, 1998. 304p. $23.95. ISBN 0-312-86619-4. In this work of historical fiction, A.J. Sowell, the narrator, gathers differing perceptions about significant events in the life of Jim Bowie, the colorful hero of the Alamo.

3.   Harrison, Michael. **Facing the Dark.** New York: Holiday House, 2000. 128p. $15.95. ISBN 0-8234-1491-4. An accused murderer's son and the murdered man's daughter join up to solve the crime. They record their perceptions of people and events in alternating chapters.

4.   Kay, Philip, Andria Estepa, and Al Desetta. **Things Get Hectic: Teens Write About the Violence That Surrounds Them.** New York: Touchstone Books, 1998. 282p. $13.00. ISBN 0-684-83754-4. **NF** In "Rocking, Bombing, Tagging…My Career as a Writer" on pages 141 to 145, an anonymous author describes the excitement and compulsion of graffiti.

5.   Wright, Cynthia. **Everything You Need to Know About Dealing with Stalking.** New York: Rosen Publishing Group, 2000. 64p. (The Need to Know Library). $17.95. ISBN 0-8329-2841-1. **NF** This source tells how to identify, prevent, and deal with stalking.

༄༅

Hamm, Mia with Aaron Heifetz. Go for the Goal: A Champion's Guide to Winning in Soccer and Life.

New York: HarperCollins Publishers, 1999. 222p. $21.00.
ISBN 0-06-019342-5. NF

Summary/Description

Although Mia Hamm speaks primarily to girls interested in soccer, her advice in Part I about working hard and sacrificing for success, following a passion, improving focus, and maintaining physical fitness encourages all young adults to work successfully for themselves and those around them. Part II talks about specific soccer skills and gives advice, specific drills, and diagrams concerning trapping the ball, passing, dribbling, shooting, heading, and goal keeping. Other players, such as Tiffeny Milbrett, Tisha Venturini, Briana Scurry, and Michelle Akers, contribute advice on their specialties. Part III again is for a larger audience. Hamm emphasizes that winning includes respect, sportsmanship, fitness, and personal balance as well as celebration. "Talk the Talk: the

Soccer Glossary" includes all the terms the reader will need to understand the technical advice and talk about the game.

Booktalk

Mia Hamm is shy, quiet, small, and a soccer terror. Mentally and physically tough, she decided at a young age to get her game together on and off the field. A "military brat" in a family of six children, Mia learned how to be part of a team and to adjust to new situations. In each new community, Mia's skill and ability to work with others helped her fit in, learn more, and enjoy success. As the "youngest player ever to suit up for the U.S. Women's National Team," she has proven that spirit and hard work win over age, sex, or size. *Go for the Goal: A Champion's Guide to Winning in Soccer and Life* is full of specific suggestions for improving a soccer game, but it isn't just for soccer players or girls. Mia Hamm wins in the game of life, and she can help you be a winner too.

Related Activities

1. Chapters 2, 3, 4, and 5 emphasize enjoyment, practice, focus, and physical fitness—qualities required for success in any endeavor. Think about an aspect of athletics or academics you wish to improve. Plan an activity in each of the four areas to improve your performance. Ask yourself how you can enjoy the task, practice the task, focus on the task, and increase your endurance to work on the task. You might want to adapt the format or style that Hamm uses to explain soccer drills.
2. Each week, record how your plan has improved your performance. Then decide what elements of the plan you will continue and what elements you will change.
3. Using the format of *Play Like a Girl* (Related Work 4), create a display of your school's athletic teams. Include quotations, pictures, and graphics.
4. Choose one sport and research women's participation in that sport. Share your findings with the rest of the group.
5. Part III defines a winner as a person who shows respect, sportsmanship, fitness, balance, focus, and celebration. It defines a champion as a person who always has another goal. Those labels go beyond athletics. Identify someone who, on the basis of these criteria, is both a winner and a champion. Explain your choice.

Related Works

1. Corbett, Sara. **Venus to the Hoop.** New York: Anchor Books, 1997. 341p. $12.95pa. ISBN 0-385-49352-5. (See full booktalk in *Book-*

talks Plus, 2001, pages 99 to 101.) **NF** This story of the women's Olympic team records the talent, dedication, and personalities that produced the winning team.

2.   Covey, Sean. **The 7 Habits of Highly Effective Teens.** (See full booktalk in chapter 4.) **NF** Covey explains how a person can improve and prepare to be a successful part of any group or team.

3.   Jemison, Dr. Mae C. **Find Where the Wind Goes: Moments from My Life.** New York: Scholastic Press, 2001. 208p. $16.95. ISBN 0-439-13195-2. **NF** Dr. Jemison, the first African-American woman to travel into space, encourages young people to pursue non-traditional means to realize their dreams.

4.   Macy, Sue and Jane Gottesman, ed. **Play Like a Girl: A Celebration of Women in Sports.** New York: Henry Holt and Company, 1999. 32p. $15.95. ISBN 0-8050-6071-5. **NF** This series of pictures of famous women athletes and quotations from the players about winning, losing, and loving the game would be an appropriate award book for women athletes.

5.   Sherman, Josepha. **Competitive Soccer for Girls.** New York: Rosen Publishing Group, 2001. 64p. (Sports Girl). $19.95. ISBN 0-8239-3405-5. **NF** Including a history of soccer and information about players, rules, gear, training, competition, and teamwork, the book also includes soccer organizations, Web sites, books, and online magazines.

6.   Walker, Niki and Sarah Dann. **Soccer in Action.** New York: Crabtree Publishing Co., 2000. 32p. (Sports in Action). $5.95pa. ISBN 0-7787-0173-5. **NF** This how-to manual is geared to middle school soccer players.

Developing Our Minds

Trembath, Don. **The Popsicle Journal.**
Victoria, BC: Orca Book Publishers, 2001. 144p. $6.95pa. ISBN 1-55143-185-8.

Summary/Description

High school student Harper Winslow reports for *The Emville Express* through a work release program in his school. When his editor assigns him a weekly column and the courthouse beat, Harper is in deep conflict. His father is running for mayor, but Harper feels that news he hears at home is off limits. He should report his older sister's DUI accident but believes the report would destroy his father's chances and betray his family. His editor and another student reporter push him to report the news, not filter it.

By the end of the novel, Harper's sister is living at the Winslow home without a job, her husband, or her children. Harper's father loses the election with no clear connection to the DUI article, and Harper decides accurate reporting is necessary in both private and public lives. His columns, reflecting on the demands of journalism and adulthood, present a maturing Harper.

Like other Harper Winslow books, *The Popsicle Journal* comes with new off-beat characters: Kip Kelly, the twenty-eight-year-old editor with a grade ten education; Dixie, the supportive but volatile forty-five-year-old office assistant; Paula, the eighteen-year-old, too-nice editorial assistant; Tom Davey, the sports-crazed, body-focused advertising salesman; and Rufus Monahan, an obnoxious but effective student reporter from a rival paper.

Booktalk

Harper Winslow is a real reporter—not the high school kind. He reports to a newsroom, has his own column *The Popsicle Journal,* and covers the courthouse beat. Life is great—until his editor discovers Harper forgot to mention something: Benjamin Winslow, Harper's father, is running for mayor. Next Harper discovers that his successful, buttoned-up sister is into alcohol and pills, a little detail his parents didn't mention for twelve years. Telling family secrets isn't as much fun as finding out about everyone else's. Harper has to decide if he has the guts to report all the news or if he should just turn his job over to Rufus Monahan, that weasel from *The Recorder* who can think up all the right questions and sell out his own mother to get the story.

Related Activities

1. In chapter 8, Harper comments that, as a reporter, he will not be writing the same old character sketches his English teachers assign, but chapter 1 is a series of character sketches of Harper's co-workers and family. Choose one of these sketches. List the elements Harper uses to describe people. Then, using the sketches as models, describe a member of your family, class, or work force.

2. Harper gets the name for his column, *The Popsicle Journal,* from his friend Billy. In chapter 2, beginning with the words, "I think you should use it…" Harper explains why the name is appropriate. Read the discussion about it that extends to the end of the chapter. Make up a name for a column you would like to write. Then explain the appropriateness of your choice. Write at least three columns and share

them with the group. You might wish to first read *How to Write Clearly* (Related Work 2).

3.　Seen only briefly, Clarissa plays a major role in the story. What issues does she represent for Harper?

4.　Harper tells his own story. Discuss his reliability as a narrator. Has his reliability increased, decreased, or stayed the same in comparison with his other novels?

5.　Read Harper's columns in the order they are written (see chapters 6, 8, and 14). Discuss what these columns reveal about Harper's personal and professional development.

6.　Truth is a major issue in this novel. Discuss why. Research how news media decide to run a story or accent one story over another. Share your information with the group.

Related Works

1.　Fraustino, Lisa Rowe. **Dirty Laundry: Stories About Family Secrets.** New York: Viking Press, 1998. 181p. $16.99. ISBN 0-670-87911-8. In each story, a discovered family secret changes the family relationships.

2.　Lipman, Michel and Russell Joyner. **How to Write Clearly: Guidelines and Exercises for Clear Writing.** San Francisco, CA: International Society for General Semantics, 1979. 15p. $4.00pa. Catalog number 1370HTWC. Although this book does not speak directly about newspaper columns, it quickly communicates principles of clear, effective writing. For more information, write International Society for General Semantics, P.O. Box 728, Concord, CA 94522-0728.

3.　Trembath, Don. **A Beautiful Place on Yonge Street.** Victoria, BC: Orca Book Publishers, 1998. 190p. $6.95pa. ISBN 1-55143-121-1. (See full booktalk in *Booktalks Plus*, 2001, pages 166 to 168.) In this third book of the series, Harper's parents send him to writing camp, where he falls in love with the artistic Sunny.

4.　Trembath, Don. **A Fly Named Alfred.** Victoria, BC: Orca Book Publishers, 1997. 138p. $6.95pa. ISBN 1-22143-083-5. (See full booktalk in *Booktalks Plus*, 2001, pages 128 to 130.) In this second book of the series, Harper uses his words to strike out at bullies and discovers that venting emotions rather than reporting can be unhealthy.

5.　Trembath, Don. **The Tuesday Café.** Victoria, BC: Orca Book Publishers, 1996. 121p. $6.95pa. ISBN 55143-074-6. (See full booktalk in *Booktalks Plus*, 2001, pages 23 to 25.) In this first book of the series, Harper expresses his anger by setting a fire in the school and begins his writing career when a judge assigns him to write an essay about his future.

ᘓᘔ

Ferris, Jean. **Bad.**

New York: Farrar Straus Giroux, 1998. 182p. $16.00. ISBN 0-374-30479-3.

Summary/Description

Sixteen-year-old Dallas Carpenter is willing to do anything her friends ask. When she agrees to hold the gun while they rob a Jiffy-Spot, she finds herself first in "Juvie" and then in Girls' Rehab. Here she encounters inmates such as Dahlia, who has a skin-head mentality; Damaris, who is willing to sell drugs, do drugs, and endure beatings to keep a boyfriend; Shatasia, who is a seventeen-year-old mother determined to go straight; and Toozdae, who believes she must prostitute herself to hold her family together. As Dallas moves through days filled with studies, athletics, support groups, bedtime stories, and confrontations, she begins to believe her actions, not her genes, determine her future. She identifies with the characters her English teacher shares with her. She ponders the bedtime story lessons she hears five days per week, and she watches how the staff and inmates treat and react to each other. Returning home, she finds that her meticulous, joyless father cannot trust her, and that her boyfriend and best friend who set her up for the crime are dating. When she leaves the Girls' Rehab, she requests placement in a group home rather than her own. With her books, her thoughts, and her now good friend Shatasia, she hopes to build a positive, happy life but realizes she could easily return to stealing and another term in rehabilitation.

Booktalk

Dallas is *Bad,* and she hangs with *Bad.* Why not? Her father always tells her that her mother was no good. The wild "skating" sprees she has with her friends give her a great rush, and she's probably one of the city's best shoplifters. She believes she's too smart to be caught, but she's not too smart to use a gun, and one day—Bam!—she's in Juvie and sentenced to Rehab. Her dad's fed up and lets her go. Her friends disappear when the fun stops. Now Dallas has to find out who she really is and who she wants to be. Her choices could lead to the most dangerous skate of all.

Related Activities

1. On page 182, Dallas lists ten books she has read in Girls' Rehab. Ask ten people to choose one of the books to read. Then discuss how the book applies to Dallas's life.

2. On pages 129 and 130, Dallas talks about the lessons in *Aesop's Fables* (Related Work 6). After reading each story, write the moral. Then explain how it does or does not apply to real life.

3. Each day in English class, the girls write a journal entry. Write your own journal entry in response to the assignment on page 143, "Write Five Wonderful Things About Yourself." Then make a list of journal topics you feel would challenge your group. Compare the topics you have chosen with topics chosen by other members of the group.

4. Nolan, the anger management group leader, gives Dallas a guidebook to Texas to show her all the wonderful features and choices available in the city for which she is named. The gift also implies that each person needs a map or guidebook to reach a goal in life. Identify a goal you wish to achieve, and write a map that tells how you will get there. Then read or show that map to the group, to your group leader, or to a counselor. Ask them to react to or help you revise what you have planned.

5. Select a book, poem, or story you would select for bedtime stories. Explain your choice.

6. Research juvenile detention systems. Identify one successful program. Share your findings with the group.

Related Works

1. Burnett, Frances Hodgson. **The Secret Garden.** New York: Tom Doherty Associates Book, 1988. 274p. $2.95. ISBN 0-812-50501-8. Mary Lennox and her cousin Colin Craven survive and thrive in spite of neglectful and sometimes harmful adults. The Afterword by Jane Yolen explains the background of the story in relation to children's literature and Burnett's life. The explanation is helpful in understanding its relationship to *Bad.*

2. Klebanoff, Susan and Ellen Luborsky. **Ups & Downs: How to Beat the Blues and Teen Depression.** (See full booktalk in chapter 3.) **NF** This book talks about how to maintain one's emotional balance when faced with problems.

3. Lubar, David. **Hidden Talents.** (See full booktalk in chapter 1.) Thirteen-year-old Martin Anderson successfully completes Edgeview Alternative School when he recognizes how to turn the almost supernatural powers of the students into positive directions.

4. Mikaelsen, Ben. **Touching Spirit Bear.** (See full booktalk in chapter 2.) Seeing the juvenile justice system as a game, a young man agrees to sentencing on an island.

5. Packer, Alex J. **Highs! Over 150 Ways to Feel Really, REALLY Good...Without Alcohol or Other Drugs.** Minneapolis, MN:

Free Spirit, 2000. 251p. $14.95pa. ISBN 1-57542-074-0. **NF** Packer includes inexpensive ways for teenagers to safely enjoy themselves and connect with other people.

6. Pinkney, Jerry. **Aesop's Fables.** New York: SeaStar Books, 2000. 87p. $11.96. ISBN 1-58717-000-0. Witty and instructive, the stories about animals with human qualities will provide lively discussions, writing prompts, and public speaking inspirations.

Bloor, Edward. Crusader.

New York: Harcourt Brace and Company, 1999. 390p. $17.00. ISBN 0-15-201944-8.

Summary/Description

Fifteen-year-old Roberta Ritter works in a virtual reality arcade (Arcane) operated by her father and uncle. Roberta's father doesn't pay his bills; and he spends most of his time with Suzie Quinn, the inept mall manager. Roberta's alcoholic uncle, a retired colonel, runs the business.

Roberta's mother was killed in an arcade robbery. Dreams about her mother's death haunt Roberta. Home alone, she finds comfort and fascination in *The Last Judgment*, a television program hosted by Stephen Cross, whose motto is "Admit the truth; ask forgiveness; find redemption."

Roberta has an internship at the local television station and writes the mall newsletter. Reporting makes her examine the truth in all messages, even her own.

Mrs. Weiss, who owns the mall's Hallmark Store, befriends Roberta. Seeing how selfish Roberta's father is, she invites Roberta to live with her. Mrs. Weiss, who lost her parents in Hitler's Germany, teaches Roberta to take responsibility for her own decisions.

In the arcade's virtual reality games, battles between good and evil are often expressed in racial terms. The newest game, *The Crusader*, portrays Arabs as evil. Nineteen-year-old Samir Samad (Sam), a Muslim who manages Crescent Electronics, experiences harassment and believes Arcane is responsible. Roberta and Sam watch the arcade every night from the empty store across the way. They discover that Roberta's uncle is trying to drive Sam and other successful businesses out of the mall so his business franchise will allow him to move and he can avoid bankruptcy.

Roberta also discovers that the mall owner wants it to fail so he can build a golf course complex. Using her journalism skills, she organizes the mall tenants to defeat the owner's plan. She discovers that her own father and Stephen Cross cooperated in her mother's death. She identifies Stephen Cross as the murderer and permanently separates herself from her father. Roberta concludes that although life does not follow the simple good versus evil pattern of the virtual reality games, honesty and caring are life's most valuable defenses. Mrs. Weiss dies and leaves Roberta the store, a condominium, a car, and a trust fund. But integrity, not money, gives Roberta, the *Crusader,* control of her life.

Booktalk

Fifteen-year-old Roberta Ritter works in her family's virtual reality arcade and can play any game for as long as she wants—a dream job. But Roberta doesn't have time to play games. You see, for Roberta, life is more complicated. Her mother, killed seven years ago, appears in Roberta's nightmares. Her father is more interested in dating the dizzy mall manager than in paying attention to business. Her glamorous cousin Kristen is as cruel as she is pretty, and her cousin Karl looks just plain dangerous.

Roberta wants to leave the virtual reality world and, as a journalist, search for truth, but she is tangled in the lies, lives, and crimes of people she never knew and people she only thought she knew. Can this *Crusader* win her war for right and justice, or do the good guys win only in virtual reality?

Related Activities

1. Read the paragraph that begins on page 43 with "Today's lecture was about the muckrakers..." and ends on page 45 with "This is what an editor would do." Discuss what Mr. Herman reveals about the journalism profession. In the discussion, be sure to consider the term muckraker and Mr. Herman's editing process, especially his restructuring of the story in a David/Goliath format. Continue to research famous muckrakers and their impact on history.
2. Arcane, the name of the virtual reality arcade, and Crusader, the name of the new virtual reality game and the novel, relate significantly to the novel's purpose. Discuss that relationship.
3. The motto of the television show *The Last Judgment* is "Admit the truth; ask forgiveness; find redemption." How is that statement central to the novel?
4. The virtual reality games in the Arcane express good and evil in racist terms. How is this expression harmful? How does it compare to the David/Goliath scenario Mr. Herman suggests to Roberta? Further research virtual reality games. Try to find out how they are constructed and the possible effects they have on the people who play them.
5. The minor characters in the novel have a significant effect on Roberta's life. List them. Explain how each affects her and how each relates to the novel's virtual reality motif.

Related Works

1. Fraustino, Lisa Rowe. **Dirty Laundry: Stories About Family Secrets.** New York: Viking Press, 1998. 181p. $16.99. ISBN 0-670-87911-8. Each story reveals a family secret that changes the narrators' lives or perceptions.

2. Harrison, Michael. **Facing the Dark.** New York: Holiday House, 2000. 128p. $15.95. ISBN 0-8234-1491-4. An accused murderers' son and the murdered man's daughter ignore the accusations against their fathers and work together to find the real murderer.

3. Mazer, Anne. "The Transformations of Cindy R." In **Stay True: Short Stories for Strong Girls,** edited by Marilyn Singer. New York: Scholastic Press, 1998. 204p. $16.95. ISBN 0-590-36031-0. When a fairy godmother arrives to physically transform her, the main character decides she must use her own assertiveness, not magic, to take control of her life. The story appears on pages 1 to 16.

4. McFarland, Rhoda. **Drugs and Your Parents.** New York: Rosen Publishing Group, 1997 rev. ed. 64p. (Drug Abuse Prevention Library). $17.95. ISBN 0-8239-2603-6. **NF** This book explains how teenagers can recognize drug abuse and how they can separate themselves from their parents' habits.

5. Morrison, Jaydene. **Coping with ADD/ADHD.** New York: Rosen Publishing Group, 1996. 96p. (Coping) $17.95. ISBN 0-8239-2070-4. **NF** Morrison defines and outlines strategies to deal with ADD/ADHD.

〈〉

Cushman, Karen. Matilda Bone.

New York: Clarion Books, 2000. 167p. $15.00. ISBN 0-395-88156-0.

Summary/Description

Deserted by her mother and orphaned by her father's death, young Matilda is raised by Father Leufredus, who teaches her that spiritual matters are more important than practical ones. When Father Leufredus travels to swear his loyalty to Edward III of England, he leaves Matilda with Red Peg, a bonesetter in Blood and Bone Alley. Matilda earns her keep with the practical tasks of fire building, cleaning, shopping, and cooking. At first she prays to the saints to solve all her problems. These saints and her knowledge of their gory lives and deaths give her little help. Gradually she learns to admire and trust people such as the eccentric bonesetter Peg, lowly doctor Margery Lewes, Peg's husband Tom, and the apothecary Nathaniel for their actions and compassion rather than for their status or knowledge of Latin. She builds a personal pride in completing practical tasks and discovers that her ability to read and write is not a mark of superiority but a skill she can use to help her friends. By the end of the novel, she trusts her own friend's life to the capable Margery Lewes and has earned the last name Bones from the people who respect her work. She no longer looks forward to Father Leufredus's return or the help of elusive saints.

An Author's Note explains medieval concepts of disease and medicine and lists the books about medieval medicine that the author consulted in writing the book. This book should have a special appeal to the younger, female teen audience.

Booktalk

When we go to a doctor today, we probably expect a waiting room, people dressed in white, a thermometer, a shot, or a prescription, and—oh yes—a diploma hanging on the wall. An ailing patient in medieval times could choose a physician, healer, bonesetter, or barber—mostly trained by trial and error. The practitioner might bleed the patient, choose an appropriate chant, set a broken bone, or pull a tooth. Or he or she might give out something to use at home—ground bone, the blood of a bull, the boiled down fat of a newly executed felon, or an eel skin.

Twelve-year-old Matilda suddenly finds herself dropped into this mysterious and confusing medical world. She is used to spending her days thinking about prayer and the horrible tortures of the saints: St. Lucy, who carries her eyes on a platter; St. Hippolytus, who was torn apart by horses; or St. Agnes, who was confined in a dark dungeon "before being led naked through the streets." Someday she hopes to be like them. But before she earns her own sainthood, she must work in Blood and Bone Alley with Red Peg, a notorious bonesetter. Matilda doesn't understand why Father Leufredus left her here to clean, build fires, and learn to buy fresh eel for dinner—all lowly, unimportant tasks. She seems better suited to the house of a real physician, such as Master Theobald, who speaks Latin, reads horoscopes, and skillfully tastes and stores his patients' urine. Such a man would understand how prayers and study rather than Red Peg's hand tricks heal. But as Matilda waits for Father Leufredus to return, she finds herself becoming, not Saint Matilda, but *Matilda Bone.*

Related Activities

1. On page 167, Cushman lists the books she consulted when researching *Matilda Bone*. Choose one of the books listed or a source from your own library's collection. Ask your librarian to help you find additional information. Find a fact about medicine practiced in the me-

dieval period. Share it with the members of the group through an oral or visual presentation.

2. List the events in the story that reveal how Matilda changes. Compare Matilda at the beginning of the story with Matilda at the end of the story.

3. Begin reading the passage on page 91 that begins "Afterward Peg said." Read to the bottom of the page. Explain the differences between Peg and Matilda.

4. Effie is a very minor character in the story. Why do you think Cushman includes her?

5. Read the duck conversation between Walter and Matilda that takes place on pages 137 and 138. In your own words, state the point Walter is making. If you had been Matilda, how would you have reacted to Walter's comments?

6. Compare Master Theobald and the healers of Blood and Bone Alley. Discuss the differences between them and how these differences reflect the changes in Matilda's life.

Related Works

1. Armstrong, Jennifer. "The Martyrdom of Monica Macallister." In **I Believe in Water: Twelve Brushes with Religion,** edited by Marilyn Singer. New York: HarperCollins Publishers, 2000. 280p. $24.89. ISBN 0-06-028398-X. After having contact with the Catholic faith, Monica tries to get her own Protestant congregation interested in the martyrs by using the garden gnomes to depict their bloody deaths. The story appears on pages 157 to 170.

2. Avi. "Oswin's Millennium." In **Second Sight: Stories for a New Millennium.** (See full booktalk in chapter 2.) An orphan who spends his life as a slave in the Abbey of St. Benedict is terrified by promises of devils and dragons as the world approaches the millennium. He finds that the predictions were wrong, runs away, and finds the joy of the real world. The story appears on pages 1 to 18.

3. Collins, Pat Lowery. **Signs and Wonders.** New York: Houghton Mifflin Company, 1999. 176p. $15.00. ISBN 0-395-97119-5. Fourteen-year-old Taswell, who feels ignored by her father and grandmother, believes she has been chosen to give birth to the new prophet for the millennium until her new stepmother makes her a part of their new family.

4. Meltzer, Milton. **Witches and Witch-hunts: A History of Persecution.** (See full booktalk in chapter 3.) **NF** Suggesting that each of us might have a little bit of the witch-hunter in us, Meltzer explains the psychology of witch-hunts and their connection with healing, religion, race, and politics.

5. Miklowitz, Gloria D. **Secrets in the House of Delgado.** (See full booktalk in chapter 3.) When fourteen-year-old Maria is given a job in the House of Delgado, she must decide whether she will be a spy for the Inquisition or a loyal friend to the family.

6. Newth, Mette. **The Transformation.** (See full booktalk in chapter 4.) Navarana and Brendan blend the spiritual beliefs of their fifteenth-century cultures to build a new world with each other. This novel is for a slightly more mature audience than the audience for *Matilda Bone.*

Avi. Midnight Magic.

New York: Scholastic Press, 1999. 256p. $15.95. ISBN 0-590-36035-3.

Summary/Description

Twelve-year-old Fabrizio serves Mangus the Magician, who has been tortured by the king and Count Scarazoni. Count Scarazoni returns to take Mangus to the castle. He wants the magician to free the princess from a terrifying ghost. Mangus does not want to claim magical powers but must answer to the court's pressure. Fabrizio accompanies him. Together they discover that the princess, the prince, and queen are trying to prevent Count Scarazoni from marrying the ten-year-old princess and gaining control of the Kingdom of Pergamontio. The Count thinks he has already killed the prince. Mangus and Fabrizio discover that the ghost is a combination of shadows, candlelight, and green glass created by the prince, who has escaped the assassination attempt and is now disguised as the kitchen boy. The queen, princess, and prince use the secret passages and the privacy of darkness to carry out their plan. Mangus employs logic to solve the mystery. Fabrizio adds the theatrical magic. When Scarazoni confesses his plot, justice is served. Mangus and Fabrizio find themselves successful and rewarded.

Booktalk

The ghost that haunts the beautiful Princess Teresina threatens to destroy her wedding day. The nervous groom summons the magician, but Mangus brings truth, not magic, to the castle—a truth that creates even bigger problems. The tarot cards, cast at midnight, promise death, not success, and now dead bodies, as well as ghosts, start to appear. Can truth and logic save the day, or will both the beautiful princess and the questionable count need a little *Midnight Magic*?

Related Activities

1. In chapter 2 and beginning with the phrase, "Distressed, Fabrizio…" Avi describes the castello through the eyes of Fabrizio. In his description he includes the building's significance to Fabrizio and the town. Using the description as a model, choose a building of significance in your own town and describe it.
2. In both *Midnight Magic* and *The Fool Reversed* (Related Work 6), tarot cards play a significant role. Explain how each author uses the device to direct the story. Continue to research the history of tarot cards and their use.
3. When Mangus says they will use only logic and truth, is he saying magic is useless? How would you describe the function of magic?
4. In Chapter 8, Mangus and Fabrizio exchange aphorisms about buying, gold, and payment. Discuss the truth of each saying. Using *Familiar Quotations* (Related Work 1), find groups of quotations that apply to a single topic. Discuss each one. Then try to create a conversation that incorporates at least three of them.
5. Both Matilda in *Matilda Bone* (Related Work 2) and Fabrizio in *Midnight Magic* work as apprentices in both the spirit and earthly worlds. Compare their experiences and what they learn about each of the worlds.

Related Works

1. Bartlett, John with Justin Kaplan, general editor. **Familiar Quotations: A Collection of Passages, Phrases, and Proverbs Traced to Their Sources in Ancient and Modern Literature. 16th ed.** Boston: Little, Brown, 1992. 1405p. $40.00. ISBN 0-316-08277-5. ⓝⓕ Many quotations classified by subject reveal perceptions of a particular topic that span several generations.
2. Cushman, Karen. **Matilda Bone.** (See full booktalk in chapter 2.) A young serving girl in the house of a bonesetter learns that practical arts are strong assets to spiritual beliefs.
3. Mandell, Jude. "princess dragonblood." In **half-human,** edited by Bruce Coville. (See full booktalk in chapter 2.) A young girl born to a human queen and a dragon king learns to balance her human and dragon powers so she can defeat evil. The story appears on pages 139 to 163.
4. Mayer, Anne. "The Transformations of Cindy R." In **Stay True: Short Stories for Strong Girls,** edited by Marilyn Singer. 65 to 85. New York: Scholastic Press, 1998. 204p. $16.95. ISBN 0-590-36031-0. After sending for a fairy godmother to physically transform her, a

busy and capable girl decides she can improve her life with her own assertiveness. The story appears on pages 65 to 85.

5. Meltzer, Milton. **Witches and Witch-hunts: A History of Persecution.** (See full booktalk in chapter 3.) ⓝⓕMeltzer emphasizes that the witch-hunt mentality can occur at any place and at any time as people try to figure out why evil happens.

6. Whitcher, Susan. **The Fool Reversed.** New York: Farrar Straus Giroux, 2000. 183p. $16.00. ISBN 0-374-32446-8. A young girl uses tarot cards to discover her future as she engages in an affair with a twenty-nine-year-old man. This novel is directed to a much older audience than *Midnight Magic.*

ᘓᘔ

Philbrick, Rodman. **The Last Book in the Universe.**

New York: The Blue Sky Press, 2000. 224p. $16.95. ISBN 0-439-08758-9.

Summary/Description

*T*he Last Book in the Universe expands the short story "The Last Book." Set in a future devoid of books and full of violence, the novel describes the journey of Spaz, a young Urb (city) normal (inferior breed) who remembers books. Because he has epilepsy, Spaz cannot use the mind probes that entertain and destroy others' minds. When Billy Bizmo, head of the Bully Bangers, sends Spaz to "bust…down" (rob) a gummy (old person) named Ryter, Spaz befriends this man who will give up his possessions to save the book he is writing. Spaz also connects with a feral street child and becomes fascinated by a proov (genetically improved person) princess who leaves her home in Eden to observe the Urb culture.

One night, a runner (illegal messenger) tells Spaz that his foster sister Bean, near death, wants to see him. Disobeying Billy Bizmo's orders, Spaz returns to his foster family's latch (territory). Ryter helps Spaz. They travel the path of an old pipe system and cross three latches controlled by separate gang leaders. The feral child follows them. In the second latch, they rescue the beautiful proov Lanaya who takes them to Spaz's family. Seeing the dying Bean, Lanaya and Ryter lead the group to Eden, where Bean receives a genetic replacement. Ryter, Spaz, and Bean return to their segregated latches, but first Ryter accuses Eden of exporting illegal mind probes to control and destroy the normals. When the proovs turn off the probes, the population turns into an angry mob. Billy Bizmo focuses them on Ryter to protect Spaz, whom Billy now reveals is his son. The mob kills Ryter and burns his book, but before he dies, Ryter names Spaz the last book in the universe. Spaz buys a voice-writer machine and changes his name to Ryter. One night he receives a message from the feral boy and Lanaya saying "the future is ours."

Booktalk

Hold up an outdated object (such as a buttonhook, a horseshoe, or a washboard). Discuss its replacement and how it affects daily life. Ask each person to write down a device that might be missing in one hundred years and its possible replacement. Discuss some responses.

Spaz is just your typical normal of the future. Well, sometimes he does fall down in a fit, but he's not high class enough to have a genetic improvement. To make it, he has to stick with his latch gang, the Bully Bangers. They tell him to steal or die. When Spaz busts down a gummy, just like his gang tells him, he discovers that the old guy will give him everything he owns except a book, and Spaz is sure nobody is going to read a book. Nobody even remembers books—except Spaz. But if Billy Bizmo, the gang leader, finds out Spaz left the book, Spaz is in big trouble. Then a message brings more trouble: Spaz's sister is dying. To see her, he has to leave his gang and his latch. Guess who wants to go with him? The old guy with the book, Ryter. Ryter knows they might never find Spaz's sister or come back alive, but telling their story might be important to someone, someone in the future. It might turn out to be *The Last Book in the Universe*.

Related Activities

1. In chapter 10, Ryter says "Memories are better than diamonds, and nobody can steal them from you." Discuss that statement in relation to the future.

2. *The Last Book in the Universe* is an expansion of a short story of the same name by Rodman Philbrick in *Tomorrowland* (Related Work 3). Read the short story and the novel. Discuss how the expansion changes the story.

3. In chapter 13, Ryter misquotes the last lines of Robert Frost's "Stopping by Woods on a Snowy Evening." Read the entire poem (Related Work 2). Then discuss the appropriateness and irony of Ryter's change in relation to the entire poem and the novel.

4. In chapter 13, Ryter alludes to the *Odyssey*, the story of a dangerous journey. In "Ulysses" by Tennyson (Related Work 2), Ulysses reflects on this journey, his old age, and his determination "to strive, to seek, to find, and not to yield." Discuss this poem's relationship to Ryter's decisions.

5. Epilepsy plays a major role in both *The Last Book in the Universe* and *Lefty Carmichael Has a Fit* (Related Work 5). Discuss how each au-

thor uses the condition to accomplish the purpose of his novel. Continue to research epilepsy. Share your findings with the group.

Related Works

1. Egendorf, Laura. **Gangs: Opposing Viewpoints.** San Diego, CA: Greenhaven Press, 2001. 170p. (Opposing Viewpoints Series). $23.00. ISBN 0-7377-0510-8. **NF** Because gangs control the society of *The Last Book in the Universe,* reading some of the articles in Egendorf's work could generate discussion about that society's relationship to our own.

2. Harmon, William, ed. **The Classic Hundred Poems: All-Time Favorites, 2nd ed.** New York: Columbia University Press, 1998. 360p. $19.95. ISBN 0-231-11259-9. **NF** "Stopping by Woods on a Snowy Evening" by Robert Frost deals with the desire to appreciate natural beauty and the pull of responsibility. It appears on pages 228 to 229. "Ulysses" by Alfred Tennyson is a reflection by Ulysses in his old age. He decides that seeking gives his life meaning. The poem, with discussion, appears on pages 165 to 168.

3. Philbrick, Rodman. "The Last Book in the Universe." In **Tomorrowland: Stories About the Future,** compiled by Michael Cart. (See full booktalk in chapter 4.) The story appears on pages 9 to 21. In the Author's Note on pages 23 to 24, Rodman explains that Spaz has much more to say.

4. Skurzynski, Gloria. **Virtual War.** New York: Simon & Schuster Books for Young Readers, 1997. 152p. $16.00. ISBN 0-689-81374-0. Fourteen-year-old Corgan, raised and trained in a box, will fight the next World War, a virtual war, to remind the world population of war's horrors and destruction.

5. Trembath, Don. **Lefty Carmichael Has a Fit.** Victoria, BC: Orca Book Publishers, 1999. 215p. $6.95. ISBN 1-55143-166-1. Fifteen-year-old Lefty Carmichael deals with epilepsy.

ᘓᘔ

Buchanan, Jane. Hank's Story.

New York: Farrar Straus Giroux, 2001. 136p. $16.00. ISBN 0-374-32836-6.

Summary/Description

Twelve-year-old Hank Donohue, an orphan, lives in Nebraska with the Olsons. Hank's older brother, Peter, ran away from the farm because of Mr. Olson's beatings, and Hank endures the bitter and abusive Olsons alone. Working constantly at farm chores, Hank cannot please the childless couple that accepted him from a New York orphanage for free labor. The town children, supported by the schoolmaster, bully and tease Hank and the other orphans who arrived here on the Orphan Train in the early 1920s.

When Hank finds a wounded bird, he also finds a new friend, Molly, the strange woman who walks the road and uses her house as an animal hospital and refuge. She helps him develop his talents for helping and healing animals. Molly and the local minister, aware of the ongoing abuse, take Hank away from the Olsons. Hank discovers that the ringleader school bully is also abused, moves in with Molly, and forms strong friendships with two of the other orphans from the Orphan Train.

Booktalk

Twelve-year-old Hank Donohue knows about being lonely. His mother and father are dead. In the 1920s New York City was overcrowded with homeless children just like Hank and his brother Peter, so the Children's Aid Society gave them a ride to Nebraska—on the Orphan Train. But his brother ran away. Now Hank is figuring out how to run away too. The Olsons who took in Hank and his brother just want free labor—the less food, water, and soap they give him the better, but they'll willingly hand out a fist and a harsh tongue. The schoolyard bullies like to make fun of orphans, and the schoolmaster tells everyone Hank is stupid. Even the New York streets seem safer and friendlier than Nebraska farms. You think you have problems? Read *Hank's Story*.

Related Activities

1. Compare Hank from *Hank's Story* and Clem from *Clem's Chances* (Related Work 5). Explain how their characters and situations are alike and different.

2. Both Hank and Clem are drawn to *Oliver Twist* (Related Work 2). Read chapters 6 and 7 from *Oliver Twist* to the group. In these chapters Noah insults Oliver's mother, and Oliver retaliates. Compare this situation and the characters' reactions to the similar bullying situation of *Hank's Story*.

3. Read the paragraph on pages 4 and 5 that begins "Hank heard the rooster…" and ends with "so early in the morning." Discuss what this paragraph reveals about Hank's situation. Describe yourself or a person you know getting up in the morning. Try to let your description reveal that person's living situation. Use the paragraph from *Hank's Story* as a model.

4. In the Author's Note, Buchanan describes the Orphan Train movement started by Reverend Charles Loring Brace. Find as much in-

formation as you can about that movement, and share your findings
with the group. You might wish to start with *We Rode the Orphan
Trains* (Related Work 7).

5. In many ways, *Hank's Story* is about coping with life's disappoint-
    ments and hardships. Discuss how each character deals with hard-
    ship and the success or failure of their coping choices. Be sure to
    consider Molly's reaction to Hank's fighting.

Related Works

1. Brooks, Martha. **Being with Henry.** New York: DK Publishing,
    Inc., 2000. 216p. $17.95. ISBN 0-7894-2588-2. In conflict with his
    stepfather, the main character is thrown out of his house, takes to the
    road, and finds another home with Henry, who gives him love and re-
    sponsibility.

2. Dickens, Charles and Don Freeman (illus.). **Oliver Twist.** New
    York: William Morrow & Company, 1994. 442p. $20.00. ISBN
    0-688-12911-0. An orphan runs away from an abusive workhouse,
    faces the dangers of the city, and finds he is part of a wealthy family.
    The first edition was published in 1867.

3. Karr, Kathleen. **The Boxer.** (See full booktalk in chapter 2.) As the
    main wage earner after his father deserts the family, John Woods de-
    cides fighting will pay him more than a sweatshop.

4. Klass, David. **You Don't Know Me.** (See full booktalk in chapter 1.)
    Abused by his mother's boyfriend, a young man tells no one, but is
    helped by a teacher who suspects he is abused.

5. Levitin, Sonia. **Clem's Chances.** (See full booktalk in chapter 1.)
    After his mother's death, Clem strikes out to find his father who de-
    serted them, overcomes physical and emotional abuse, and discovers
    that his father is a selfish man with little interest in Clem.

6. Tifft, Wilton S. **Ellis Island.** Chicago, IL: Contemporary Books,
    1990. 239p. $35.00. ISBN 0-8092-4418-7. **NF** On page 74, a full-page
    picture shows young boys being sent to homes in America's Wild
    West, compliments of the Children's Aid Society.

7. Warren, Andrea. **We Rode the Orphan Trains.** Boston, MA:
    Houghton Mifflin Company, 2001. 132p. $18.00. ISBN 0-618-
    11712-1. **NF** These true stories of children who rode the Orphan
    Trains begins with information about Charles Loring Brace, the
    movement's founder, and Clara Comstock, one of the agents who su-
    pervised the children. The seven adults interviewed recall the good
    and bad experiences of their lives. Warren provides sources for addi-
    tional information.

❧❦

Konigsburg, E. L. Silent to the Bone.

New York: Atheneum Books, 2000. 261p. $16.00. ISBN 0-689-83601-5.

Summary/Description

Thirteen-year-olds Connor Kane and Branwell Zamborska are two super-intelligent best friends. Branwell stops talking after an "accident" that threatens the life of Nicole, his six-month-old half-sister. Vivian Shawcurt, the family's young English *au pair*, accuses Branwell of having an unhealthy fascination with the baby and dropping her. Visiting Branwell in the detention center each day, Connor sets up a communication system with him and discovers, with the help of Margaret, Connor's older half-sister, that the *au pair* abused the baby and sexually manipulated Branwell while she conducted a love affair with the pizza deliveryman. As Branwell realizes that Connor can discover the truth and that Vivian can go on to hurt other children, he recovers his voice. Then Branwell and his parents begin to resolve many of the problems that led to the neglect, accident, and misunderstanding. Mature content might be objectionable to some audiences.

Booktalk

Thirteen-year-olds Connor Kane and Branwell Zamborska have been friends from nursery school. They faced school, family, and stepfamily adjustments together. Suddenly Branwell is distant and different. Then Branwell's half-sister, six-month-old Nicole, slips into a coma, and Branwell, in the middle of a 911 call, stops talking completely. Vivian Shawcurt, the family's English *au pair*, says Branwell dropped Nicole. Branwell, now in custody, won't say anything.

Connor wants to believe in his friend, but Vivian is both attractive and believable. Why won't Branwell defend himself? Connor discovers a way for them to communicate, and when he does, Branwell reveals the secrets, the shame, and the treachery that keep him *Silent to the Bone.*

Related Activities

1. Connor uses a system of cards for communication. Make up a system of your own that allows you to communicate with a friend or family member without language. Explain your system and how it is related to your relationship with that person. You might wish to research communication systems that use pictures and codes before doing so.
2. The relationship between Connor and his sister Margaret is also an issue in the novel. Discuss why you think Konigsburg includes it.

3. Yolanda plays a small but significant role in the novel. Why is she important beyond providing information for the investigation?
4. Essentially Vivian Shawcurt sexually abuses Branwell. Compare his experience and reaction to those described in *Speak* (Related Work 1) and *Learning to Swim* (Related Work 7).
5. In both *Silent to the Bone* and *You Don't Know Me* (Related Work 6), the main characters make assumptions about those around them that could destroy their lives. Compare these assumptions, the problems they create, and their clarifications. Discuss how situations in both novels apply to lives that do not involve sexual manipulation or physical abuse.

Related Works

1. Anderson, Laurie Halse. **Speak.** (See full booktalk in chapter 2.) Raped by a high school football star, Melinda Sordino relies on nonverbal behavior to communicate with those around her.
2. Cobb, Carlene. **Coping with an Abusive Relationship.** New York: Rosen Publishing Group, 2001. 108p. (Coping). $18.95. ISBN 0-8239-2822-5. Cobb explains how to recognize an abuse victim and what the abuse victim can do to cope with the abusive relationship.
3. Cormier, Robert. **The Rag and Bone Shop.** New York: Delacorte Press, 2001. 154p. $15.95. ISBN 0-385-72962-6. Accused of murdering a seven-year-old girl, innocent twelve-year-old Jason is bullied into a confession by an expert interrogator.
4. Frank, E.R. **Life Is Funny.** (See full booktalk in chapter 2.) Teens who are friends and neighbors battle through various problems with and without the help of their parents, but most of them never know that all the people around them are having difficult experiences.
5. Fraustino, Lisa Rowe. **Dirty Laundry: Stories About Family Secrets.** New York: Viking Press, 1998. 181p. $16.99. ISBN 0-670-87911-8. This short story collection emphasizes that full disclosure is the best policy.
6. Klass, David. **You Don't Know Me.** (See full booktalk in chapter 1.) A young man, abused by his mother's live-in boyfriend, does not reveal the abuse and almost dies because of his silence.
7. Turner, Ann. **Learning to Swim.** New York: Scholastic Press, 2000. 128p. $14.95. ISBN 0-439-15309-3. **NF** In a series of poems, the author tells about how a neighbor boy molested her as a child and how she felt powerless to overcome it.

Dedication: We Battle the Forces Against Us

The Forces of Good and Evil Complicating Our Lives

Pullman, Philip and Leonid Gore (illus.).
Clockwork: Or All Wound Up.

New York: Arthur A. Levine Books, 1998. 112p. $14.95. ISBN 0-590-12999-6.

Summary/Description

In "A Note About Clocks," Pullman describes the clock as both normal and horrible and then compares it to a story. He notes that once either the clock or the story is set, the end of each is inevitable. When Part I opens, Karl, the clock apprentice, sits brooding in the tavern. He has not made the required figure for the town clock. This task, signaling the end of his apprenticeship, must be completed by the next day. Fritz, the novelist, begins to tell a ghost story, which he also has not finished, about Prince Florian and his father, Prince Otto. In the story, Otto and Florian return from a hunting trip. Otto's corpse has a clock instead of a heart, and Baron Stelgratz has disappeared with the rest of the hunting party. Prince Florian is fine. As Fritz introduces the character Dr. Kalmenius of Shatzberg, the "philosopher of the night," into the story, the real Dr. Kalmenius enters the tavern. Then fiction and reality blend as Kalmenius offers Karl a figure of a knight for the clock. The figure kills when it hears the word "devil" and stops its attack when it hears a certain song. Afraid of disgrace, Karl accepts the knight. Part II reveals that Prince Florian is actually a silver mechanical figure made by Kalmenius to replace Otto's son who died at birth. Otto returned to Kalmenius when the boy began to rust. Kalmenius told Otto that Florian needed a human heart to live, and Otto sacrificed his own. When Karl realizes that the prince is also mechanical, he decides to increase his riches by keeping the knight, and he places Florian in the clock. The knight figure kills Karl. Gretl, the young barmaid, realizes that Karl has placed the prince in the clock. Her love saves them both and makes him human.

Booktalk

Karl, the clock apprentice, sits brooding in the tavern. He must have his clock made by the next day or he won't pass his apprenticeship. Fritz, the storyteller, has something unfinished also. Dreaming about a dead man with a clock instead of a heart, he began to weave a plot that now seems to have no end. As he tries to finish the story in the tavern, the most evil character in this mysterious tale comes through the door. Now that character, the threatening and marvelous Dr. Kalmenius who makes fantastic mechanical figures, blends the fact and fiction of life. Who will end the tale? Who can control the love, the hate, and the fear that Kalmenius's carefully fashioned knight and prince create? Can anyone—the writer, the apprentice, or the magician—direct the motion once the figures are *All Wound Up* and the *Clockwork* begins?

Related Activities

1. Read "A Note About Clocks" on pages ix to xi. Discuss how the details in this passage anticipate the story. In the library and on the Internet, research clocks and the role they have played in history.
2. In the last chapter, Pullman explains what happens to every character except Dr. Kalmenius. Discuss why Pullman says, "He was only a character in a story, after all."
3. Discuss whether Dr. Kalmenius is the source of good and evil in the story. Use specifics from the story to support what you say.
4. When Dr. Kalmenius gives Florian a human heart, he warns, "The heart that is given must also be kept." Pullman refers to the statement in the last paragraph of the novel. Discuss what it means and how it affects the story.
5. Gore's illustrations reflect the tone of the story as well as its contents. Discuss the illustrator's choices in relation to the story.

Related Works

1. **Grimm's Grimmest.** San Francisco, CA: Chronicle Books, 1997. 142p. $22.95. ISBN 0-8118-1675-3. Maria Tatar, in the introduction

to this collection of Grimm's most gruesome tales, describes the stories as "the stuff of nightmares" and the "ancestors of our urban legends." Comparing them to the dark battle between good and evil presented in Pullman's story would be interesting.

2. Napoli, Donna Jo. **Beast.** New York: Atheneum Books for Young Readers, 2000. 260p. $17.00. ISBN 0-689-83589-2. Changed into a beast because he has abused a beast in sacrifice, a young Persian prince is brought back to human form through a woman's true love.

3. Skurzynski, Gloria. "Nethergrave" in **On the Edge: Stories at the Brink,** edited by Lois Duncan. New York: Simon & Schuster Books for Young Readers, 2000. 211p. $17.00. ISBN 0-689-82251-0. The real world and virtual worlds blend when an eighth grader becomes a jaguar in the world of Nethergrave. The story appears on pages 25 to 39.

4. Silverman. **Mirror Mirror: Twisted Tales.** New York: Scholastic Incorporated/The Chicken House, 2002. 192p. $15.95. ISBN 0-439-29593-9. In the story "Satanium," on pages 76 to 90, a scientist makes a pact with a demon so he can become famous. But his tears of regret, saved in an "I'm sorry" bottle, eventually are used to reverse the harm he has done.

5. Springer, Nancy. **I Am Mordred: A Tale from Camelot.** New York: Philomel Books, 1998. 184p. $16.99. ISBN 0-399-23143-9. Telling his story as a raven, the form that now holds his soul, Mordred reveals the battle between father and son that requires both men to cooperate with evil as they follow their destinies.

ᏗᏗ

Thesman, Jean. The Other Ones.
New York: Viking Press, 1999. 181p. $15.99. ISBN 0-670-88594-0.

Summary/Description

Bridget Raynes shares her aunt's magical difference. Aunt Cait is rumored to be the town witch. Cait and Bridget's threshold guardian is trying to persuade Bridget to accept and use her own magical powers. Bridget's mother and father encourage her to live only a normal life. Then the high school in-group bullies Bridgett, her friends, and Althea, the mysterious new girl. Bridgett wants to get even. Although her parents suggest she ignore the problems, her aunt and threshold guardian urge her to tap into her positive forces, not the negative ones, and solve them. To connect with her strengths, she must meet *The Other Ones* in the woods. To help her best friend Jordan, who has been abused and abandoned by his father, and to aid Althea's family, who are "shape-shifters," Bridget goes to the woods. Here she discovers that *The Other Ones* are sensitive people she meets every day. She uses her power to free Jordon from his terrible life and help the shape-shifters escape. At the end of the novel, she is complete with broom (sweeping her father's store) and familiar (a complaining cat).

Booktalk

Do witches always wear black pointed hats, ride brooms, keep cats, and cast evil spells? Not always. Maybe that normal-looking person sitting next to you has powers you don't know about—supernatural powers.

Bridget knows all about that. She's different, as different as her aunt whom everyone calls the town witch. Bridget would rather be normal and solve problems in normal ways, but when teachers let the bullies control the classes, shape-shifters move into town, and it looks like her best friend might die, Bridget makes some tough decisions. Will she be like her parents and say, "Not my problem"? Or will she share the power and responsibility of *The Other Ones?*

Related Activities

1. Trace Bridget's journey to accepting her powers. Discuss when and why she finally accepts them.
2. In *The Other Ones,* magic could be considered a metaphor. Discuss the relationship Thesman establishes and why.
3. Althea Peale, the shape-shifter, plays a major role. Describe that role and discuss how it complements Bridget's.
4. *The Other Ones* is an ambiguous title. Discuss how it might refer to more than just witches.
5. In *The Other Ones,* Bridget's parents want Bridget to hide her powers. In "The Woman with the Green Hair" (Related Work 2), the main character claims knowledge and supernatural powers she does not have. After reading both works, discuss each character's decision and the decision's appropriateness.
6. In *The Other Ones,* it takes supernatural powers to handle bullies. Ask your librarian to help you research the causes of bullying and the skills a person needs to cope with it. Share your information with the group.

Related Works

1. Atwater-Rhodes, Amelia. **In the Forests of the Night.** New York: Delacorte Press, 1999. 147p. $8.95. ISBN 0-385-32674-2. Rachel Weatere moves into the negative supernatural world when she becomes a vampire and ultimately must face her brother, who has be-

come part of the positive supernatural world. Both appear as ordinary people.

2. Canales, Viola. "The Woman with the Green Hair." In **Orange Candy Slices and Other Secret Tales.** Houston, TX: Piñata Books, 2001. 122p. $9.95. ISBN 1-55885-332-4. When the town witch dies, the people she harassed discover she was both bald and blind. The story is on pages 87 to 90.

3. Coville, Bruce. **Odder than Ever.** New York: Harcourt Brace and Company, 1999. 146p. $16.00. ISBN 0-15-201747-X. Each story deals with unusual experiences, both natural and supernatural, that help young people clarify their thinking.

4. Rowling, J. K. **Harry Potter and the Prisoner of Azkaban.** New York: Arthur A. Levine Books, 1999. 431p. $19.95. ISBN 0-439-13635-0. (See full booktalk in *Booktalks Plus*, 2001, page 183.) Men moving from human to animal form challenge Harry's supernatural powers. Harry finally prevails by drawing on his family's positive magic.

5. Vande Velde, Vivian. **Never Trust a Dead Man.** New York: Harcourt Brace and Company, 1999. 194p. $17.00. ISBN 0-15-201899-9. When Selwyn Roweson finds himself falsely accused of murder, he turns for help to a witch and the ghost of the man he was supposed to have killed.

⓪⓫

Roberts, Katherine. Spellfall.

England: The Chicken House, 2000. New York: Scholastic, 2001. 256p. $15.95.
ISBN 0-439-29653-6.

Summary/Description

Hawk is a spellmage who wishes to invade and destroy Earthaven, a parallel world sheltering creatures "threatened by modern technology." He kidnaps Natalie Marlins. Hawk killed Natalie's mother, an Earthaven Spell Lady, but her spirit still lives in Oq, the soultree that is the heart of the kingdom. In her efforts to save the tree and her mother's spirit, Natalie is joined by the bumbling and timid Merlin, Hawk's abused son. Realizing the similarity between Oq's root system and the Internet, Merlin thwarts Hawk's attempts to infect and destroy the tree.

In the human world, Tim (Natalie's resentful stepbrother), Mr. Marlins (Natalie's alcoholic father), and Jo (Natalie's good friend) try to find and rescue Natalie. In the search, they bond and clarify their own lives. Good triumphs over evil, and the Earthaven realizes it must combine magic with new technology to survive. The Guide to Earthaven at the end of the novel explains terms common to Earthaven and the use of spells.

Booktalk

Natalie doesn't believe in magic, even though she could use a miracle right about now. Her mother is dead, her father is trying to drink away his grief, and her stepbrother is making her life miserable. But one day she sees a paper shimmering in the grocery store's parking lot. When she stoops to pick it up, a strange stick with a bird head winds around her arm. An old man hisses something about her ancient blood, and soon she is surrounded by spells, familiars, and zombie-like creatures that are all part of the old man's plan to destroy an "enchanted realm, parallel to our own world." He needs Natalie to help him. Natalie never knew this other world existed. Now she discovers that she, her family, and her friends might all die with it. How can she prevent *Spellfall*, and whom can she trust, in either world, to help her?

Related Activities

1. Sight and perception are major themes in this story. Discuss how each affects the novel's outcome.
2. Several issues are left open at the end of the novel. How will Natalie explain this experience to her stepmother? Will she ever see Merlin again? Will she be expected to carry on her mother's work? Describe the sequel to *Spellfall* that you would like to read next.
3. The character perceiving Oq as a computer is named Merlin. Research the name Merlin. On the basis of the information you find, discuss how the name choice aids the author's purpose.
4. Although much of the novel centers on Natalie's relationship with her mother and her mother's death, two father/son relationships are also prominent. Merlin defeats his father, a man who abuses and uses everyone around him. Tim wants attention from his stepfather. Discuss how the author uses the father characters to achieve her purpose.
5. Animals are central in the novel. List the animals, and discuss the purpose and power of each one.

Related Works

1. Atwater-Rhodes, Amelia. **In the Forests of the Night.** New York: Delacorte Press, 1999. 147p. $8.95. ISBN 0-385-32674-2. Rachel Weatere, born in 1684, becomes a vampire named Risika who roams the modern New York streets to seek out her own prey.
2. Karr, Kathleen. **Playing with Fire.** New York: Farrar Straus Giroux, 2001. 185p. $16.00. ISBN 0-374-23453-1. A young girl must distin-

guish fraud, magic, and mystical power when her mother and "uncle" agree to help very wealthy people speak with loved ones they have lost.

3. Peck, Richard. **Ghosts I Have Been.** New York: Viking Press, 1977. 214p. $20.00. ISBN 0-670-33813-3. Blossom Culp discovers she has the second sight and the power to calm ghosts.

4. Pierce, Tamora. **Briar's Book.** New York: Scholastic Press, 1999. 258p. $15.95. (Circle of Magic Quartet). ISBN 0-590-55359-3. Briar Moss, part of the magic quartet of students living in Winding Circle Temple, has a near-death experience that forces him to reflect on the importance of discovering and using his magical powers with plants.

5. Rowling, J. K. **Harry Potter and the Sorcerer's Stone.** New York: Arthur A. Levine Books, 1997. 509p. $17.95. ISBN 0-590-35340-3. (See full booktalk in *Booktalks Plus*, 2001, pages 181 and 182.) In this first book of the Harry Potter series, Harry discovers he has magical powers.

Russell, Barbara Timberlake. **The Taker's Stone.**

New York: DK Publishing, Inc., 1999. 231p. $16.95. ISBN 0-7894-2568-8.

Summary/Description

Fourteen-year-old Fischer dreads spending the summer with his aggressive, intimidating cousin David. When David talks Fischer into going with him to spy on hoboes, they think they see a man and a young boy guarding red stones. Fischer, wanting to impress David, grabs three of the stones and runs.

Who David and Fischer actually see are Solomon and Thistle. This father and daughter are the Keepers of stones that "are about everything good in this world, and how strong, yet fragile, that good can be." When Fischer grabs the stones, he becomes a Taker and sets in motion a battle between good and evil expressed through natural disasters—earthquakes, tornadoes, and floods. Belial, the personification of evil, seeks to control Fischer, the stones, and the world. When David and Fischer wish on two of the stones, Fischer feels compelled to ask for Thistle. She appears, explains the significance of their action, and tells them what they must do to correct it. The three travel to the center of the United States to unite with Thistle's father. During the journey, Fischer remembers he has seen Thistle in his dreams, discovers he has special spiritual powers, and realizes his cousin David has more bluster than true strength. When Fischer and Thistle find Solomon, Belial appears and tempts Fischer to join him. Fischer defeats Belial by returning the stones to Solomon. Fischer and David reunite and return home. The ending implies that Fischer has entered a spiritual "flow" with Solomon and Thistle.

Booktalk

What did you do last summer? Fourteen-year-old Fischer changed the world. His summer started out all too normal. His father was gone again, and his mother had too much to do to have him around the house. So Fischer visited his aunt, uncle, and overpowering, obnoxious, know-it-all cousin David. Trying to impress his cousin, Fischer stole a few bright stones from a couple of hoboes. Suddenly, he finds himself in a battle between good and evil. Suddenly, he finds himself protecting a girl named Thistle he never met before. Suddenly, humanity's survival depends on Fischer. Why? Because when Fischer decides to steal the stones he becomes a Taker, and now he holds the power of *The Taker's Stone*.

Related Activities

1. Read again the prologue to the story. Explain how it sets the tone and prepares the reader for the events of the story.
2. Discuss whether the story needs an epilogue. List what such an epilogue might include.
3. Discuss the role Fischer's grandfather plays in the novel even though he does not appear in the story.
4. Discuss the significance of the wooden nickel David receives when he wishes for riches.
5. Describe what David and Fischer will be like in ten years. Base your explanation on the facts of the story.
6. Research the name Belial and its significance in relation to good and evil. Then research the other character names and identify their possible relationships to Belial.

Related Works

1. Crossley-Holland, Kevin. **The Seeing Stone: Book One.** New York: Scholastic Press, 2001. 368p. (Arthur Trilogy). $17.95. ISBN 0-439-26326-3. When the magical Merlin enters his life, thirteen-year-old Arthur, left-handed and inept, believes he might have significant powers and an important destiny.
2. McCaughrean, Geraldine. **The Stones Are Hatching.** New York: HarperCollins Publishers, 1999. 230p. $15.95. ISBN 0-06-028765-9. Living with an older abusive sister, Phelim discovers he has been appointed to save the world from the evil Stoor Worm and its Hatch-

lings. On his hero's journey, he discovers magical friends and, like Fischer, a new relationship with his father.

3. Paulsen, Gary. **The Transall Saga.** New York: Delacorte Press, 1998. 248p. $15.95. ISBN 0-385-32196-1. (See full booktalk in *Booktalks Plus,* 2001, pages 192 to 193). Thirteen-year-old Mark Harrison finds himself transported to another world where, through heroic battles, he prepares himself for adult life.

4. Rowling, J.K. **Harry Potter and the Sorcerer's Stone.** New York: Arthur A. Levine Books, 1997. 509p. $17.95. ISBN 0-590-35340-3. (See full booktalk in *Booktalks Plus,* 2001, pages 181 to 182). An orphan who discovers he has wizard blood and power decides to go into training.

5. Sleator, William. **The Boxes.** New York: Dutton Children's Books, 1998. 196p. $15.99. ISBN 0-525-46012-8. (See full booktalk in *Booktalks Plus,* 2001, pages 189 to 192.) After opening mysterious boxes left by her uncle, Annie Levi finds herself responsible for controlling the good and evil in the natural and supernatural worlds.

❧❧

Pullman, Philip. The Golden Compass: His Dark Materials Trilogy.

New York: Alfred A. Knopf, 1995. 399p. $20.00. ISBN 0-679-87924-2.

Summary/Description

Lyra, an orphan raised by the scholars in the Jordan School of Oxford, discovers that Lord Asriel, who she thought was her uncle, is her father and that the beautiful Mrs. Coulter, with whom she will now live, is her mother and the leader of the Gobblers, a group of child stealers who separate children from their daemons, or alter egos, in order to control them. Before Lyra leaves the school, the Master gives her a golden alethiometer to help her divine the truth about the powers competing for her life. She discovers that these powers are her parents. Her father, a heretic, wishes to explore the unknown. Her mother, a supporter of the established church, wishes to control behavior throughout the world. Their battle focuses on Lyra and a magical Dust to which children, and Lyra in particular, seem connected. Lyra runs away from her mother and allies herself with the gyptian people who wish to rescue the stolen children. The gyptians and her truth meter lead her to witches, a renegade bear, and a balloon pilot who free the captured children. At the end of the story, Lyra is determined to discover the mysterious, magical Dust that both her mother and father pursue.

Booktalk

Ask each person in the group to give an example of a necessary as well as an unnecessary rule. Make two short lists and discuss reasons for the classifications.

Lyra grew up in the Jordon School of Oxford. Rules surround her—so many that she doesn't follow any of them. The night she breaks into the Retiring Room reserved only for Scholars, the men scholars, she sees a murder attempt and a severed head kept in ice. She hears stories about stolen children in the North, victims of terrible experiments. Lyra thinks none of the gore applies to her, but suddenly she finds herself leaving school, running away, and traveling north. She makes her own rules now. Each may have life and death consequences. *The Golden Compass*, which only she can read, will guide her journey and perhaps the universe's journey through the kindness and treachery of strangers.

෴

Pullman, Philip. **The Subtle Knife: His Dark Materials Trilogy.**
New York: Alfred A. Knopf, 1997. 326p. $20.00. ISBN 0-679-87925-0.

Summary/Description

Twelve-year-old Will leaves his mother to find his father. Fleeing men he believes are his father's enemies, he enters an alternative reality and meets Lyra. With help from her, the witches, and the balloon man of *The Golden Compass*, Will finds his father and his own role in the universe, the keeper of the *The Subtle Knife* that allows men to travel from one world to another. At the end of the story, Lyra is missing, probably stolen by her evil mother, and Will becomes the hope of humankind who must carry the compass and knife to Lord Asriel, now waging the war between those who desire man's complete submission and those who support man's spirit of discovery.

Booktalk

Twelve-year-old Will Parry has problems. His mother is afraid to leave her home because she thinks people watch her. His father, John Parry, deserted the family when Will was just a baby, and now strange men are hanging around Will's house. When they break in, Will kills one. Then he knows he has to escape, and does, into a completely new world. It happens to be Lyra's world. Because she likes murderers, she really likes Will. But destiny, not accident, brings these two people, a knife, and a compass together. Lyra will support Will. The compass will guide them, but Will must carve his own fate, a fate that forces him to face thieves, kidnapping, Specters, death, and—worst of all—a painful truth fashioned by *The Subtle Knife*.

CRYPTID SYMBOLS

Pullman, Philip. **The Amber Spyglass: His Dark Materials Trilogy.**

New York: Alfred A. Knopf, 2000. 518p. $19.95. ISBN 0-679-87926-9.

Summary/Description

K nowing that Lyra is the new Eve and that Metatron will want to destroy or control her, Mrs. Coulter hides her daughter in a cave. Will decides to find her. With the help of two minor angels, Iorek Byrnison, and Asriel's spies and soldiers, Will and Lyra unite and escape. They journey to the underworld, where they find Roger, Scoresby, and John Parry. Under Lyra's leadership, the ghosts tell their true stories to the Harpies who guard the underworld. The Harpies lead the ghosts to freedom. The ghosts battle the Specters and joyfully mix their molecules with nature. Fighting Metatron, who wishes to control Lyra and thus the world, Mrs. Coulter and Lord Asriel sacrifice themselves as they drag him into the abyss.

Mary Malone, the physicist from *The Subtle Knife*, enters the world of the mulefas, benevolent creatures who maintain the balance of nature. The church marks her as the tempter in the prophecy about Lyra and Will. Father Gomez is sent to kill her. She discovers, by building *The Amber Spyglass* and listening to the mulefa history, that Dust leaks out through the doors among worlds. The Spyglass allows her to study the problem. Alerted by a dream, Mary welcomes Will and Lyra when they escape from battle in the other world and knows they hold part of the answer to the Dust problem. She shelters them and allows them to express their physical love. Two inspirational visitors come to this world also. From the witch Serafina Pekkala, they discover that their trip to the Underworld gave them witch powers. From the angel Xaphania, they learn that openings between worlds must be closed to preserve the Dust and prevent the Specters from increasing. Sealing all the doors means Lyra and Will can never see each other again. Mary Malone helps Lyra and Will combine inspiration, knowledge, and love so they might complete their duties in their own worlds. Lyra returns to Oxford with a new appreciation for her teachers. She studies the truth meter, which she no longer can read, with Dean Hannah. Will returns to his own world. He lives with Mary and gets help for his mother. Following the advice of John Parry's ghost, all will build heaven where they are.

Booktalk

Will and Lyra are fighting a final battle for their own lives and the world. Mrs. Coulter, Lord Asriel, and Iorek Byrnison appear again, along with angels, witches, miniature spies, dragonflies, mulefa, and of course—the Specters. Armed with *The Golden Compass* and *The Subtle Knife*, Lyra and Will descend to the world of the dead and escape to even more new worlds of the living. But this campaign to save the universe is different. This time, a quiet physicist, Mary Malone, enters their world with a frightening weapon of uncompromising knowledge rather than brutal might. This time the church sends a lone and determined assassin to kill them all. Will one, two, or all three be killed? Can their worlds or anyone else's ever be safe again? The answers are in the visions that come through *The Amber Spyglass*.

Related Activities

1. Lord Asriel and Mrs. Coulter represent completely different points of view. Pullman characterizes these as freedom of thought and acceptance of authority. List the characters that represent each viewpoint. Then discuss whether these two ideas should be translated as good and evil.

2. In *The Golden Compass*, Lyra discovers that Iofur Raknison has killed his own father. On page 341, she turns his deed into a compliment by telling him he must have the strength of a god. After researching the father/son relationship in Greek and Roman mythology, explain why her comment is appropriate. Then discuss whether you would interpret it as a compliment.

3. Both Lyra and Will discover parents they did not know they had. Explain the relationship each character has with each parent and how that relationship affects the children's lives.

4. The gyptians, the witches, the Specters, and the balloon man all play minor but important roles in the stories. Explain the function and meaning of each.

5. In *The Amber Spyglass*, Pullman again draws heavily on Greek and Roman mythology when Lyra and Will descend to the Underworld. In the library or on the Internet, research the Greek and Roman underworlds. Then discuss Pullman's changes and what they add to the story.

6. *The Golden Compass*, *The Subtle Knife*, and *The Amber Spyglass* are obviously key objects in the novels. Discuss why Pullman describes

the compass as golden and the knife as subtle. Discuss how the construction of the spyglass is appropriate to its function.

7. On page 181, Iorek tells Will that in doing what Will intends, the knife is also doing what it intends. Then Iorek asks Will if he can see the sharpest edge of the knife. State the idea that Iorek is trying to communicate. Explain how Iorek's warning proves true and how it applies to inventions in our world also.

8. Make a chart of all the characters in the trilogy. In the chart, group the characters. Then, using the relationship of the characters, explain how the physical, spiritual, and mental aspects of this trilogy world interact.

9. Define allegory. Discuss whether Pullman's trilogy is an allegory.

10. Pullman draws extensively on the story of Adam and Eve. Discuss how he uses the allusion in his trilogy. How is Lyra a different Eve? How is Will a different Adam? Why is Mary labeled the tempter? How does the story of Adam and Eve fit into the Harpies' desire to hear only true stories? Be sure to include the mulefa version on page 224 in your discussion. You might wish to consult a summary of *Paradise Lost*. Check the Web site *Paradise Lost, Study Guide* (Related Work 3).

Related Works

1. Hamilton, Edith (text) and Steele Savage (illus.) **Mythology.** New York: Little, Brown, 1998. 497p. $13.00pa. ISBN: 0-316-19152-3. This is an excellent basic source for information about myths and mythical characters.

2. Lewis, C. S. **The Chronicles of Narnia.** New York: HarperCollins Publishers, 1994. 7 vol. $34.65pa. ISBN 0-06-447119-5. Lewis's fantasy world expresses his spiritual beliefs and the relationship between good and evil.

3. *Paradise Lost, Study Guide.* Available: www.paradiselost.org/ (Accessed September 2002). This Web site includes an overall summary of the epic, summaries of the individual books, and the specific Biblical allusions on which Paradise Lost is based.

4. Rowling, J. K. **Harry Potter and the Chamber of Secrets.** New York: Arthur A. Levine Books, 1998. 341p. $17.95. ISBN 0-439-06486-4. (See full booktalk in *Booktalks Plus*, 2001, page 182.) In this second book in the series, Harry saves Ginny Weasley from the evil Draco Malfoy.

5. Rowling, J. K. **Harry Potter and the Goblet of Fire.** New York: Arthur A. Levine Books, 2000. 734p. $25.95. ISBN 0-439-13959-7. (See full booktalk in *Booktalks Plus*, 2001, pages 184 to 185.) In this fourth adventure, Harry battles evil and his own flaws.

6. Rowling, J. K. **Harry Potter and the Prisoner of Azkaban.** New York: Arthur A. Levine Books, 1999. 431p. $19.95. ISBN 0-439-13635-0. (See full booktalk in *Booktalks Plus*, 2001, page 183.) In this third book in the series, Harry draws help from his father's spirit.
7. Rowling, J. K. **Harry Potter and the Sorcerer's Stone.** New York: Arthur A. Levine Books, 1997. 509p. $17.95. ISBN 0-590-35340-3. (See full booktalk in *Booktalks Plus*, 2001, pages 181 to 182.) In this first book, Harry discovers he is a wizard.

Disease and Injury
Threatening to Limit Our Abilities

ເŷ°ວ

Altman, Linda Jacobs. **Plague and Pestilence: A History of Infectious Disease.**
Springfield, NJ: Enslow Publishers, Inc., 1998. 128p. (Issues in Focus). $17.95.
ISBN 0-89490-957-6. **ℕ𝔽**

Summary/Description

*P*lague and Pestilence: *A History of Infectious Disease* explains the relationship between humans and disease as a series of movements and mutations. Humans explore other worlds or change their life-styles and carry a dormant or endemic disease that becomes an epidemic in a new environment, hides again, or rapidly mutates. Humans sometimes blame a new element in the environment, usually the victim, for the disease. Sometimes the victim becomes angry about his or her fate and infects healthy people. Altman asks if disease should be treated scientifically, spiritually, or morally and implies that the answers affect everyone.

Altman traces the history of disease outbreaks and the detection of their sources from the Bronze Age to the present, and she explains the impact of Black Death, tuberculosis, leprosy, yellow fever, malaria, cholera, influenza, polio, AIDS, and the newly discovered filoviruses such as Marburg and Ebola. She describes the people and discoveries controlling these diseases and draws parallels between diseases that have emerged in different time periods.

Further Reading provides books and Internet sources. A topic and name index provides easy access to information.

Booktalk

Are AIDS and Ebola new diseases? Maybe not. Scientists know that bacteria and viruses caught on to recycling long before humans. Diseases attack humans. Humans attack diseases. The diseases hide and return—stranger and more dangerous. They might be living in us, our pets, our food, or the next airplane we board. *Plague and Pestilence* tells the history of infectious disease, but shows that infectious diseases aren't history. Read this book. Then learn to think a little more clearly about how to protect yourself and your world.

Related Activities

1. Research and find more information about any of the following people: Hippocrates, Galen, Andreas Vesalius, William Harvey, Hans and Zacharias Janssen, Antoni van Leeuwenhoek, Edward Jenner, John Snow, Edwin Chadwick, Louis Pasteur, Alice Catherine Evans, Joseph Lister, Robert Koch, Walter Reed, Jonas Salk, Elizabeth Kenny, Albert Sabin, Luc Montagnier, Robert Gallo, Gertrude Belle Elion, and George Herbert Hitchings. Share your information with the other members of the group through an oral presentation, a timeline, or a visual display.
2. Define and continue to research viruses. Prepare an informative chart or display that distinguishes one type of virus from another.
3. Read one of the books listed for further reading. Ask your librarian to help you find more sources. Visit one of the Web pages listed on pages 122 to 124. Report to the group any useful information you find. Continue to check the Web site periodically and continue to report to the group.
4. Define the following terms. Use each word in a sentence. Include a context clue that reveals its meaning: etiology, miasma, endemic, epidemic, pandemic, and pathogen.
5. *Plague and Pestilence, Invisible Enemies* (Related Work 1), and *The Black Death* (Related Work 5) discuss disease from three distinct perspectives. Ask three different people to choose one of the three sources, read it, and then share the information with the group. Discuss how each perspective affected your thinking about disease or tragedy.

Related Works

1. Cefrey, Holly. **AIDS**. New York: Rosen Publishing Group, 2001. 64p. (Epidemics: Deadly Diseases Throughout History). $19.95. ISBN 0-8239-3344-X. **NF** Cefrey defines the disease and describes its transmission, its consequences, its stigma, and its possible relationship to polio vaccine.

2. Cefrey, Holly. **The Plague**. New York: Rosen Publishing Group, 2001. 64p. (Epidemics: Deadly Diseases Throughout History). $19.95. ISBN 0-8239-3343-1. **NF** Opening with a diary entry from a plague witness, Cefrey explores the history, cause, treatment, misconceptions, and modern day means of prevention.

3. Cefrey, Holly. **Yellow Fever**. New York: Rosen Publishing Group, 2002. 64p. (Epidemics: Deadly Diseases Throughout History). $19.95. ISBN 0-8239-3489-6. **NF** *Yellow Fever* explains the disease, its history, and its control.

4. Donnelly, Karen. **Leprosy (Hansen's Disease)**. New York: Rosen Publishing Group, 2002. 64p. (Epidemics: Deadly Diseases Throughout History). $19.95. ISBN 0-8239-3498-5. **NF** Donnelly defines the disease, explains its transmission, discusses its relationship to plague and tuberculosis, and explains the social implications for the victim.

5. Draper, Allison Stark. **Ebola**. New York: Rosen Publishing Group, 2002. 64p. (Epidemics: Deadly Diseases Throughout History). $19.95. ISBN 0-8239-3496-9. **NF** Draper describes the disease, explains its transmission, and gives several examples of battling its outbreaks.

6. Draper, Allison Stark. **Polio**. New York: Rosen Publishing Group, 2001. 64p. (Epidemics: Deadly Diseases Throughout History). $19.95. ISBN 0-8239-3348-2. **NF** Tracing the history of the disease and treatment, Draper points out polio's potential for biological terrorism.

7. Farrell, Jeanette. **Invisible Enemies.** New York: Farrar Straus Giroux, 1998. 224p. $17.00. ISBN 0-374-33637-7.(See full booktalk in *Booktalks Plus*, 2001, pages 146 to 148.) **NF** Telling the story of seven diseases, Farrell emphasizes that prejudice, fear, and misconception are the most effective allies of disease.

8. Hayhurst, Chris. **Cholera**. New York: Rosen Publishing Group, 2001. 63p.(Epidemics: Deadly Diseases Throughout History). $19.95. ISBN 0-8239-3345-8. **NF** In describing the sources of cholera, Hayhurst emphasizes that it is a continuing threat that someday might be controlled through genetic engineering.

9. Isle, Mick. **Malaria**. New York: Rosen Publishing Group, 2001. 64p. (Epidemics: Deadly Diseases Throughout History). $19.95. ISBN 0-8239-3342-3. **NF** Isle presents malaria as a significant problem for the modern world. It may never be conquered, but it can be controlled.

10. Meltzer, Milton. **Witches and Witch-hunts: A History of Persecution.** (See full booktalk in chapter 2.) **NF** In chapter 6, Meltzer explains how women healers were often persecuted as witches.

11. Nardo, Don, ed. **The Black Death.** San Diego, CA: Greenhaven Press, 1999. 173p. (Turning Points in World History). $31.20. ISBN 1-56510-995-3. **NF** This collection of essays explains why the Black Death changed the world. It is part of the Turning Points in World History series.
12. Ramen, Fred. **Tuberculosis**. New York: Rosen Publishing Group, 2001. 64p. (Epidemics: Deadly Diseases Throughout History). $19.95. ISBN 0-8239-3349-0. **NF** Ramen discusses the resurgence of tuberculosis and its relationship to Black Death and AIDS.
13. Ramen, Fred. **Influenza**. New York: Rosen Publishing Group, 2001. 64p. (Epidemics: Deadly Diseases Throughout History). $19.95. ISBN 0-8239-3347-4. **NF** Beginning with the influenza epidemic that changed the course of World War I, Ramen explains the history of the disease and the rapid mutation that makes the virus difficult to control.

McCormick, Patricia. **Cut.**

Ashville, NC: Front Street, 2000. 168p. $16.95. ISBN 1-886910-61-8.

Summary/Description

Fifteen-year-old Callie is a patient at Sea Pines, where she has been sent for cutting herself. She refuses to talk. When she smuggles a pie pan out of the cafeteria and uses it as a knife, the bleeding and pain frighten her enough to start talking to her therapist and fellow residents. She feels responsible for her brother Sam's asthma condition, but as she talks to her therapist, Callie reveals dysfunctional parents who push too much responsibility on her. Her mother spends her time visiting Callie's grandmother in the nursing home or working on crafts. She lets her fears about everyday life, her marriage, and her son's condition overwhelm her. Callie's father says he is calling on customers but spends his free time in bars. Callie feels shut out, almost invisible. When she finally runs away from Sea Pines, she calls her father, who has not visited her during her rehabilitation. He comes to pick her up, finally admits to her that he, not Callie, should have been home to take care of Sam when Sam had the episode that precipitated his asthma, and tells her that both he and her mother are trying harder. Callie, now encouraged and focused, decides she will return to Sea Pines and work to get better.

Booktalk

Callie doesn't want to talk about what everyone calls her "issue." The other girls are the ones with the big problems, such as eating disorders and substance abuse. Callie just cuts herself once in a while. It gives her a good feeling, a rush. And she doesn't do it all the time. Besides, Sam, her eight-year-old brother, is the sick one. His asthma is so bad he can't go to school. Her dad has to work day and night to pay all the medical bills, and her mother has to make sure the house and car will be clean enough, quiet enough, and safe enough for Sam. So Callie really doesn't belong at Sea Pines, the place her roommate calls "Sick Minds." Everybody else has problems, not her, and she can get away from anything that bothers her with just a little *Cut*.

Related Activities

1. On page 12, start reading the paragraph that begins with "Twice a day we have 'loony bin.'" Discuss the language or word choice. How is Sidney using language, and how is Sea Pines using language? Is one side telling more of the truth than the other?

2. Callie tells her own story. Is she a reliable narrator? Discuss what she reveals about herself as she tells her story.

3. For a long time, Callie remains silent in individual sessions and group therapy. Do these sessions affect her or not? Support your answer with specifics from the novel. Compare her reaction to her therapist and the thoughts of the speaker in "Insomnia—A Journal Entry" on pages 35 and 36 of *Ophelia Speaks* (Related Work 5).

4. When Callie gives the metal strip she has stolen to the therapist, the therapist does not throw it away. She says Callie will have to decide what to do with it. Discuss your reaction to the therapist's answer.

5. In *Cut, Dancing on the Edge* (Related Work 4), and *Life Is Funny* (Related Work 2), characters hurt themselves to prove they still exist. Compare how adults in each of the novels influence the mutilation. Continue to research the problem of self-mutilation and the treatment programs used to address it.

6. In *Speak* (Related Work 1), *Cut,* and *You Don't Know Me* (Related Work 3), the main characters tell no one about their problems. Compare the characters in each of the novels. Discuss how they are alike even though their problems are different.

Related Works

1. Anderson, Laurie Halse. **Speak.** (See full booktalk in chapter 2.) The main character, raped at a party, spends the year in silence. She sees herself as shunned and refuses to talk about what happened.

2. Frank, E. R. **Life Is Funny.** (See full booktalk in chapter 2.) Eleven teenagers grow up dealing with the problems created by their abili-

ties, attitudes, families, schools, and neighborhoods. Two of the girls cut themselves.

3. Klass, David. **You Don't Know Me.** (See full booktalk in chapter 1.) A teenager, abused by his mother's live-in boyfriend, tells no one about the abuse until he is almost killed.

4. Nolan, Han. **Dancing on the Edge.** (See full booktalk in chapter 1.) Because her entire family ignores her, the main character bruises herself in violent dances to prove she still exists.

5. Shandler, Sara. **Ophelia Speaks.** New York: Harper Perennial, 1999. 285p. $12.95pa. ISBN 0-06-095297-0. (See full booktalk in *Booktalks Plus*, 2001, pages 126 to 128.) **NF** In the chapter "Self-Inflicted Wounds," Shandler includes one essay and three poems that address self-mutilation.

꿍꿍

Klebanoff, Susan, Ellen Luborsky, and Andy Cooke (illus.). Ups & Downs: How to Beat the Blues and Teen Depression.

New York: Price Stern Sloan, 1999. 90p. $9.95pa. (Plugged In).
ISBN 0-8431-7460-9. **NF**

Summary/Description

Ups & Downs begins with two negative reactions to the same situation. These reactions illustrate the difference between sadness and depression. The book gives the signs of depression and suicide, defines trauma, and lists the triggers of depression. These triggers are organized by the topics of loss, rejection, anger, and low self-esteem. Each term is explained. The authors also describe the physical signs of depression, which include stomach disorders, eating disorders, drinking, drugs, and sex. After defining and explaining the causes of depression, the authors provide an action plan section that includes inventories for general health and mental attitude. It also suggests ways to handle stress independently and with support. The authors include the names and numbers of specific hotlines and names and addresses of organizations that deal with depression and organizations that help with depression-related problems.

Booktalk

Do you ever wonder how some people just seem to float through the problems that seem to be drowning you? In *Ups & Downs*, other teenagers describe their problems, and they show us that everyone can develop a way to cope with life. This book has self-help quizzes, suggestions, and people sources. Examples even help you figure out if you or a friend is just sad or really depressed.

Get control of the forces that seem to be controlling you. Start with happier days and plan for a more hopeful tomorrow. *Ups & Downs* will help you get that life you are always hearing about.

Related Activities

1. Contact the organizations listed in *Ups & Downs* and *When Nothing Matters Anymore: A Survival Guide for Depressed Teens* (Related Work 1). Ask them for additional information that describes depression and explains how to fight it. Ask your librarian to help you find additional sources.
2. Answer the questions listed in the inventories for general health and mental attitude. Describe yourself as you are now. Describe how you would like to be. List the steps you will take to become the person you would like to be or explain why you like the person you are.
3. Explain what you do to relieve stress. Ask your friends to describe how they cope with stress. Then make up a journal that describes the keys to healthy and acceptable stress-relieving activities.
4. In *The 7 Habits of Highly Effective Teens* (Related Work 2), Sean Covey talks about how to secure and maintain a positive life. Relate the steps he identifies and describes to the suggestions given in *Ups & Downs*. Describe the overlaps you find. Then discuss the differences.
5. *Ups & Downs* emphasizes attitude. The authors also acknowledge that the word "attitude" has some heavy connotations for teenagers, who are often accused of showing a bad attitude if they object to someone or something. Each time you hear the word attitude used in the next few weeks, describe the context in which you hear it. Then write an extended definition of the word that uses the illustrations you have gathered. You might want to compare notes with someone else who is working on the same project.

Related Works

1. Cobain, Bev. **When Nothing Matters Anymore: A Survival Guide for Depressed Teens.** Minneapolis, MN: Free Spirit, 1998. 164p. $13.95. ISBN 1-57542-036-8. **NF** Written by the cousin of Kurt Cobain, who committed suicide in 1994, the book is divided into two major parts: "What's Wrong?" and "Getting Help and Staying Well." The sections include definitions, illustrations, survival tips, and ways to actively build strong physical and mental health.
2. Covey, Sean. **The 7 Habits of Highly Effective Teens.** (See full booktalk in chapter 4.) **NF** In this teen version of *The 7 Habits of*

Highly Effective People, Covey uses illustrations from teen experiences to outline a positive and proactive life-style.

3. Hamm, Mia with Aaron Heifez. **Go for the Goal: A Champion's Guide to Winning in Soccer and Life.** (See full booktalk in chapter 2.) **NF** Although a great deal of the book focuses on specific soccer techniques, Hamm also emphasizes developing a good head game that will ensure life successes.

4. Packer, Alex J. **Highs: Over 150 Ways to Feel Really, REALLY Good…Without Alcohol or Other Drugs.** Minneapolis, MN: Free Spirit, 2000. 251p. $14.95pa. ISBN 1-57542-074-0. **NF** Packer explains free to expensive ways to improve your environment and therefore your emotional and physical health.

5. Robinson, Sharon. **Jackie's Nine: Jackie Robinson's Values to Live By.** (See full booktalk in chapter 2.) **NF** Robinson identifies the nine values that helped Jackie Robinson overcome disappointments and prejudice. She illustrates these values with essays by and about her father and other celebrities.

Fleischman, Paul. Mind's Eye.

New York: Henry Holt and Company, 1999. 108p. $15.95. ISBN 0-8050-6314-5.

Summary/Description

Described as a "novel in play form," *Mind's Eye* records the conversation of sixteen-year-old Courtney and eighty-eight-year-old Elva. Both live at the Briarwood Convalescent Home. Courtney has been in an accident that has severed her spinal cord. Her father deserted her, and her mother died. She shares a room with Elva and May, an Alzheimer's patient. Although other characters do speak with Courtney, their conversations illustrate only the developing relationship between Courtney and Elva. Elva taught high school English and drama for thirty-two years. All her life, she memorized literature. As a child, her sister Rose organized the family and neighborhood for fantasy trips and plays. These inner resources sustain her in the bleak world of Briarwood.

Courtney is the youngest resident in the home. She has no family, reading background, or spiritual experience. After Elva persuades her to tour Italy via travel books, Courtney begins to realize her own worth and power. In the last chapter, after Elva's death, Courtney tells her new roommate about her own fantasy world. It encompasses the beauty of the Italian countryside, a blind boyfriend who shares the beauty with her, and her parents, Elva and Emmett. The novel includes discussions of mature issues that might be considered controversial.

Booktalk

Sixteen-year-old Courtney lived for malls, television, parties, drinking, friends, and lots of boyfriends. Then she severed her spinal cord. Now she spends most of her day with two roommates. Elva is eighty-eight, and May has Alzheimer's. May can't even remember how old she is. The television in the room doesn't work. Courtney's friends don't come around much anymore, and when they talk about their parties and boyfriends, Courtney isn't sure she wants to listen. How will she keep from losing her mind? But after Courtney starts talking to Elva, she discovers what having a mind can mean. Courtney decides to take a trip with Elva. Together they find a new world, a world Courtney never knew existed, in her own *Mind's Eye.*

Related Activities

1. On page 6, Elva compares life at Briarwood to the poem "Snowbound" (Related Work 5). Read the poem several times over a period of several days. After each reading, mark or write the lines that express Elva's vision of life. Explain why you have chosen those lines.
2. Compare the lines you have chosen from "Snowbound" (Related Work 5) and your reflections about them with other members of the group who have completed the same activity.
3. On page 11, Elva refers to the "sixth window." Read the passage. Discuss whether you agree with her point of view.
4. Courtney focuses on Medusa. Using the library resources and the Internet, research the myth. Trace the use of this myth throughout the novel. Discuss the conflicts it creates and the many ways Courtney might be identifying with the myth.
5. *Mind's Eye, Snake Dreamers* (Related Work 1), and "becoming" in *half-human* (Related Work 4) employ Medusa as a central allusion. Discuss how each author uses the allusion to accomplish the work's purpose.
6. Using the poetry section of your library, choose a poem you feel expresses Courtney's feelings. Explain your choice.
7. Select or write a poem that reflects your own feelings. Explain your choice. Memorize the poem. Record it in your notebook. Share your poem and/or explanations with others who have chosen to complete the same exercise.

8. With two other people and your library's resources, create your own fantasy trip. Present your trip to the rest of the group and explain what you expect to do and see at each stop.

Related Works

1. Galloway, Priscilla. **Snake Dreamer.** (See full booktalk in chapter 2). Medusa's sisters find her head and attach it to her body. A young girl, plagued by snake dreams, discovers that Medusa is a protector rather than a monster.
2. Hamilton, Edith (text) and Steele Savage (illus.). **Mythology.** New York: Little, Brown, 1998. 497p. $13.00pa. ISBN: 0316191523. **NF** This classic source explains Medusa in relation to other myths, legends, and stories.
3. Janeczko, Paul B. **How to Write Poetry.** New York: Scholastic Incorporated, 1999. 117p. (Scholastic Reference). $12.95. ISBN 0-590-10077-7. (See full booktalk in *Booktalks Plus, 2001,* pages 215 to 217.) **NF** Janeczko takes the poet through all the steps of the writing process from recording in a journal to producing specific poetry forms to share with others.
4. Springer, Nancy. "becoming." In **half-human,** compiled and edited by Bruce Coville. (See full booktalk in chapter 2.) Dusie Gorgon discovers she is part of a mythological dynasty when snakes spring from her head the day after she begins menstruating. Her mother, a famous sculptress, then explains beauty and love to her in relation to her new identity.
5. Whittier, John Greenleaf. "Snow-Bound." In **John Greenleaf Whittier's Poetry: An Appraisal and a Selection,** by Robert Penn Warren. Minneapolis: University of Minnesota Press, 1971. 208p. $4.48. ISBN 0-8166-0604-8. **NF** Whittier's poem, appearing on pages 167 to 187, re-creates the scenes and culture of Whittier's boyhood.

かいり

Dominick, Andie. Needles.

New York: Scribner, 1998. 220p. $22.00. ISBN 0-684-84232-7. **NF**

Summary/Description

Andie Dominick tells about her life with diabetes. Watching her older sister Denise cope with the disease and playing with her sister's discarded needle, Andie is knowledgeable about diabetes and injections before she has the disease. When Andie is nine, she develops the disease and her life changes dramatically. Andie describes getting her blood and urine checked constantly; the long hospital stays; rebellious periods of denial that include drinking, drug abuse, and dieting; teasing from peers; loss of sight; pregnancy; abortion; sterilization; and marriage. In Andie's life journey, she realizes that her sister Denise, whom she finds dead from a lethal mix of cocaine and insulin, had a death wish. Falling in love and marrying, Andie believes she can separate herself from her sister's destructive tendencies, and she decides that taking care of her body will help her live a longer and happier life. Andie's narrative gives a graphic picture of juvenile diabetes and the demands it places on the entire family.

Booktalk

Andie and her brother have water battles—with their sister's discarded hypodermic needles. Their older sister Denise is so smart and so pretty that Andie wishes she could be like Denise in every way—even down to having her diabetes. Then Andie's wish comes true: at nine years old, she finds she is diabetic too. But how bad can this disease be? Andie knows more about giving shots than most nurses. She even knows the signs of insulin shock and what to do about it. What she doesn't know is how hard it is to own the shots and shocks for real. But Denise will be her guide. Denise will show her how to cheat the *Needles*, fool their parents, and face off the doctors who try to tell them how to live. Andie just has to figure out if the disease or Denise will kill her first.

Related Activities

1. Read the paragraph on page 149 that begins "I say nothing..." and ends with the sentence *"You're not going blind right now."* How does that paragraph signal a turning point for Andie? How does it relate to the advice her friend gives her on page 159, that in her blindness she will gain vision?
2. In *Needles*, a nonfiction account, and *Lefty Carmichael Has a Fit* (Related Work 5), a novel, the main character must face a life-long illness in the teen years. Compare the problems each character faces and how other people help or fail to help them deal with those problems.
3. Read "Jessica: Diabetes" on pages 20 to 29 in *Young People and Chronic Illness: True Stories, Help, and Hope* (Related Work 3). Discuss Jessica's attitude toward her disease. Compare her comments and attitude to Andie's and Denise's attitudes.
4. In Part 2, "Learning to Cope," of *Young People and Chronic Illness: True Stories, Help, and Hope* (Related Work 3), the first seven chapters discuss the different aspects of dealing with a chronic illness in

teen years. Ask seven people to choose one chapter to read. Tell them, as they read the chapter, to note any communication skills suggested.

5. After they have completed activity four, ask the seven people to compare the skills they have identified. Discuss how these skills might be helpful in coping with any stressful or difficult situation. Ask them to present their conclusions to the group.

6. Pages 30 and 31 of *Young People and Chronic Illness: True Stories, Help, and Hope* (Related Work 3) and pages 60 to 62 of *Everything You Need to Know About Diabetes* (Related Work 1) list organizations, books, and Web sites for more information about diabetes. Ask your librarian to help you find additional information. Examine one of the sources. Evaluate the information you receive or find and share that information and your opinion about the information with the group. Explain how that information relates to Andie Dominick's story.

Related Works

1. Apel, Melanie Ann. **Everything You Need to Know About Diabetes.** New York: Rosen Publishing Group, 2000. 64p. (The Need to Know Library). $17.95. ISBN 0-8239-3090. ⓝⓕ Apel explains the disease and the maintenance it requires.

2. Dessen, Sarah. **Dreamland.** (See full booktalk in chapter 2.) The main character, who tries to define herself in terms of her sister, falls into drugs, sex, and abuse for her life answers.

3. Huegel, Kelly. **Young People and Chronic Illness: True Stories, Help, and Hope.** Minneapolis, MN: Free Spirit, 1998. 198p. $14.95pa. ISBN 1-57542-041-4. ⓝⓕ Written by a person with Crohn's disease who decided to hide rather than discuss her disease, this book uses case studies and communication techniques to persuade a young person that being open about chronic illness is a healthy policy.

4. Mikaelsen, Ben. **Petey.** New York: Hyperion Press, 1998. 280p. $15.95. ISBN 0-7868-0426-2. (See full booktalk in *Booktalks Plus*, 2001, pages 6 to 8.) This fictional account of a man born with cerebral palsy shows how even the most severely challenged person can build a worthwhile life.

5. Trembath, Don. **Lefty Carmichael Has a Fit.** Victoria, BC: Orca Book Publishers, 1999. 215p. $6.95pa. ISBN 1-55143-166-1. When a teenager discovers he has epilepsy, he begins to realize that those around him might also be coping with chronic illnesses and problems.

CR ED

Anderson, Laurie Halse. **Fever, 1793.**

New York: Simon & Schuster, 2000. 251p. $16.00. ISBN 0-689-83858-1.

Summary/Description

Fourteen-year-old Mattie Cook works unwillingly in her mother's Philadelphia coffeehouse. In the summer of 1793, a yellow fever epidemic sweeps the city, killing thousands. Those who can, including President Washington, flee. Mattie's mother comes down with fever and insists that Mattie and her grandfather go to the country, but they are thrown off the wagon because the grandfather is sick. Trying to get help, Mattie is overcome with fever and regains consciousness in a French hospital established in Pennsylvania's countryside. Her grandfather, suffering from heart disease, not fever, is there to help her, but without healthy adults to support her, Mattie faces the possibility of having to sell the coffeehouse for a dowry, live in an orphanage, or become a scullery maid. When she and her grandfather return to the city, they find her mother's house ransacked. Robbers break in again during the night. The confrontation kills the grandfather, and Mattie buries him. Searching for food and help, she finds a little orphan girl, Nell. They meet Eliza, a freewoman who worked in the coffeehouse and now, through the Free African Society, helps fever victims. Mattie and Nell join Eliza, her brother, and her twin nephews. When the three children become ill, Mattie and Eliza take them to the cooler building where Mattie's mother had her coffeehouse. The children recover. The fever abates with the frost, and Mattie decides she and Eliza will run the business as partners. Their enterprise is well underway when Mattie's mother returns, weakened from the fever. In the Epilogue, Mattie is the household's early riser who happily gets each business day started.

An appendix at the end of the novel explains the epidemic, the conflicting medical opinions about dealing with it, the mass graves, and the events, people, and organizations of the times surrounding and affected by the fever. It also explains how often Congress and the capital moved in the early days of the Republic, the fear and panic that the fever caused, and the status of yellow fever today.

Booktalk

At fourteen, Mattie must work hard in her mother's coffeehouse and begin looking for a husband. She doesn't want to do either. She has her own ideas about running a coffeehouse, and she would rather spend her time with the dreamy artist Nathaniel than with one of the snobby Ogilvie sons—good catches according to her mother. The year is 1793. When *Fever* hits, Philadelphia is in panic. Everyone's world turns upside down. People aren't worried about life's everyday details anymore; they're just trying to stay alive. Mattie is forced to leave the city, her mother, and the fever behind. But death, disease, and violence follow her, and her struggle-filled journey brings challenges, heartaches, strengths, and plans she never would have imagined.

Related Activities

1. *Fever, 1793* is also about the social classes of the period. Explain the class structure revealed at the beginning of the book. Compare it to the class structure at the end of the book.
2. On pages 19 and 20, the term "miasma" is used. Define it and explain how it applies to the story.
3. Anderson describes *Fever, 1793* as plot-driven. List the significant plot events. Then explain how the choices presented in each event reveal and change Mattie.
4. After researching yellow fever, discuss the appropriateness of Anderson's plot and character choices. Especially consider the role of Eliza. You might wish to start with *Yellow Fever* (Related Work 1) by Holly Cefrey.
5. Quotations and recipes introduce each chapter. Discuss how each anticipates the purpose of the chapter and reveals the time period. Contrast the use of recipes in *Fever, 1793* with the use of recipes in *Sunshine Rider: The First Vegetarian Western* (Related Work 2).
6. Although written about very different times and cultures, *Fever, 1793*, *Homeless Bird* (Related Work 6), and *Ties that Bind, Ties That Break* (Related Work 4) are all about young girls who, in the face of death and disaster, challenge tradition and become independent businesswomen. Read the three novels. Compare and contrast the patterns in each novel.

Related Works

1. Cefrey, Holly. **Yellow Fever.** New York: Rosen Publishing Group, 2002. 64p. (Epidemics: Deadly Diseases Throughout History). $19.95. ISBN 0-8239-3489-6. **NF** Opening with a description of a yellow fever victim, *Yellow Fever* explains the disease, its history, and its control. *Fever, 1793* is included in "For Further Reading."
2. Hardman, Ric Lynden. **Sunshine Rider: The First Vegetarian Western.** New York: Laurel-Leaf Books, 1998. 343p. $4.99pa. ISBN 0-440-22812-3. In this humorous coming-of-age novel, sixteen-year-

old Wylie Jackson discovers his manhood and his real father when he signs on with a cattle drive. A recipe introduces each chapter and keys the time, place, and mood.

3. Hill, Christine. "Laurie Halse Anderson Speaks: An Interview." *VOYA.* (December 2000) 325–327. **NF** Anderson contrasts the writing processes of *Fever, 1793* and *Speak.* She says *Fever, 1793* is plot-driven and *Speak* is character-driven.

4. Namioka, Lensey. **Ties That Bind, Ties That Break.** (See full booktalk in chapter 1.) Ailin grows up in China during the first quarter of the twentieth century. Her indulgent parents allow her to refuse foot binding. That decision begins her pattern of fighting traditions and developing a new way of life.

5. Litwin, Laura Baskes. **Benjamin Banneker: Astronomer and Mathematician.** Berkeley Heights, NJ: Enslow Publishers, Inc., 1999. 112p. (African-American Biographies). $20.95. ISBN: 0-7660-1208-5. **NF** Setting the scene in chapter 5, Litwin explains the allusion Anderson makes to Blanchard's balloon. Throughout the book, she emphasizes the abolitionist movement in Philadelphia and the part the Quakers played in it.

6. Whelan, Gloria. **Homeless Bird.** (See full booktalk in chapter 4.) When Koly, a widow at thirteen, is abandoned, she uses her skills and the love of a young rickshaw driver to build a new, independent, and unconventional life.

Hate and Prejudice
Trying to Shut Us Out

ﾃﾔ

Hesse, Karen. **Witness.**

New York: Scholastic Press, 2001. 176p. $16.95. ISBN 0-439-27199-1.

Summary/Description

Hesse describes the Ku Klux Klan invasion of a small Vermont town through the eyes of eleven of its citizens—the doctor, the town constable, a female farmer, two shop owners, a restaurant owner and rum runner, a newspaper editor, a clergyman, a twelve-year-old African-American girl, a six-year-old Jewish girl, and an eighteen-year-old Klan recruit. The characters are pictured on the opening pages, and each person expresses his or her opinions in verses organized in five acts. Esther Hirsh and Leanora Sutter, because of their religion and race, become the targets of Klan hatred. The clergyman, punished by the Klan for impregnating a young girl, tries to regain their good graces by killing Esther and her father. He manages only to wound the father, and then he commits suicide. Merlin Van Tornhout, the Klan recruit, does not carry out his assignment to poison the Sutter well because Leanora's bravery and Mr. Hirsh's kindness have touched him. He leaves town but returns because he thinks the clergyman (whom he does not realize has died) is following him. Eventually, the Klan invasion is defeated by the small acts of kindness from the Sutters, the Hirshes, and the people who accept them. Set in 1924, the narratives also discuss the re-election of Calvin Coolidge, the Leopold and Loeb trial, women's independence, and running of illegal liquor.

Booktalk

Show the pictures at the beginning of the novel. Ask the people in the group to speculate about each person's character. Ask them to guess which people are active participants in the Klan. Discuss their choices.

The year is 1924. The Ku Klux Klan is burning crosses, closing businesses, and preaching sermons in Vermont. Most people in the town think the Klan will just go away. But for some people, joining the Klan means money. For others, it's a way to feel they're a little better than someone else is. For most of the members it just means finding someone to blame for all their troubles. The Klan decides to target twelve-year-old Leanora Sutter, an African-American, and six-year-old Esther Hirsh, a Jew. Neither girl has a gun, a knife, or a guard dog. What could possibly protect them? The Klan finds out. When accidents, poisoning, shooting, and suicide unfold in a small Vermont town, eleven people *Witness* and tell their stories.

Related Activities

1. Johnny Reeves, Merlin Van Tornhout, Leanora Sutter, and Reynard Alexander give their reactions to the burning cross. Discuss what each reaction reveals about the person.
2. The movie *The Birth of a Nation* (Related Work 1) and the Leopold and Loeb trial are significant allusions in the story. Research the two allusions. Share your information with the class, and then explain how the two references support Hesse's purpose.
3. Ask people in each group to reread only the poems for a particular person. Then ask them to explain that person's character in terms of what the person wants, what forces are against the person's getting what he or she wants, and what the person is willing to do to overcome those forces.

4. Each day, read aloud a small group of the poems in the order in which they are presented. The readers might be the people who analyzed an individual character in activity 3. Then discuss the relationship among the poems and the significance of each.
5. Classify the characters in as many ways as possible. You might use age, sex, political views, or status in the town. Then explain each classification and how each group relates to the novel's purpose. In your explanation, be sure to consider the novel's title.
6. Mr. Field, Mary, and Mr. Hirsh have no poems of their own but make a significant impact on the speakers. Explain how each character is important to the novel's outcome. Using the other poems as models, write one or two poems for each of the three characters.

Related Works

1. **The Birth of a Nation.** Produced by KVC Entertainment, 1991. 130 min. Videocassette. Black and white. $24.95. ISBN 1555267580. Based on the novel *The Clansman* by Thomas Dixon and originally titled *The Clansman* when it was first produced in 1915, the movie depicts life after the Civil War: the conflict between the Southerners and the carpetbaggers as well as the evolution of the Ku Klux Klan.
2. Cormier, Robert. **Heroes.** (See full booktalk in chapter 2.) Like the clergyman who preaches against sin and then impregnates a young girl, Larry LaSalle, a respected youth leader and winner of the Silver Star, kills himself when he realizes others know about his molesting and raping of young girls.
3. Ellis, Rex M. **With a Banjo on My Knee: A Musical Journey from Slavery to Freedom.** New York: Franklin Watts, 2001. 160p. $26.00 ISBN 0-531-11747-2. **NF** In tracing the roots of the banjo, Ellis also follows the history of minstrel stereotyping and lynching associated with the instrument.
4. Fradin, Dennis Brindell and Judith Bloom Fradin. **Ida B. Wells: Mother of the Civil Rights Movement.** (See full booktalk in chapter 4.) **NF** Wells used the media and equal rights organizations to fight prejudice and the lynching that resulted from it.
5. Hesse, Karen. **Out of the Dust.** New York: Scholastic, 1997. 227p. $4.99pa. ISBN 0-590-37125-8. (See full booktalk in *Booktalks Plus*, 2001, pages 30 to 32.) In a series of poems, fourteen-year-old Billie Jo tells her story in the context of the Oklahoma Dust Bowl.
6. Masters, Edgar Lee. **Spoon River Anthology: An Annotated Edition,** edited by John E. Hallwas. Chicago: University of Illinois Press, 1992. 436p. $27.95. ISBN 0-252-06363-5. **NF** Hallwas's introduction explains why this anthology is so important to American lit-

erature and reveals why, as an expression of small-town tensions, it was an inspiration to Hesse in her writing of *Witness*.

☙❧

Paulsen, Gary. Sarny: A Life Remembered.

New York: Bantam Doubleday Dell Books for Young Readers, 1997. 180p. $4.99pa.
ISBN 0-440-21973-6.

Summary/Description

At age ninety-four, Sarny tells the story of her life from slavery through Reconstruction. Her first marriage, in slavery, produces two children, who are then sold. After her husband dies and the Union Army frees her, Sarny and her friend Lucy journey to New Orleans to find them. On the road, they encounter Miss Laura, who hires them and helps Sarny find her children. Laura dies and leaves her money to Sarny. When Sarny arrives in New Orleans, she continues to share the gift of reading that Nightjohn gave her. Her first school in the free South draws Klan resistance, and when her second husband fights back, he is killed. Finally, with her children grown and successful and her husband and Miss Laura dead, Sarny leaves New Orleans for Texas, where she founds more than twenty schools before her death. This composite character, in telling her own story, explores the situations of black women during slavery and post-emancipation—the slave girl, the free black woman in the South, the free black woman in the North, and the black female entrepreneur who is successful because of her ability to pass as white.

Booktalk

Sarny, born a slave, lives to see the Great Emancipation. But Nightjohn, a great teacher and slave, freed her mind before Lincoln freed her body. Sarny knows she should have the right to marry. She knows she should have the right to keep her own children, and she knows she can spread her mind and life far beyond the plantation. But for many in the South, another war is starting—a war of bitterness, jealousy, and intimidation, a war of Reconstruction. No Union Army can win it. Former slaves must fight it every day. Sarny proves to be one of the strongest soldiers. With ninety-four years of giving, learning, and loving—weapons stronger than guns—her life is her victory.

Related Activities

1. *Sarny* explores the roles of women in the South during slavery and emancipation. Find as much factual information as possible about

black women who lived through slavery, stayed in the South after slavery, and migrated North after slavery. Report to the class any information you find that supports the characters developed by Paulsen.

2. Read *Nightjohn.* List the values Nightjohn teaches Sarny.

3. Choose a person in your own life who has taught you values. Cite specific actions you take because of those lessons. Discuss those values and actions with others in the group.

4. In *Sarny,* Paulsen has created a composite character. His Afterword states that everything in the book is historically true but it didn't happen to one person within a specific period of time. Choose another historical event or period. Using factual information as a base, develop your own composite character who lives through and reacts to that period of history.

5. In *Zack* (Related Work 1), Zack Lane reports on the life of slave and Revolutionary War hero Richard Pierpoint. After reading this report on pages 75 to 83 of *Zack,* compare his character to those of Nightjohn and Sarny. Make a list of qualities that allowed these three people to overcome adversity.

Related Works

1. Bell, William. **Zack.** New York: Simon & Schuster, 1999. 192p. $16.95. ISBN 0-689-82248-0. On pages 75 to 83, Zack tells about the survival and triumph of Richard Pierpoint, slave and Revolutionary War soldier who fought for the British.

2. Ellis, Rex M. **With a Banjo on My Knee: A Musical Journey from Slavery to Freedom.** New York: Franklin Watts, 2001. 160p. $26.00. ISBN 0-531-11747-2. Tracing the banjo from its African roots, Ellis explains why it became associated with the pain and shame of slavery and persecution.

3. Fradin, Dennis Brindell and Judith Bloom Fradin. **Ida B. Wells: Mother of the Civil Rights Movement.** (See full booktalk in chapter 4.) Born during slavery and growing up during the Reconstruction, Ida B. Wells fought for equal rights and against lynching.

4. Paulson, Gary. **Nightjohn.** New York: Delacorte Press, 1993. 92p. $14.95. ISBN 0-385-30838-8. Sarny tells the story of Nightjohn, who gives up his freedom and subjects himself to torture and mutilation so he can teach slaves to read.

5. Rinaldi, Ann. **Cast Two Shadows.** New York: Gulliver Books, 1998. 276p. $16.00. ISBN 0-15-200881-0. (See full booktalk in *Booktalks Plus,* 2001, pages 46 to 48.) Rinaldi's composite character experi-

ences the conflict of two countries during the Revolutionary War and the conflict of two races within herself. Her father is a slave owner, and her mother is a slave who was sold when Caroline came to live in her father's house.

ᏍᎦᏋᏋ

Miklowitz, Gloria D.
Secrets in the House of Delgado.
Grand Rapids, MI: Eerdmans Books for Young Readers, 2001. 182p. $16.00.
ISBN 0-8028-5206-8.

Summary/Booktalk

When orphaned fourteen-year-old Maria Sanchez seeks refuge from the church, she is sent by Fra Adolfo to be a servant/spy in the Delgado household. The Delgados are Conversos, Jews who converted to the Catholic faith rather than leave Spain. Maria is supposed to report suspicious activity in the Delgado household to Fra Adolfo. Maria finds the Delgados to be kind and generous. Her charge—the headstrong, adventuresome, and loving twelve-year-old Angelica—teaches her how to read and play the harpsichord. Angelica's mother gives Maria beautiful dresses. Juan Pablo, Angelica's older brother, protects both girls. Maria mistakes his attentions for love. When she discovers he is betrothed to another Converso, jealousy motivates her to report trivial information to Fra Adolfo that can be construed as evidence. Angelica's father is taken away, and Maria believes his arrest is her fault. When he returns to the house after extensive torture, the family decides to flee. Juan Pablo asks Maria, their most trusted servant, to help them mask their escape with his wedding. Maria tries to make up for her betrayal, and when a ship captain betrays them, she persuades her uncle, also a ship captain, to give the couple passage. Eventually she discovers that Dr. Delgado's efforts to help a Jew, not her information, caused his arrest. She stays in Spain with Leon, another former servant in the House of Delgado, who encourages her to use the skills she learned from the Delgado family to rise above servitude.

Booktalk

Fourteen-year-old Maria Sanchez has lost her entire family. All she has now are a sack full of possessions and her Christian faith. That faith takes her to a monk, Fra Adolfo. He finds her a wonderful new job in the House of Delgado, the house of the Queen's physician. But Fra Adolfo wants one small favor: Maria must spy on the family she serves.

They are Conversos, Spanish Jews whose ancestors agreed to become Catholics. In 1492, Queen Isabella and King Ferdinand have already driven out the Moors and the Jews. Now, with the help of the Inquisition, they can eliminate any false Conversos and give their country back to the "pure" Catholics. Maria has a chance to be part of this great cleansing if she will only tell the *Secrets in the House of Delgado.*

Related Activities

1. On page 28, chapter 5, Maria uses shells in a simile. Identify the simile. Discuss its appropriateness in the story.
2. Chapter 7, "Trouble," reveals the knowledge and ignorance of both girls. Reread the chapter and discuss why it might be pivotal to the story. In your discussion, be specific about what each girl knows and does not know. Explain how each piece of knowledge and ignorance is related to the entire story.
3. Leon is a minor but significant character. Maria describes him as a practical man. Explain his function in the story. Be sure to discuss his function in relation to Fra Adolfo, another minor character whom Leon never meets.
4. In a major portion of the book, Maria has negative feelings toward Jews. Give reasons why she holds and finally rejects her prejudice. Discuss how her betrayal of the Delgado family is related or not related to that prejudice.
5. In 1492, both the exploration of the New World and the Inquisition are significant issues in Spain. Divide the group into two parts. Ask one group to research the Inquisition and the other to research Christopher Columbus's exploration. Bring the groups together. Ask them to share their information and discuss whether these events, one that is religious and the other that is monetary, are related. You might wish to begin your research by viewing the videos *Christopher Columbus: Explorer of the New World* (Related Work 1) and *The Inquisition* (Related Work 3).

Related Works

1. **Christopher Columbus: Explorer of the New World.** Produced by A&E Television Networks, 1996. 50 min. Videocassette. Color. (Biography). $14.95. AAE-14049. Christopher Columbus carries the thinking of divine destiny, greed, and the right of domination to the New World as he searches for a passage to China.
2. Cushman, Karen. **Matilda Bone.** (See full booktalk in chapter 2.) Like Maria, Matilda begins to rely on her own practical experiences rather than on the world of the church.

3. **The Inquisition.** Produced by A&E Television Networks, 1999. 100 min. Videocassette. Color. $29.95. AAE-40486. Tracing the 600-year history of the Inquisition, this documentary includes the persecution of the Conversos that occurred because of their successful integration into Spanish society.

4. Meyer, Carolyn. **Isabel: Jewel of Castilla.** New York: Scholastic Incorporated, 2000. 240p. (The Royal Diaries). $10.95. ISBN 0-439-07805-9. Fifteen-year-old Isabel writes about the sins of those around her as she prepares to be queen.

5. Staples, Suzanne Fisher. **Shiva's Fire.** New York: Frances Foster Books/Farrar, Straus, and Giroux, 2000. 276p. $17.00. ISBN 0-374-36824-4. Both a talented dancer and a Raja's son embrace and develop their practical talents rather than the mysticism that surrounds them and plan to meet again when they are educated, accomplished adults.

6. Whelan, Gloria. **Homeless Bird.** (See full booktalk in chapter 4.) Abandoned by her mother-in-law in the city of widows, thirteen-year-old Koly befriends a young rickshaw driver. Together they learn to rely on their skills and hard work rather than traditions to direct their lives and relationship.

ぐ弓を

Meltzer, Milton. Witches and Witch-hunts: A History of Persecution.

New York: The Blue Sky Press, 1998. 128p. $16.95. ISBN: 0-590-48517-2. ⓝⓕ

Summary/Description

Meltzer first explains the psychology of witch-hunts. After a person sees how an event happens, he or she continues to look for the "why" in order to control future events. Many times the "why" is related to bitterness or hate in the person's life, to stereotypes, or to jealousy. Differences in belief, appearance, thinking, age, nationality, race, or politics all might place a person or group in danger. The author then defines witches, with lists of observable behaviors. Most of the book reports specific cases such as the too-prosperous Lady Alice Kyteler of fourteenth century Ireland, the Salem witch trials, Hitler's persecution of the Jews, McCarthyism, and witchcraft persecution in modern South Africa. Meltzer discusses the disproportionate number of women persecuted, the role of Christianity in persecution, and the modern perceptions of Satanism and Paganism. Inserts explain Joan of Arc, The Witches' Sabbath, the relationship between poisoning and delusional thinking, and the thoughts and feelings behind witchcraft.

Chapter 4 includes the letter from Johannes Junius, the mayor of Bamberg, Germany. The letter explains his torture and the impossibility of anyone's presenting a personal defense against witchcraft. Explanatory notes accompany each chapter, and a four-page bibliography provides additional resources. Throughout his book, Meltzer emphasizes the need for tolerance, knowledge, and understanding to prevent future witch-hunts.

Booktalk

Witches! They cast spells, keep cats, ride brooms, and have a black, pointed hat waiting in the closet. Right? Even the glamorous television versions can make big trouble for the person who decides to cross them. Now *Witches and Witch-Hunts* gives you the real story behind that picture. Milton Meltzer tells you about witches and witch-hunts from all countries and times and also about some witch-hunts that threatened entire civilizations. He even suggests there might be a little witch and witch-hunter in each of us.

Related Activities

1. Meltzer lists the criteria for recognizing a witch on pages 16 and 17. After reading the criteria, discuss how these signs might be misinterpreted.
2. Meltzer distinguishes between witches and witch-hunts, a much broader term. Define a witch-hunt. Explain how you might recognize a witch-hunt.
3. Meltzer's introduction emphasizes that people begin witch-hunts to uncover the "why" of a disastrous event and protect themselves from future danger. Identify a situation from your community or current events that could be construed as a witch-hunt. Explain why the situation could be characterized as a witch-hunt. Then discuss if you agree or disagree with that characterization.
4. Chapter 8 discusses witchcraft in the American colonies, and chapter 10 describes the McCarthy era. "The Crucible" (Related Work 5) uses the theme of witchcraft in the colonies to attack actions in the McCarthy era. After reading the play and researching the McCarthy era, discuss the appropriateness of Miller's choices.
5. The Harry Potter Series presents witches in a positive light. For this reason, the books have been censored. Discuss Rowling's portrayal of witchcraft and magic in relation to *Witches and Witch-hunts*. You might wish to start with *Harry Potter and the Sorcerer's Stone* (Related Work 7).

Related Works

1. Avi. **Midnight Magic.** (See full booktalk in chapter 2.) Targeted and persecuted by a high government official who wishes to hide his own evil plans, Mangus the magician must solve the mystery of a ghost.
2. Branford, Henrietta. **The Fated Sky.** Cambridge, MA: Candlewick Press, 1999. 156p. $16.99. ISBN 0-7636-0775-4. When the main character's mother dies while under the care of a witch, both the witch and the main character are sentenced to die. The girl is miraculously saved but must spend the rest of her life running and hiding.
3. Hawthorne, Nathaniel. **The Scarlet Letter.** Philadelphia, PA: Courage Books/Running Press, 1991. 201p. (Courage Classics). $4.98. ISBN 1-561-38036-9. Hawthorne weaves the ideas of good and evil in relation to the dark arts. Mistress Hibbins tempts Hester to join her in the forest to sign "the Black Man's book." The first edition appeared in 1850.
4. LaMachia, John. **So What Is Tolerance Anyway?** New York: The Rosen Publishing Group/Rosen Central, 2000. 48p. (A Student's Guide to American Civics). $17.95. ISBN 0-8239-3097. **NF** This volume defines tolerance, explains its history within the United States, and illustrates how it was used and abused. Different perceptions and examples show how tolerance might be acted on in everyday life.
5. Miller, Arthur. "The Crucible." In **The Portable Arthur Miller,** edited by Christopher Bigsby. New York: Penguin Books, 1995. 575p. $16.95pa. ISBN 0-14-024709-2. Choosing the setting of the Salem witch trials, Miller wrote his play to protest the anti-communist McCarthy hearings of the 1950s. The play appears on pages 132 to 252.
6. Napoli, Donna Jo. **Zel.** New York: Dutton Children's Books, 1996. 227p. $15.99. ISBN 0-525-45612-0. In this revised version of Rapunzel, Zel, the main character, discovers her mother is a witch.
7. Rowling, J.K. **Harry Potter and the Sorcerer's Stone.** New York: Arthur A. Levine Books, 1997. 509p. $17.95. ISBN 0-590-35340-3. Harry discovers his positive magical powers. This is the first book in the series.
8. Thesman, Jean. **The Other Ones.** (See full booktalk in chapter 3.) Bridget Raynes must decide to accept the magical powers that have labeled her aunt the town witch.

Napoli, Donna Jo. Stones in Water.

New York: Dutton Children's Books, 1997. 209p. $15.99. ISBN 0-525-45842-5.

Summary/Description

*S*tones in Water is a coming-of-age survival novel set in Italy after the Japanese attack on Pearl Harbor. Thirteen-year-old Roberto goes to an American film with his older brother and two friends. German troops march the boys away and herd them onto a train. One boy, Samuele, is Jewish. To protect himself, he masquerades as a Catholic. Roberto and Samuele stay together in work details. They build a holding area for Jewish prisoners. Moved by the desperation of the Jews, the boys share their food and steal more. When Roberto is caught, Samuele also confesses, and the Germans send them to a work camp in the Ukraine, where they find tougher boys and more compassionate guards. Roberto and Samuele steal leather boots from dead German soldiers. Boys in the camp attack them for the boots and kill Samuele. Roberto knows the Germans will discover that Roberto has been protecting a Jew. He escapes and tries to return to Italy.

Aided by Samuele's knowledge and stories, Roberto has two significant encounters. The first is with a seven-year-old Ukrainian boy whose entire village has been killed. They gather supplies and travel together to the next village. Here Roberto is the enemy. He is shot, but the boy gives him boots and helps him escape. Roberto discovers a boat, and because his father, a gondolier, has taught him boating skills, he is confident he can make it home. The second is a confrontation with a young Italian deserter who tries to kill him and take the boat, but eventually they too become friends, help each other survive, and decide to fight with the resistance. Roberto learns that the power of a strong spirit joined with other strong spirits triumphs.

Booktalk

Roberto wants to go to the movies. Since the attack on Pearl Harbor, American movies in Italy are rare, and his older brother, his friend Memo, and his Jewish friend Samuele want to go too. But before the movie starts, German soldiers, Italy's allies, march into the theater and take everyone away. Now Roberto enters a new world he wishes were a bad movie. He can't go home. He can't even understand the other boys in the work camp, but he does understand that no one must find out Samuele is a Jew. Against brutality and terror, Roberto and Samuele decide they will not only survive, they will also make a difference. They will be *Stones in Water* that, like the stones of Venice, allow a city to rise and stand against the waves of war and hate.

Related Activities

1. To strengthen the spirit, Samuele tells stories. Roberto brings Samuele back to his memory through these stories. On page 114,

Roberto recalls the story of Moses on Mount Sinai. Discuss why this story is appropriate at this particular time.

2. Choose one story you have read or heard that you feel would strengthen the spirit. Tell the story, and then explain why you feel it is important.

3. Stones are central in the story. Roberto values the gift stone from the Jewish girl, and he explains the strength of good people through a comparison to stones. Read his explanation on page 208. Begin with "Power surged through Roberto…" and read to the end of the chapter. Discuss the implications of the comparison.

4. Use your library's resources and the Internet to research Italy's participation as an Axis Power in World War II and the role of the Ukraine in World War II. Share your findings with the group.

5. Define communist and fascist. Using the information you found in activity 4, explain how those terms applied to Europe before and during World War II.

Related Works

1. Byers, Ann. **The Holocaust Camps.** Berkeley Heights, NJ: Enslow Publishers, Inc., 1998. 128p. (The Holocaust Remembered Series). $20.95. ISBN 0-89490-995-9. **NF** Byers describes the evolution of the German camp system, which ranged from work camps to extermination camps.

2. Hughes, Dean. **Soldier Boys.** (See full booktalk in chapter 1.) A teenage American soldier loses his life in trying to save a wounded teenage German soldier. The novel illustrates the Reich's indoctrination of German youth. Like *Stones in Water,* that indoctrination included work camps.

3. Nir, Yehuda. **The Lost Childhood: A World War II Memoir.** New York: Scholastic Press, 2002. 288p. $16.95. ISBN 0-439-16389-7. **NF** This memoir of a Polish Jew explains in chapters 2 and 3 how the Ukrainians joined the Nazis and massacred Jews. Chapter 21 describes the author's life in the German work camps. Like Samuele, he and his family pretended to be Catholics.

4. Opdyke, Irene Gut with Jennifer Armstrong. **In My Hands: Memories of a Holocaust Rescuer.** (See full booktalk in chapter 4.) **NF** Like the fictional Roberto, Opdyke, a Catholic, protects Jewish friends from the Germans.

5. Osborne, Mary Pope. **My Secret War: The World War II Diary of Madeline Beck.** New York: Scholastic Incorporated, 2000. 192p. $10.95. ISBN 0-590-68715-8. Eighth grader Madeline Beck records

her World War II experience—a sharp contrast to the experiences of European teens.

ᏟᏠ

Bennett, Cherie and Jeff Gottesfeld.
Anne Frank and Me.

New York: GP Putnam's Sons, 2001. 288p. $19.99. ISBN 0-399-23329-6.

Summary/Description

For Nicole, a student from an affluent family, school is a social center. She ignores her English reading assignment, *The Diary of a Young Girl* by Anne Frank, and a classroom speaker, Mrs. Litzger-Gold, who lived through the Holocaust in Paris, France.

Then a freak accident transports Nicole to a parallel world—1942 in Paris, France, where she becomes Nicole Bernhardt. Her 1990s English teacher and high school principal are her mother and father. Her annoying sister, Little Bit, is now Liz-Bette. Her best friend Mimi and her school crush Jack are twins. Instead of communicating from her self-absorbed 1990s Web site, "Notes from Girl X," she writes a series of reflective, defiant, encouraging, and anonymous letters and leaves them on park benches and stuffed in cracks.

French society closes its doors to Nicole Bernhardt. She sees her Jewish friends arrested. Her father joins the resistance. The family goes into hiding, and Jack betrays them. Separated from her mother and knowing her father is dead, Nicole and her sister are transported to Birkenau, where they meet Anne Frank. When Nicole's time travel ends, she returns to the present and gets a second chance. She finishes *The Diary of a Young Girl*, accepts her sister's feelings, and listens to the "Star Spangled Banner" with new understanding. She tries to find the speaker from English class and discovers that Mrs. Litzger-Gold died of a heart attack. In the funeral display, Nicole discovers a note from Girl X that inspired the woman to face the hardships of her times and look forward to friends, family, and freedom. This discovery confirms the truth of Nicole's time travel just as scholarly organizations have fought to confirm Anne's existence.

This based-on-fact coming-of-age novel, emphasizing the need to learn about the Holocaust and check historical facts, responds to the many denial Web sites denouncing the Holocaust and Anne Frank's diary. It alludes to additional Holocaust literature within the text and provides a historical timeline and list of sources at the end of the novel. Dates on some of the chapters show how the historical events affect Nicole's situation.

Booktalk

Reading about the Holocaust won't teach me how to make more money. It won't improve my social life. It's such ancient history that there isn't much point in even talking about it, especially when I'm planning my weekend.

That's what popular and pretty Nicole Barnes thought until a freak accident transported her back to 1942 Paris, France. As Nicole Bernhardt, a Jew, she sees things differently. She's still in love, she still has friends, and her family still gives her a hard time. But bit-by-bit the Nazis rob her of her world, her dreams, her love, and her life. What does she think now? Saving the future is up to *Anne Frank and Me.*

Related Activities

1. After reading both *The Diary of a Young Girl* (Related Work 3) and *Anne and Me*, list the similarities you find between Anne and Nicole. Discuss your reaction to these similarities.

2. The June 12, 1942, entry of Anne's diary from *The Diary of Anne Frank: the Definitive Edition* (Related Work 3) could be an introduction for many young adult diaries. Discuss what the entry implies about the writer and the world in which the writer lives. Discuss how it could also apply to Nicole's world.

3. Nicole Bernhardt's mother and father in Nicole's time travel are Nicole Barnes's English teacher and high school principal. Discuss possible reasons for this choice.

4. Further research the life of Sarah Bernhardt and her protests against anti-Semitism.

5. Read the play *Anne Frank and Me* (Related Work 1) by Cherie Bennett. Discuss the differences between the play and the novel. Discuss if and how those changes affect the story's purpose.

6. Read or reread *The Devil's Arithmetic* (Related Work 7). What do the similarities and differences between *Anne Frank and Me* and *The Devil's Arithmetic* suggest about the purpose of *Anne Frank and Me?*

Related Works

1. Bennett, Cherie. **Anne Frank & Me.** Woodstock, IL: The Dramatic Publishing Co., 1997. 88p. $12.00. ISBN 0-87129-701-9. The novel is adapted from this play. Scripts are $5.60 each, and a study guide is available from the company for $25.00.

2. Comer, Melissa. "Anne and Me: A Frank Talk with Writers Cherie Bennett and Jeff Gottesfeld." *The ALAN Review.* (Spring/Summer, 2002) 20–23. **NF** In the interview, the husband and wife writing team

emphasize the difficulty of writing a historical novel involving Anne Frank and the meticulous attention it required to accurately depict Anne and the Nazi occupation of France.

3. Frank, Anne. **The Diary of a Young Girl: The Definitive Edition.** Edited by Otto H. Frank and Mirjam Pressler. Translated by Susan Massotty. New York: Doubleday, 1991. 340p. $25.00. ISBN 0-385-47378-8. **NF** This new edition contains approximately thirty percent more material and is based on the scholarship of *The Diary of Anne Frank: The Critical Edition.*

4. Levine, Ellen. **Darkness over Denmark.** New York: Holiday House, 2000. 164p. $14.95. ISBN 0-8234-1755-7. **NF** Although this book relates the details of the Danish rather than the French resistance, it describes the important part letters and underground newspapers played in inspiring and organizing the resistance fighters.

5. Levitsky, Holli. "Notes from Girl X: Anne Frank at the Millennium." *The ALAN Review.* (Winter 2002) 11–15. **NF** The article identifies the novel *Anne Frank & Me* as a tool for viewing history "through the prism of a contemporary Anne Frank."

6. Müller, Melissa. **Anne Frank: The Biography.** Translated by Rita and Robert Kimber. New York: Henry Holt and Company, 1998. 330p. $14.00pa. ISBN 0-8050-5997-0. **NF** Cited in the sources list of *Anne Frank and Me*, this work places Anne Frank in a family, social, and political context.

7. Yolen, Jane. **The Devil's Arithmetic.** New York: Viking Press, 1988. 170p. $13.00. ISBN 0-670-81027-4. Hannah's time travel experience acts as an allusion for Nicole Barnes's time travel. The contrasts highlight the truth theme in the novel *Anne Frank and Me.*

☙❧

Durrant, Lynda. The Turtle Clan Journey.
New York: Clarion Books, 1999. 180p. $15.00. ISBN 0-395-90369-6.

Summary/Description

In *Echohawk*, Echohawk discovers that he is really Jonathan Starr and that his Mohican father killed his white parents and then found and adopted him. In the sequel, *The Turtle Clan Journey*, Echohawk, his Indian father, Glickihigan, and his Indian brother, Bamaineo, find that their tribe has been wiped out by the white man's disease, so they must journey to a new territory. When they stop at a farm to rest, the family warns them that the government will pay a ransom for white captives. Echohawk hides but is captured and sent to live with his aunt, Ruth Starr.

His Mohican father and brother return to get him and then leave again for the new territory. As they flee, the Mohawk and Iroquois capture them. The captors plan to return Echohawk to the whites for ransom. An Iroquois woman who has lost her own child will adopt Bamaineo. Glickihigan will experience a long and painful death. But Glickihigan's spirit-helper creates a diversion that allows the clan to escape. As they near their destination, other members of The Turtle Clan help them complete the journey. Echohawk then reflects on everything that has happened since his Mohican mother died and finds that the white men and red men have changed each other. He also realizes he has confronted the same cruelties, kindnesses, and attitudes while living in both the white and Native American communities. Finally he concludes, "We are all the same," and decides that each man must learn to live in both worlds. In *Turtle Clan Journey,* Durrant includes an Afterword that explains the historical context of the story and the characters within it. She also includes a bibliography of her sources.

Booktalk

When the white man's disease wipes out Echohawk's tribe, The Turtle Clan must find a new home and maybe a new life. White settlers want to make Echohawk Jonathan Starr again. They will "civilize" him and teach him to live the right way, the white way. Warring tribes want to kill him or sell him. If they are successful, he will again experience the savagery that first joined him to the Lenape. Echohawk knows he is the only one who can map his life journey so closely tied to *The Turtle Clan Journey.* He must look to his mind, his spirits, and his heart to find out what to change or what to hide. But even Echohawk cannot know what future his choices will bring.

Related Activities

1. Read aloud, on pages 166 to 168, Echohawk's reflections on his life since his mother's death. Discuss his conclusion and how that conclusion relates to personal responsibility.
2. Read *Standing in the Light* (Related Work 2). Compare the experience of Catherine Carey Logan to the experience of Echohawk.
3. Each day, read a passage from *In a Sacred Manner I Live* (Related Work 3). Discuss the belief the passage presents and how that perception relates to *Echohawk* (Related Work 1) and *The Turtle Clan Journey.*
4. *Echohawk* (Related Work 1) and the *The Turtle Clan Journey* center on the issue of captives becoming part of their capturing culture. Continue to research the topic of white captives living in Indian nations. You might want to start with the discussion in Stefoff's *Tecum-*

seh and the Shawnee Confederation (Related Work 4) and then ask your librarian for additional sources.

5. Describe a time in your own life when you changed your opinion about someone. Explain the events that influenced that change. You might want to brainstorm with three columns: "I used to think that," "But now I think," and "Because." After describing your experience, explain why you think it was important.

Related Works

1. Durrant, Lynda. **Echohawk.** New York: Clarion Books, 1996. 181p. $14.95. ISBN 0-395-74430-X. This is the first book about Jonathan Starr's place between two worlds. It ends with Jonathan understanding and forgiving the murder of his parents.
2. Osborne, Mary Pope. **Standing in the Light: The Captive Diary of Catharine Carey Logan.** New York: Scholastic Incorporated, 1998. 184p. (Dear America). $10.95. ISBN 0-590-13462-0. Catherine Carey Logan tells about being captured by the Lenape. While living with the tribe, she learns to admire their culture and falls in love with Snow Hunter, who was captured at about the age of four.
3. Philip, Neil, ed. **In a Sacred Manner I Live: Native American Wisdom.** (See full booktalk in chapter 1.) **NF** This book is a collection of belief statements by Native Americans across the continent.
4. Stefoff, Rebecca. **Tecumseh and the Shawnee Confederation.** New York: Facts on File, 1998. 138p. (Library of American Indian History). $25.00. ISBN 0-8160-3648-9. **NF** Indian captives were central to Tecumseh's life. Pages 24 and 25 explain the "complex" topic of Indians and their captives.
5. Turner, Ann. **The Girl Who Chased Away Sorrow: The Diary of Sarah Nita, a Navajo Girl.** New York: Scholastic Incorporated, 1999. 182p. (Dear America). $10.95. ISBN 0-590-97216-2. As Sarah Nita and her people complete their forced walk to Fort Sumner, Sarah discovers the good and evil in both white people and Navajo people.

Family Conflicts Forcing Us to Define Ourselves

Barrett, Tracy. **Anna of Byzantium.**
New York: Delacorte Press, 1999. 209p. $14.95. ISBN 0-385-32626-2.

Summary/Description

Anna Comnena has been confined to a convent by her brother, the ruler of Byzantium. In her dull surroundings, she recalls her betrothal feast and her father's promise that she would rule Byzantium. When the nuns, with the permission of Anna's brother, allow Anna to copy for the convent, she takes the opportunity to record her life of love, lies, and treachery.

Anna's grandmother and mother battle over which child should ascend the throne. The mother, who advocates the law of love wishes Anna to marry Constantine Ducas to unite the Comnenus and Ducas families. Then Anna will be empress, and the mother's family will once again be rulers.

The grandmother, who favors power and manipulation, decides to train Anna. When the grandmother cannot control Anna, she turns her attention to John, Anna's brother. Anna's hatred and resentment of John convince their father that John, not Anna, should rule. Anna, under the direction of Simon, a slave, becomes a scholar. The grandmother trains John to spy on Anna and discredit her to the king. When Constantine Ducas is killed in battle, Anna's chances of ruling diminish. She is betrothed to a scholar, a famous historian. Throughout the intrigues, Simon counsels Anna to learn the lessons of history. Sophia, her personal slave, keeps Anna's secrets.

Anna's father returns from battle a sick and dying man. When he refuses to change the succession, Anna and her mother attempt to assassinate John. Simon reveals the plot because he does not want Anna to suffer in a chain of revenge. But John will not give in to revenge. He isolates his mother and sister but does not kill them. Anna's mother loses her mind. Anna is sent to the convent, where she becomes a writer and healer, but before she leaves, she uses her last wish to free Sophia. Anna never forgives John. When John ascends the throne, he rejects his grandmother's counsel. Sophia, Sophia's husband, and their baby find Anna again. Anna discovers that her servants are her true family. This based-on-fact novel contains a map of the Byzantine Empire under Alexius I Comnenus (1081 to 1118), a genealogy of the Comnenus and Ducas families, and a list of emperors from 1057 to 1118. The Author's Note distinguishes fiction from nonfiction.

Booktalk

Ask what people plan to be when they grow up. Then ask what might happen to change those plans.

Anna of Byzantium had her life planned. She lived in a beautiful castle where everyone adored her. She looked forward to being a ruler and shaping the Byzantine world of the twelfth century. But others wanted that powerful place, and Anna was just a woman. So she fought to keep her position, ignored the petty subjects who defied her, and defied the royal figures who tried to betray her. She knew all the answers.

Now she is alone—in a convent. Here Anna discovers a whole new set of questions, and she doesn't even know if there are any answers. Without riches or pageantry, she begins again. Here her leadership is based on talent, knowledge, and compassion rather than birth. Here Anna finds that sometimes the weak are the most wise and the lowly the most loving. Here Anna finds that who you become might be more important than what you hoped to be.

Related Activities

1. On pages 34 and 35, Simon and Anna discuss the story of Icarus. In the discussion, Simon suggests a deeper metaphorical meaning. He uses his interpretation to warn Anna about her relationship with her grandmother. Read the story of Icarus. You might wish to use Hamilton's *Mythology* (Related Work 1). Discuss whether you agree with Simon's interpretation.

2. Read the story of Prometheus. As in activity 1, you might wish to use Hamilton's *Mythology* (Related Work 1). Discuss how the story also might be used as a metaphor. Apply the metaphor to a modern situation.

3. On pages 57 and 58, Anna studies the story of Priam and Achilles. On page 167 she studies the story of King Thyestes. What do these stories have in common? Why is her mother's interpretation of Achilles' story ironic?

4. In *Mary, Bloody Mary* (Related Work 2), Queen Mary reflects on her abusive childhood, including her imprisonment. Chapter 6 of *Behind the Mask: The Life of Queen Elizabeth I* (Related Work 3) talks about Elizabeth's imprisonment under Mary Tudor. List what Mary and Elizabeth learned from their difficulties. In the library and on the Internet, further research the lives of the two queens. Which of the difficulties or lessons might have helped Anna of Byzantium?

5. In both *Elske* (Related Work 4) and *The One-Armed Queen* (Related Work 5), a woman must seize the throne from a deceptive and treacherous brother. Compare these two rulers with Anna. Discuss how each story defines success.

Related Works

1. Hamilton, Edith, and Steele Savage (illus.). **Mythology.** New York: Little, Brown, 1998. 497p. $13.00pa. ISBN 0-316-19152-3. **NF**

Hamilton's comprehensive treatment of mythology includes the stories of Icarus, Achilles, and Thyestes.

2. Meyer, Carolyn. **Mary, Bloody Mary.** New York: Gulliver Books, 1999. 227p. $16.00. ISBN 0-15-201906-5. Caught in the intrigue and turmoil of Henry VIII's court, Mary learns bitter lessons. Like Anna, the power and promise of her childhood are easily threatened.

3. Thomas, Jane Resh. **Behind the Mask: The Life of Queen Elizabeth I.** (See full booktalk in chapter 4.) **NF** This biography emphasizes Elizabeth's intelligence and power. It also explains how difficult it was for her, as a woman, to reign.

4. Voigt, Cynthia. **Elske.** (See full booktalk in chapter 2.) In an imaginary Anglo-Saxon-like time period, Elske, the granddaughter of a tribe captive, escapes her fate of death and helps a troubled princess claim her kingdom from her deceitful and treacherous brother.

5. Yolen, Jane. **The One-Armed Queen.** New York: TOR, 1998. 329p. $23.95. ISBN 0-312-85243-6. In this continuation of the saga of the Chronicle of Great Alta, Scillia, the thirteen-year-old adopted daughter of Queen Jenna and King Carum, confronts her ill-prepared brother and takes over the responsibility of the kingdom.

ෆ෯ඁ

Pennebaker, Ruth. **Both Sides Now.**

New York: Henry Holt and Company, 2000. 202p. $16.95. ISBN 0-8050-6105-3.

Summary/Description

Liza, a hardworking, high-achieving sophomore, knows how to solve every problem. She is so mature that her journalism teacher assigns her the school newspaper's advice column, "Dear Deborah." However, Liza needs help with her own life. Having just completed a series of chemotherapy treatments, Liza's mother is diagnosed with cancer again and undergoes a bilateral mastectomy. She has been the pessimistic parent. She once wrote a book, became distraught about rejections, burned it, and gave up on writing. Liza feels that her mother is unnecessarily pessimistic about her cancer, also. Liza's father supports these feelings. A lung specialist, her father has taught Liza to stay positive and focused. He pressures his wife to accept aggressive treatment.

Liza's narrative reveals her denial, turmoil, and acceptance of her mother's illness. She writes off her little sister's more emotional reaction as a bad puberty experience. She focuses on a boy with whom she is infatuated rather than on her crumbling home life. She tells no one that her mother's cancer has recurred and thinks she can prove her strength to her father.

Reality breaks through her denial. Liza screams at her sister, totals the driver-training car, forgets to screen a controversial article for the school newspaper, and gets her journalism teacher fired. Her parents fight constantly, and when she accepts a date with her new "love," she drinks too much and panics because she can't remember what happened.

As Liza loses control, her mother gains it. She demands that Liza should talk to her and look at the mastectomy scars. Standing up to her husband, she decides to refuse the treatment and remain as strong and as healthy as possible for the rest of her life. Ironically, the criticism of her rejected novel was that it lacked a consistent voice. Liza's mother finally discovers her own voice and helps Liza accept life rather than make it perfect.

Booktalk

Liza has the perfect life. She has enough money to do anything she wants. She is popular, gets top grades in the top classes, and, like her father, will probably attend Stanford. But then her mother develops cancer—for the second time. Liza isn't worried. Her father, a specialist, knows the best treatments. Things like this don't have to be disasters. They just make positive people stronger.

But it's getting harder for Liza to stay positive. Her little sister is falling apart about everything. Her parents are fighting, her friends are fighting, and she is making some major mistakes with cars, liquor, and love that she would rather keep secret. Everything in Liza's life used to be so good. Suddenly she sees *Both Sides Now*.

Related Activities

1. Liza's mother's book is criticized because it lacks a consistent voice. Define voice. Then discuss what each character's voice reveals.
2. Liza's grandfather seems to play a relatively minor role in the novel. Discuss why Pennebaker might have chosen to include him.
3. Define pessimistic, optimistic, and realistic. Discuss how each term applies to the characters in the novel. Using the Internet and library resources, research the effect attitudes can have on health. Discuss the information you find in relation to *Both Sides Now*.
4. In several situations, Liza loses control. List those situations and the circumstances that influence their outcomes.
5. Discuss the role that the character of Rory plays in the novel.
6. In *Both Sides Now* and *The Year They Burned the Books* (Related Work 3), the main characters' personal lives affect their positions on the school newspaper. Discuss how the combination is used in each novel. Be sure to discuss the role of personal and public communication in each novel.

Related Works

1. Abelove, Joan. **Saying It Out Loud.** New York: DK Publishing, Inc./Richard Jackson, 1999.136p. $15.95. ISBN 0-7894-2609-9. A self-centered, selfish, and perfectionist father refuses to talk with his daughter about her mother's terminal illness.
2. Bauer, Joan. **Hope Was Here.** (See full booktalk in chapter 4.) A young waitress finds the father she always hoped for and then loses him to cancer.
3. Garden, Nancy. **The Year They Burned the Books.** New York: Farrar Straus Giroux, 1999. 247p. $17.00. ISBN 0-374-38667-6. Jamie Crawford, the editor of the high school paper, finds herself in turmoil over the paper's position on the school's health curriculum and her own realization that she is gay.
4. Hobbs, Valerie. **Tender.** New York: Francis Foster Books/Farrar Straus Giroux, 2001. 256p. $18.00. ISBN 0-374-37397-3. Liv deals with the cancer of her father's girlfriend, a person to whom she is much closer than she is to her father.
5. Jacobs, Thomas A. **Teens on Trial.** Minneapolis, MN: Free Spirit, 2000. 196p. $14.95pa. ISBN 157542-081-3. **NF** Pages 108 to 114 discuss the issue of student newspaper censorship.

ᘓᘔ

Holubitsky, Katherine. **Alone at Ninety Foot.**
Victoria, BC: Orca Book Publishers, 1999. 169p. $5.95pa. ISBN 1-55143-129-7.

Summary/Description

Fourteen-year-old Pamela Mary Collins spends a great deal of time at Ninety Foot, a "natural pool in Lynn Creek which runs through Lynn Canyon." The high rock walls on either side of the canyon give the formation its name. Pamela's mother jumped off a bridge in this canyon and killed herself. Pamela is overwhelmed with grief. Now her father is dating again. When the story begins, Pam criticizes everyone, but by the end of the story she sorts the phonies from the genuine article. Danielle, the most popular classmate, seems to monopolize Pam's friends and attract the best dates. By the end of the novel, Pam reclaims her friendships and catches the attention of the boy she likes. When the story begins, Pam seems to think all her teachers are clueless. By the end of the novel, she is starting to like even Mr. Bartell, her English teacher. When the story begins, Pam thinks all her father's girlfriends are strange. By the end of the novel, she accepts his latest and best friend, Jennifer Reid, and respects her as a focused and confident career woman. Most important, by watching the conflicts, cruelties, and kind acts around her, Pam starts to accept her mother's death and begins to build a new sense of family and self-esteem.

Booktalk

Pam's mother committed suicide, and she didn't even do it quietly: she jumped off a bridge. Pam wants to know why her mother killed herself, but Pam's father is moving on with his life. He's dating again, and some of his choices are real losers. Pam's friends are moving on too. They are trying to be popular, but the popular people seem pretty phony. Pam wishes her teachers would move on, but they seem to stick around, no matter how old, odd, or rule-crazy. The only place Pam seems to fit is in the canyon that took her mother. When everyone else seems to be getting together, Pam finds herself *Alone at Ninety Foot*.

Related Activities

1. On pages 1 to 5, Pamela describes the canyon. How does that description set the tone of the novel?
2. *Crusader* (Related Work 1), *The Spirit Window* (Related Work 5), *Dancing on the Edge* (Related Work 4) and *Alone at Ninety Foot* all focus on a young girl who has lost her mother. Discuss how each author uses that situation in accomplishing the novel's purpose.
3. In both *You Don't Know Me* (Related Work 2) and *Alone at Ninety Foot*, the main character must deal with pressures at home and school that they can't discuss. Both characters experience an embarrassing meltdown in school. Read pages 44 to 47 in *Alone at Ninety Foot*. Compare it to the description on pages 201 to 202 in *You Don't Know Me*. Discuss how each author has used the emotional scene to define or clarify the character and the character's world.
4. In chapter 11, Pamela describes Mrs. Marshall searching for her dead daughter. Read that chapter aloud. Discuss what Pamela might be learning by watching her.
5. In chapter 9, Pamela gets to know Jennifer, her father's new friend. What does Pamela reveal about herself in her description of Jennifer?
6. Emily Carr is an outstanding Canadian artist to whom Pamela refers in the novel. Using your library's resources and the Internet, research Carr's life and work. Then share your findings with the group and discuss why that allusion is appropriate.

Related Works

1. Bloor, Edward. **Crusader.** (See full booktalk in chapter 2.) Roberta discovers that her father is responsible for her mother's death.

2. Klass, David. **You Don't Know Me.** (See full booktalk in chapter 1.) The main character wants to date the most beautiful girl who belongs to the in-group and discovers she can be as abusive and as manipulative as his mother's boyfriend. He also discovers that the teachers he mistrusted are really his best friends.

3. Klebanoff, Susan and Ellen Luborsky. **Ups & Downs: How to Beat the Blues and Teen Depression.** (See full booktalk in chapter 3.) **NF** This book explains the difference between sadness and depression and how to work through both.

4. Nolan, Han. **Dancing on the Edge.** (See full booktalk in chapter 1.) A young girl whose family ignores grief by translating tragedy into mystical happenings discovers that her mother committed suicide.

5. Sweeney, Joyce. **The Spirit Window.** New York: Delacorte Press, 1998. 243p. $15.95. ISBN 0-385-32510-X. (See full booktalk in *Booktalks Plus*, 2001, pages 19 to 21.) Miranda, now part of her father's new family, enables her father to keep the love of his mother, wife, and new daughter by helping him work through conflicts he has refused to face.

෪෮

Powell, Randy. **Tribute to Another Dead Rock Star.**
New York: Farrar Straus Giroux, 1999. 215p. $17.00. ISBN 0-374-37748-0.

Summary/Description

Grady Innis Grennan (GIG) is the son of Debbie Grennan, who was a famous rock star. On the weekend of his mother's memorial concert by the musical group Tantrum, Grady's grandmother and his new step-grandfather drop Grady off and make if clear that he will be living with someone else while they pursue a new life. Grady is to do a talk show interview arranged by his mother's former friend and manager. Then he will visit his stepbrother and family. A limousine will pick up Grady and take him to the concert, where he will deliver a memorial. Grady's stepbrother Louie is mentally retarded. Louie was born when Grady's mother was drinking, taking drugs, and living with her boyfriend Mitch. Mitch is now married to Vickie, and they have two children in addition to Louie. They are trying hard to maintain a stable, Christian family unit. Even though Mitch is not Grady's biological father, he is the only father Grady remembers. When Grady visits, he tries to disrupt that unit because he resents Vicki's rules. He is angry that Louie considers Vicki, not Debbie, his mother. Grady finds that Louie replaced his Tantrum and Debbie Grennan posters with Christian Rock posters. Grady thinks Vicki is attempting to brainwash Louie. When Louie discovers that Grady will be a guest at Debbie's memorial concert, he wants to go. Vickie feels the concert will upset Louie and then the family. Again Grady resents her strong-arm decisions, and they confront each other. When Grady does attend the concert, he realizes that he cannot embrace his mother's world. Vicki and Mitch discuss inviting Grady to be part of their family. Grady and Vicki decide to work together. Grady's efforts to shock Vicki might be considered offensive.

Booktalk

Grady Grennan's mom is a rock star, so he's a celebrity. Well, he's a celebrity, and his mom *was* a rock star; now she is dead. Now she's a legend—a legend that's a lot different than the person he knew. Everybody wants to crowd around him and get his autograph, but nobody wants to live with him. Grady loves his brother Louie, but they have different families with different rules. Besides, being around Louie can be pretty embarrassing. And when Grady tries to liven things up at Louie's house, Louie's Christian stepmother decides to get in Grady's face.

This is Grady Grennan's big weekend. He has to find a place to live, make it on a talk show, and find out who his friends really are, and he has to figure it all out before he gives his final *Tribute to Another Dead Rock Star.*

Related Activities

1. Louie, Grady's half brother, is the center of much of the novel's conflict. Discuss why.
2. Nicole, from *Keeping the Moon* (Related Work 3) and Grady, from *Tribute to a Dead Rock Star,* both deal with celebrity mothers. Discuss how each parent's celebrity affects each child's life.
3. In both *Tribute to Another Dead Rock Star* and *Run, If You Dare* (Related Work 5), young men reject the life-style of their immature parents. After reading each book, write a letter from the main character's point of view to each of the parents. The letter should show acceptance of the parent but not of the life-style.
4. Research the history of rock culture. You might wish to start with chapters 11 through 13 of *Art Attack* (Related Work 1). Share your findings with the group.
5. In *Tribute to a Dead Rock Star,* the band playing the memorial concert is named Tantrum. After reading *Art Attack* (Related Work 1), discuss why the title is appropriate.

Related Works

1. Aronson, Marc. **Art Attack: A Short Cultural History of the Avant-Garde.** New York: Clarion Books, 1998. 192p. $20.00. ISBN 0-395-79729-2. **NF** The index entry "rock" under "Music" guides the

reader to several entries dealing with the history of rock and its relation to other art forms. Chapter 11, however, begins with a description of the Woodstock Nation and describes the positives and the extremes of the rock movement in relation to modern culture.

2. Cobain, Bev. **When Nothing Matters Anymore: A Survival Guide for Depressed Teens.** Minneapolis, MN: Free Spirit, 1998. 164p. $13.95. ISBN 1-57542-036-8. **NF** Written by the cousin of Kurt Cobain, who committed suicide in 1994, the book defines depression and explains how to control it.

3. Dessen, Sarah. **Keeping the Moon.** (See full booktalk in chapter 2.) Nicole Sparks feels deserted when her celebrity mother sends her to live with Nicole's aunt for the summer.

4. Hurwitz, Jane. **Coping in a Blended Family.** New York: Rosen Publishing Group, 1997. 102p. $17.95. ISBN 0-8239-2077-1. (See full booktalk in *Booktalks Plus,* 2001, pages 170 to 172.) **NF** The book is based on the premise that any group can be a family and deals with the skills needed to build a good communication unit.

5. Powell, Randy. **Run If You Dare.** (See full booktalk in chapter 1.) A young man decides he doesn't want to become like his immature father.

6. Shoemaker, Joel. "Is Writing Sports Action Like Writing a Sex Scene?" *VOYA.* (June 2000) 94–97. **NF** In this interview, Randy Powell discusses *Tribute to Another Dead Rock Star,* as well as his other books. He explains his process of writing and his journey to becoming a young adult writer. A bibliography at the end of the article lists other Powell young adult novels.

ಭಿ

Rinaldi, Ann. **The Coffin Quilt: The Feud Between the Hatfields and the McCoys.**

New York: Harcourt Brace and Company, 1999. 228p. $16.00. ISBN 0-15-202015-2.

Summary/Description

On December 3, 1889, the day the innocent "half-wit" Ellison Mounts hangs for a vicious attack on the McCoys' home, sixteen-year-old Fanny McCoy begins a journal chronicling the feud between the Hatfields and the McCoys. The feud begins in 1880 with the theft of a pig but escalates when Fanny's favorite sister, Roseanna, runs off with Johnse Hatfield. Love denied generates enough hate to kill most members of both families. Fanny McCoy develops from a small girl who lies for the beautiful sister with whom she shares a room to a wise young woman who realizes the destruction Roseanna holds. Each dated chapter recalls a pivotal event in which the objective Fanny reveals how her own family as well as the Hatfield family destroys. Fanny's visions of the Yeller Thing, a combination of beauty and evil, signal each tragedy. The coffin quilt Roseanna uses to record the deaths of both families and wants to will to Fanny finally proves to Fanny that Roseanna is an instrument of death. In the Author's Note, Rinaldi explains the fact base of the novel and provides an extensive bibliography.

Booktalk

Ask how many people in the group have heard of the Hatfields and the McCoys. Ask what they have heard.

Fanny McCoy isn't one of the gun-toting, Hatfield-hating McCoys we hear about in the stories or the songs. In fact, Fanny worries more about defending herself from the McCoys than from the Hatfields. Her older sister Alifair, who has the "light of holiness," keeps trying to drown her. Her father might shoot her if he finds out she lies for her beautiful sister Roseanna. And Fanny's mother seems to have the power to send Fanny to hell. Then there is that evil-smelling but kind of pretty Yeller Thing that keeps showing up just before something happens bad enough to tear out Fanny's heart. Someday Fanny will inherit *The Coffin Quilt* from Roseanna to cover her with all the death and family sadness stitched together. Fanny doesn't seem to have any way out, but Mr. Cuzlin, her teacher, tells her "sometimes we don't have to leave in order to get away. Sometimes all we have to do is choose."

Related Activities

1. Discuss what you feel the Yeller Thing, the coffin quilt, and the pebbles of the saved and the damned contribute to the story.
2. Rinaldi compares the beautiful Roseanna to Helen of Troy. Find out more about Helen of Troy. You might wish to start your research with the videocassette, *The Odyssey of Troy* (Related Work 4). Agree and/or disagree with the comparison.
3. On page 223 of the Author's Note, Rinaldi points out that she has researched the when and where of her novels and, as a writer of historical fiction, she has supplied the emotions behind the events: the why. Choose a brief news report from a current newspaper or magazine. Then describe the emotions you think influenced the event.
4. Alifair is an especially puzzling character. List her personal qualities and the specifics from the novel that illustrate the qualities. Then discuss how Rinaldi uses this character in her novel. Be sure to consider the concluding paragraph on page 13.
5. Rinaldi's Author's Note traces the feud as an outgrowth of the Civil War, in which people were conditioned to kill an enemy. In this

framework she presents Fanny McCoy, whose personal choices eventually pull her out of the conflict. In *Amelia's War* (Related Work 5), Rinaldi presents a Civil War character who must also make choices in conflict. After reading the two novels, compare Fanny and Amelia. Outline what each character wants, the forces against them, and what each is willing to do to overcome those forces.

6. In *The Coffin Quilt* and *Clem's Chances* (Related Work 2), both characters have family members whom they love but from whom they must detach themselves. Fanny separates herself from Roseanna, and Clem separates himself from his father. Discuss whether each separation is justified or necessary.

Related Works

1. **Hatfields and McCoys: An American Feud.** Produced by A&E Television Networks, 1996. 50 min. Videocassette. Color. $14.95. AAE 14106. This documentary disagrees with the romantic idea that the feud began with Roseanna and Johnse. It maintains that misunderstanding, politics, and greed played much bigger parts in fueling the battle.

2. Levitin, Sonia. **Clem's Chances.** (See full booktalk in chapter 1.) Clem goes west to find his father and discovers a cold, distant, and irresponsible man.

3. McGlinn, Jeanne M. **Ann Rinaldi: Historian & Storyteller.** Lanham, Maryland: The Scarecrow Press, 2000. 94p. (Scarecrow Studies in Young Adult Literature, No. 2). $29.50. ISBN 0-8108-3678-5. **NF** Although *Coffin Quilt* is only briefly summarized in the Afterword, McGlinn explores Rinaldi's themes and characters thoroughly and much of the analysis applies to *Coffin Quilt.*

4. **The Odyssey of Troy.** Produced by Multimedia Entertainment, 1995. 50 min. Videocassette. Color. (Ancient Mysteries). $14.95 AAE-95064. Like *Hatfields & McCoys: An American Feud,* this documentary explores the difference between the myth and the reality.

5. Rinaldi, Ann. **Amelia's War.** (See full booktalk in chapter 1.) Living in Maryland, a state that sees itself as Southern but not rebel and pro-union but not pro-Yankee, Amelia tries to stay out of the war but is eventually pushed to a decision that saves the town.

6. **Vigilantes.** Produced by A&E Television Networks, 1999. 50 min. Videocassette. Color. (History's Mysteries). $19.95. AAE-42602. In the videocassette *Hatfields & McCoys: An American Feud,* poor law enforcement is cited as a primary reason for the extended feud. According to this documentary, similar conditions produce vigilantes.

Legacy: We Are Remembered

Entertaining and Creating

Almond, David. **Kit's Wilderness.**
New York: Delacorte Press, 2000. 229p. $15.95. ISBN 0-385-32665-3.

Summary/Description

Thirteen-year-old Kit Watson and his parents move to Stoneygate, a coal-mining town filled with legends and family histories, to care for Kit's aging grandfather. Here he meets Allie Keenan, the good-bad ice girl, and John Askew, a talented artist who plays the game of Death. Invented by Askew and rooted in the history of child labor, the game requires the chosen one to stay in an abandoned mine hole until he or she comes back to life. Kit joins the group, and although the other players fake their reactions, he finds himself drawn into a trance-like state. Adding to this mystical tone, his grandfather tells him the story of "Little Silky," a mischievous mine ghost. Kit writes the story for English class, and Askew illustrates it. Kit's enjoyment of the creative process and the praise he receives for the story motivate him to develop the legend of Lak, a primitive boy trying to keep himself and his baby sister alive in the harsh northern winter. Both fictional worlds entwine with Kit's reality. His grandfather becomes increasingly weak and forgetful and refers to each trance-like episode as following Silky. Askew, thrown out of school for his part in the Death game, runs away from his abusive father. Kit sees both himself and Askew in Lak's survival struggles, two sensitive artists fighting to stay alive in a cold and harsh world.

In Part Two: Winter, Kit, and Askew confront each other in the primitive home Askew has made for himself. They become blood brothers and, with the help of Allie, who is enthralled with acting, they decide to deal with their problems and return to their families.

Part Three: Spring sees Askew back in school part-time for art classes and Kit accepting the death of his dear grandfather. All three friends learn to look for the positive elements in their lives so they can deal with the negative.

Booktalk

Thirteen-year-old Kit Watson holds "ancient stories in [his] head and ancient pebbles in [his] palm." When his family moves to Stoneygate to take care of his widowed grandfather, Kit meets John Askew, "the blackened boy with bone necklaces and paintings on him" and Allie Keenan, "the good-bad ice girl with silver skin and claws." Together they play the game of Death as Kit learns about the ghosts of the Stoneygate coal mines from his grandfather and sees his own name already carved on a tombstone. Suddenly he is part of the town's legends, strengths, and sorrows. And as he begins to explore this wilderness, soon to become *Kit's Wilderness,* he must struggle to survive or join all the other young souls buried in the pits of the mines.

Related Activities

1. Read page 3 again. Discuss how this very bizarre introduction relates to the rest of the novel.
2. Magic and its relationship to good and evil or happiness and sadness are major issues in the novel. Reread chapters 15, 16, and 17 in Part Two: Winter. Then explain what Allie and Kit learn about magic and its relationship to life.
3. Discuss how the stories of Little Silky and Lak relate to the real-life events in the novel.
4. Both Kit and his grandfather find reality and fantasy blending. Cite various points in the story where this blending occurs. Discuss why Almond might have chosen to use this parallel between the youngest and oldest members of the family.
5. Kit is a writer, Askew is an artist, and Allie is an actress. Discuss how these talents support their friendship and help them survive.
6. Child labor is a grim backdrop to the story. England and the United States shared harsh labor practices in the past. Further research the history of child labor in either England or the United States. Share your information with the group and explain how your information relates to the themes of *Kit's Wilderness.*

Related Works

1. Almond, David. **Skellig.** (See full booktalk in chapter 2.) When a young boy moves into a new house and his family focuses on his premature baby sister, he discovers Skellig, a mystical figure who helps him and his new friend Mina deal with the crises of life.

2. Bartoletti, Susan Campbell. **Kids on Strike!** Boston: Houghton Mifflin Company, 1999. 208p. $20.00. ISBN 0-395-88892-1. **NF** Bartoletti traces the child labor movement from the early nineteenth century to the early twentieth century and emphasizes that the ability to protest distinguished the laborer from the slave.

3. Nolan, Han. **Dancing on the Edge.** (See full booktalk in chapter 1.) Ignored, isolated, and abused, Miracle McCloy begins to live in the fantasy world her controlling grandmother constructs for her.

4. Rice, Ben. **Pobby and Dingam.** New York: Alfred A. Knopf, 2000. 94p. $16.00. ISBN 0-375-41127-5. Fantasy and reality blend in an opal mining community when a young girl's imaginary friends begin to have real consequences for her family and town.

5. Wynne-Jones, Tim. "The Pinhole Camera." In **Lord of the Fries and Other Stories.** New York: DK Publishing, Inc., 1999. 214p. $17.95. ISBN 0-7894-2623-4. A young boy seeks refuge in an imaginary world when he enrolls in a new school and discovers that a school outcast has an imaginary world of his own centered on the same real site. The story appears on pages 150 to 172.

✿✿

Holt, David and Bill Mooney (comp.).
Spiders in the Hairdo: Modern Urban Legends.
Little Rock, AR: August House Publishers, Inc., 1999. 111p. $7.95pa.
ISBN 0-87483-525-9. **NF**

Summary/Description

The fifty-five short urban legends organized by themes such as "Jerks," "Scams and the Conspiracy Theories," and "The Old College Try" are the stories that "have happened to a friend of a friend," the FOAF tales. Readers will recognize stories they have heard and told themselves, such as the one about the boy who loses his tongue on the railroad tracks or the woman who smuggles a Mexican Hairless across the border only to discover it's a Mexican rat. The introduction defines the urban legend, explains its popularity, and speculates about its future. "The Danger of Urban Legends," a thumbnail summary of all the legends, concludes the collection. A bibliography shows the readers where they can find even more.

Booktalk

Does the vanishing hitchhiker really exist? If you go to Las Vegas, could you lose your kidney? Do poisonous snakes really live in leather coats? *Spiders in the Hairdo: Modern Urban Legends,* tell all those "true" stories that happened to a friend of a friend. Some will make you laugh, and others will make you check under the bed at night. But laughing or shaking, you probably can't read just one.

Related Activities

1. After reading *Spiders in the Hairdo,* use the "Further Resources" section to find more urban legends. Search the Internet or ask your librarian to locate even more legends. Copy the legends you find most interesting. Group them by theme or structure.
2. Plan a storytelling program made up of urban legends. Be sure to memorize the stories.
3. Urban legends warn people about consequences of their behavior. Make up your own urban legend that warns someone about a danger in the city.
4. Write down unusual stories you hear or read. Match them with an urban legend or make up your own legend about them.
5. *In the Forests of the Night* (Related Work 1), *Spellfall* (Related Work 4), *The Taker's Stone* (Related Work 5), and *The Boxes* (Related Work 6) all could be extended urban legends. Ask four different people to read one of the books. Then ask them to write a paragraph that expresses the possible urban legends contained in these novels. They should try to imitate the style of Holt and Mooney.

Related Works

1. Atwater-Rhodes, Amelia. **In the Forests of the Night.** New York: Delacorte Press, 1999. 147p. $8.95pa. ISBN 0-385-32674-2. A three-hundred-year-old vampire becomes part of the modern day crime scene.
2. Davis, Donald. **Telling Your Own Stories: For Family and Classroom Storytelling, Public Speaking, and Personal Journaling.** Little Rock, AR: August House Publishers, Inc., 1993. 127p. $10.00. ISBN 0-87483-235-7. **NF** Davis asks questions that spark stories about personal experiences, but each question can be adapted to apply to others.

3. **Grimm's Grimmest.** San Francisco, CA: Chronicle Books, 1997. 142p. $22.95. ISBN 0-8118-1675-3. In the introduction, Maria Tatar describes the Grimm fairy tales as the ancestors of our urban legends. Comparing the tales and legends might be an interesting class exercise.

4. Roberts, Katherine. **Spellfall.** (See full booktalk in chapter 3.) A young girl discovers she is part of a modern magic world centered on nature.

5. Russell, Barbara Timberlake. **The Taker's Stone.** (See full booktalk in chapter 3.) Fourteen-year-old Fischer and his cousin steal some red stones that set all the forces of good and evil into motion.

6. Sleator, William. **The Boxes.** New York: Dutton, 1998. 196p. $15.99. ISBN 0-525-46012-8. (See full booktalk in *Booktalks Plus*, 2001, pages 189 to 192). A young girl's curiosity leads her into a supernatural world that threatens fatal consequences.

ः

Vande Velde, Vivian. **The Rumpelstiltskin Problem.**

New York: Houghton Mifflin Company, 2000. 116p. $15.00. ISBN 0-618-05523-1.

Summary/Description

In the Author's Note, Vande Velde analyzes the illogical fairy tale of Rumpelstiltskin. The stories that follow retell the tale in six different ways. "A Fairy Tale in Bad Taste" explains how a cannibalistic Rumpelstiltskin manipulates the miller's daughter and king into marriage so he can eat their first-born child but destroys himself instead. In "Straw into Gold," a reliable Rumpelstiltskin rescues the miller's daughter from a self-absorbed king. In "The Domovoi," Rumpelstiltskin is a spirit who protects the king's house and leaves when he discovers that the residents perceive crisis as happiness. In "Papa Rumplestiltskin," the miller brags about his daughter and then decides to save her by impersonating a magical troll. "Ms. Rumpelstiltskin" is a lonely and homely girl who tries to steal a baby to love. "Good as Gold" tells the story of a prince who avoids marriage to a persistent and greedy miller's daughter. Each witty and entertaining version will also provide excellent models for a similar writing assignment.

Booktalk

Remember Rumpelstiltskin? The ugly little man who demanded payment in gold for showing how to spin gold? Did you ever wonder where a poor miller and his daughter ever got the gold? Why a troll wanted her first-born child? Or why the miller's daughter consented to marry a king who said "Spin gold or die"? Well, Vivian Vande Velde asks all those questions too, and she rewrites the story six times to get the answers. According to Vande Velde, Rumpelstiltskin might have been a cannibal, a knock-down gorgeous elf, a furry little man living under the porch, or a homely girl who just couldn't get a date. What is the truth behind the tale? Take a little vacation from your own illogical world and ponder *The Rumpelstiltskin Problem.*

Related Activities

1. Read the original fairy tale of Rumpelstiltskin (Related Work 1). Discuss what you believe the purpose to be. Then read the Author's Note by Vande Velde. Do you agree with her observations?
2. Choose the version of Rumpelstiltskin you prefer. Explain the reasons for your choice.
3. Choose another fairy tale. Like Vande Velde, ask yourself questions about the story. Then write your own essay about the fairy tale.
4. Write a new version of the tale that answers the questions you made up in activity 2.
5. Further research fairy tales and the people who gathered them. You might want to begin your search by referring to *The Brothers Grimm: Two Lives, One Legacy* (Related Work 2), the life story of two men who dedicated their lives to gathering German stories, one of which is Rumpelstiltskin. Share the information you find with the group.
6. One of Vande Velde's versions, "Straw into Gold," and Schmidt's novel *Straw into Gold* (Related Work 4) focus on the king's abuse of family. Compare the two versions and discuss how the original tale supports each.
7. Read one or several of Aesop's fables (Related Work 3)—also fictional. Then try to explain the difference between a fairy tale and a fable.

Related Works

1. *Grimm's Fairy Tales.* Available: www.cs.cmu.edu/~spok/grimmtmp /044.txt (Accessed September 2002). In this version, Rumpelstiltskin shows humanity and affection even though he wishes to take the baby from the queen. He refuses her offer of gold because he feels humans are more valuable than gold. The story is one of several Grimm tales that are being studied.
2. Hettinga, Donald R. **The Brothers Grimm: Two Lives, One Legacy.** New York: Clarion Books, 2001. 180p. $22.00. ISBN 0-618-

05599-1. **NF** Hettinga lists all the brothers' publications and the tales they gathered. On page 70, Hettinga relates that Jacob wanted the stories written down just as told "even if the story didn't make sense."

3. Pinkney, Jerry. **Aesop's Fables.** New York: SeaStar Books, 2000. 87p. $17.96. ISBN 1-58717-000-0. The fables offer more didactic stories, less open to interpretation.

4. Schmidt, Gary D. **Straw into Gold.** New York: Clarion Books, 2001. 172p. $15.00. ISBN 0-618-05601-7. Rumpelstiltskin brings his foster son, Tousle, to the king's celebration. Tousle and a companion, the blind Innes, must solve the king's riddle in seven days or die.

5. Yolen, Jane and Shulamith Oppenheim. **The Fish Prince and Other Stories: Mermen Folk Tales.** New York: Interlink, 2001. 160p. $29.95. ISBN 1-56656-389-5. In chapter 2, the story "The Sea King and Vasilisa the Wise" tells about a prince given tasks by the Sea King. He marries Vasilisa the Wise, who saves him.

✧✧

Whelan, Gloria. Homeless Bird.

New York: HarperCollins Publishers, 2000. 216p. $15.95. ISBN 0-06-028454-4.

Summary/Description

Thirteen-year-old Koly marries so her family can have her portion of the family food. Her new husband is terminally ill. His parents use her dowry for a trip to the Ganges. When her husband dies, Koly serves her in-laws, who take Koly's widow's pension and valuables. Her mother-in-law berates her. Her father-in-law, a passive man, will not challenge his wife's authority but secretly teaches Koly to read. Koly discovers how she has been cheated and starts to think about her ability to become independent. When Koly's sister-in-law marries and her father-in-law dies, Koly travels with her mother-in-law to the city of widows. The mother-in-law abandons her to the streets, but Koly befriends a young rickshaw driver who takes her to a shelter for abandoned young widows. The director helps her find honest work in the city, and Koly's embroidery talent and quick mind earn her a good paying job, independence, and respect. She and the rickshaw driver, who has saved money to buy farmland, decide to marry. Both have sifted through the good and bad of traditional and modern ways in India and find happiness. The Author's Note explains the historical background and provides a glossary.

Booktalk

Thirteen-year-old Koly is from a poor Indian family. She must marry because her family cannot afford to feed her anymore. Her bridegroom is sick and weak, all a poor girl can hope for. He dies. Koly must die with him or live with a mother-in-law who hates her and a father-in-law who is too timid to defend her. Her family's poverty, her country's customs, and her in-laws' cruelty cage her, but Koly decides that someday she too will be free. Her fingers can't stop stitching the beautiful images that dance in her memory of home. Her mind starts to decipher what the magic symbols on paper say. She searches for knowledge, love, and respect, but Koly, a *Homeless Bird*, could perish in the streets if she dares to fly higher than she, a poor girl, ever imagined.

Related Activities

1. Trace the events that lead Koly to the pride and confidence she demonstrates at the end of the novel.
2. One of the issues in the novel is the changing Indian society. List some of these changes. Then list the characters' reactions to the changes. Discuss which reactions are positive and which ones are destructive.
3. List some of the changes in your own family, town, or society that make your life different from your parents' lives.
4. Koly's life in India is much different from an American teenage girl's life. Continue to research Indian life and culture. Make a comparison/contrast chart that illustrates the similarities and differences.
5. Discuss the universal themes involved in the novel. You might consider the themes of personal choice, independence, or tradition.
6. Skill, knowledge, and hard work are emphasized throughout the *Homeless Bird, Shiva's Fire* (Related Work 5), *Ties that Bind, Ties that Break* (Related Work 2), *The Transformation* (Related Work 3), and *Esperanza Rising* (Related Work 4), all books that question tradition. Ask five people to choose one novel each. Point out how the values produce good results in each novel. Then find instances in your own life or observations where these values give or fail to give positive results. Discuss the books in reference to your own experience.

Related Works

1. Jordon, Sherryl. **The Raging Quiet.** (See full booktalk in chapter 1.) Forced into a loveless marriage to save her family, Marnie is blamed for the death of her husband and finds love with the village outcast.
2. Namioka, Lensey. **Ties That Bind, Ties That Break.** (See full booktalk in chapter 1.) Refusing to accept her culture's restrictions and estranged from her family after her father's death, a young girl comes to America and builds a new life with a husband of her choice.

3. Newth, Mette. **The Transformation.** (See full booktalk in chapter 4.) With her parents dead, Navarana must hunt the family food and discovers a young man from another culture with whom she falls in love.

4. Ryan, Pam Muñoz. **Esperanza Rising.** (See full booktalk in chapter 1.) Accustomed to being the pampered daughter of a wealthy landowner in Mexico, Esperanza is forced to flee her home and build a new life in the United States.

5. Staples, Suzanne Fisher. **Shiva's Fire.** New York: Farrar Straus Giroux/Frances Foster Books, 2000. 276p. $17.00. ISBN 0-374-36824-4. Gifted with unusual talents, a young girl decides to completely develop her abilities before entering marriage.

ℭℑ℥

Carroll, Joyce Armstrong and Edward E. Wilson, comp. **Poetry After Lunch: Poems to Read Aloud.**
Spring, TX: Absey & Co., 1997. 164p. $17.95. ISBN 1-888842-03-2. **NF**

Summary/Description

Grouping poems through the metaphor of a meal, *Poetry After Lunch* celebrates the joy of poetic sound and sense rather than its analysis. It begins with "Troubleshooting" by William Stafford, in which he warns against choosing the analytic rather than the romantic approach. Then three Bread poems, six Appetizer poems that talk about new experiences, and an entire menu of poems—Beverages, Light Snacks, Pastas, Sandwiches, Salads, Daily Specials, Entrees, Children's Menu, Desserts, and Fruits & Cheeses—follow. The Repast "The Purpose of Poetry" by Jared Carter concludes with a graphic and convincing illustration of why poetry must "be" the experience—re-create it rather than tell about it. Contributors include outstanding poets such as May Swenson, Robert Frost, Robert Penn Warren, Archibald MacLeish, Joyce Armstrong Carroll, Shel Silverstein, and Gary Soto. Two indexes, one of poems and one of poets, are included.

Booktalk

Ask how many people like poetry. Talk about the negatives and positives in the group. Ask how many people like to eat.

Here is a poetry book for people who like to eat. When you order from this menu, there will be no bill—not even an analysis paper or discussion questions delivered later. These poems—appetizers, entrees, desserts—and more are here to just digest and enjoy. Let's try a few together.

Read a few of the shorter poems as an illustration. You might want to try "The Poem as Striptease" by Phillip Dacey on page 129, "Sister Girl" by Olga Samples Davis on page 10, "While Dissecting Frogs in Biology Class Scrut Discovers the Intricacies of the Scooped Neckline in His Lab Partner's Dress" by George Roberts on page 23, or "Epitaphs" by David Wagoner on pages 28 and 29. Then pass the book around the room.

Related Activities

1. Read one poem aloud each day. If members of the listening group wish to write a reaction to it in their journals, fine.
2. Carroll and Wilson use a food metaphor to organize the poems. Collect poems and choose a metaphor of your own to organize them. You might want to consider an athletic event, a school day, a workday, or seasons as possible metaphors.
3. Choose five poems from *Poetry After Lunch*. Illustrate them or find pictures that would be appropriate companions.
4. Choose appropriate background music for each chapter.
5. After listening to all the poems in *Poetry After Lunch: Poems to Read Aloud,* choose those you feel are most appealing to the ear. Organize them into a dramatic reading. You might want to ask other readers to join you. Then make a presentation to a local organization, perhaps after the organization's scheduled luncheon meeting. When planning the presentation, you might want to consult "Responding to Poetry by Performing" in *Teaching Poetry in High School* (Related Work 5).
6. Choose one of the poets whose work is included in *Poetry After Lunch: Poems to Read Aloud.* Using your library's resources, research the writer's life and work. Share the information you find with the group. Read to the group more poems by that writer that you find pleasing to the ear.

Related Works

1. Franco, Betsy, ed. **You Hear Me? Poems and Writing by Teenage Boys.** Cambridge, MA: Candlewick Press, 2000. 107p. $14.99. ISBN 0-7636-1158. **NF** Although some of these poems might be considered controversial, all are quite performable and will appeal to a young audience.
2. George, Kristine O'Connell (text) and Kate Kiesler (illus.). **Old Elm Speaks: Tree Poems.** New York: Clarion Books, 1998. $15.00. ISBN 0-395-87611-7. **NF** These tree statements combine the oral and visual. "Knotholes" is at the tongue-twister level.

3. Mora, Pat. **My Own True Name: New and Selected Poems for Young Adults, 1984-1999.** Houston, TX: Piñata Books, 2000. $11.95pa. ISBN 1-55885-292-1. **NF** These poems lend themselves to oral presentations, and some are written in both English and Spanish.

4. Nam, Vickie, ed. **Yell-Oh Girls!** (See full booktalk in chapter 4). **NF** This collection of essays and poems capturing the voices of Asian-American girls contains powerful messages suitable for dramatic performance—prose as well as poetry.

5. Somers, Albert B. **Teaching Poetry in High School.** Urbana, IL: National Council of Teachers of English (NCTE), 1999. $19.95pa. ISBN 0-8141-5289-9. **NF** In the section "Responding to Poetry by Performing," Somers describes performance options that include oral interpretation, memorization, slams, chants and choral reading, line reading, two-part reading, multiple-part reading, antiphonal reading, mime, and creative dramatics.

Trusting

✿✿

Dessen, Sarah. **Someone Like You.**
New York: Viking Press, 1998. 281p. $15.99. ISBN 0-670-87778-6.

Summary/Description

Halley, a high school junior attending an improvement camp for young women, receives an emergency call from her best friend Scarlett Thomas, whose summer boyfriend Michael has died in a motorcycle accident. At the funeral, Halley meets Macon Faulkner, Michael's best friend. Eventually he asks Halley out. He's exciting, daring, and rebellious—the opposite of anyone Halley's mother wants Halley to date. Scarlett discovers she is pregnant with Michael's baby. Although Scarlett's mother wants her to have an abortion, Scarlett decides to keep the baby. Halley continues to date Macon, who pressures her to have sex. She and Macon decide New Years Eve will be the big night, but Halley, overcome by the party's drinking, drugs, and sex, insists on going home. An angry Macon and apologetic Halley wind up in an accident. An ambulance takes Halley to the hospital, but Macon disappears. Halley breaks off her relationship. Halley also tells her dominant mother/therapist to trust Halley's decisions before jumping in to control the situation. The novel ends at the prom, the evening Scarlett and Halley have fantasized about for years. Scarlett attends with a new student, Cameron, who has become her shy defender and supporter. Halley dates the "safe" family friend who shows up drunk and rips her dress. In the Ladies' Room, trying to repair the dress, Halley gets an emergency call: Scarlett is having the baby. With the limousine not returning until midnight and Cameron passing out, Macon and his date drive Halley to the hospital. Halley's mother forces Halley to stay with Scarlett through the labor, and Scarlett delivers a baby girl, Grace Halley. As Halley leaves the hospital waiting room jammed with prom and party dates, she reflects on the sorority into which Grace has been born: her own grandmother Halley (named after the comet and after whom Halley was named); her super strong mother who has fought to keep her safe; Scarlett, her best friend; Scarlett's mother, the alcoholic, depression-prone woman who is herself a single mother; and Halley, an older and wiser girl who embraces but respects the challenges of independence.

Booktalk

Dating, parties, pep assemblies, and proms—that's what high school juniors should think about. But fun times and *Seventeen* magazine fantasies can turn into drug habits, dropping out, and unexpected pregnancies. Anything can happen to *Someone Like You*, and it does happen to Scarlett and Halley as they spend their year dating the wild boys instead of the safe ones and then facing the consequences. Along with their mothers, they are trying to find out what those three little words "I love you" really mean, anyway.

Related Activities

1. *Someone Like You* and *Keeping the Moon* (Related Work 5) both include strong female support groups. Explain how the group in each novel functions and aids the novel's purpose.
2. Read the two passages on page 200, beginning with "Nope." Halley and Scarlett discuss doing the right thing. How does that discussion apply to their actions throughout the story?
3. In *Someone Like You* and "Rice Pudding Days" (Related Work 1), mothers of teenagers have abortions. Discuss the circumstances of each woman's decision and each daughter's reaction.
4. *Someone Like You* and *Smack* (Related Work 2) include rebellion against parents, unstable homes, peer group support, teenage pregnancy, and drug abuse. Yet one novel is much more sinister than the other. After reading both, discuss the tone and realism of each.
5. Read the poem "Origen" on page 1 of *The Year of Our Revolution* (Related Work 3). Describe the speaker and why the speaker feels compelled to make the demand in the poem. Discuss the implication

of the phrase "heirs of carelessness" and the responsibilities it presents to both the speaker's audience and the speaker.
6. Using the library resources, research the consequences of teenage mothers having children. Share with the group any information you find about quality of life for both mother and child. Then discuss that information in relation to *Someone Like You*.

Related Works

1. Bartoletti, Susan Campbell. "Rice Pudding Days." In **Dirty Laundry: Stories about Family Secrets,** edited by Lisa Rowe Fraustino. New York: Viking Press, 1998. 181p. $16.99. ISBN 0-670-87911-8. A young girl discovers that her mother had an abortion because the pregnancy would have kept her from returning to school. The story appears on pages 18 to 39.
2. Burgess, Melvin. **Smack.** New York: Henry Holt and Company, 1998. 327p. $16.95. ISBN 0-8050-5801-X. Teenagers who form a new family away from adults experiment with drugs and sex with disastrous results.
3. Cofer, Judith Ortiz. **The Year of Our Revolution: New and Selected Stories and Poems.** Houston, TX: Piñata Books, 1998. 101p. $16.95. ISBN 1-55885-224-7. In the poem "Origen" on page 1, the speaker expresses each person's need to know if his or her conception was intended or accidental.
4. Dessen, Sarah. **Dreamland.** (See full booktalk in chapter 2.) A young girl who gives in to her boyfriend's controlling demands almost dies from drug use and abuse.
5. Dessen, Sarah. **Keeping the Moon.** (See full booktalk in chapter 2.) Isabel, Morgan, and Aunt Mira present Nicole Sparks with enough advice and positive examples to help her develop a stronger self-concept during her fifteenth summer.
6. O'Dell, Katie. "Ringing True: The Authentic Voice of Sarah Dessen." *VOYA* (June 2002) 100–102. **NF** Dessen discusses how much girls identify with the characters in *Someone Like You*. A book discussion guide for *Someone Like You* appears on page 102.

Ferris, Jean. **Eight Seconds.**

New York: Harcourt Brace and Company, 2000. 186p. $17.00. ISBN 0-15-202367-4.

Summary/Description

Sixteen-year-old Gentleman John Ritchie discovers he is gay. Pressured by his girlfriend, John breaks up with her and welcomes the opportunity to go to rodeo camp with his best friend, Bobby Bryant, and the school bully, Russ Millard. His entire focus will be staying on an angry bull's back for eight seconds. At camp, he meets Kit Crowe, a football star whom all the girls in high school, including his older sister Caroline, wanted to date. Kit, harassed by Millard, emerges as the top performer and most popular cowboy. He takes an interest in John, and John experiences a strong physical and emotional attraction. After camp, the group meets at Kit's house and at rodeos. Caroline, attending college with Kit, reveals that he belongs to the politically active gay group. John, confused by his feelings, tries to stay away from Kit and date girls. Russ Millard, jealous of Kit's success on the rodeo circuit, follows and harasses Kit and John. Millard spreads the rumor that John is gay. In a three-way confrontation among Russ, John, and Kit, John turns on Kit and blames him for involving him in false rumors. Kit rejects John. John realizes that dealing with his sexuality will be as difficult as learning to ride the bull, but he can defeat this fear just as he confronted his fear of bull riding—*Eight Seconds* at a time.

Booktalk

Everybody knows gay men are artists and interior decorators. They don't show up in any of the "manly" stuff such as football, fighting, or rodeos. That's what sixteen-year-old John Ritchie thinks. When John leaves his four sisters and nagging girlfriend to attend a rodeo camp, he looks forward to sorting out manly things. He does. With his friends, John conquers the most dangerous rodeo event, the eight-second bull ride. One person who helps John is Kit Crowe, the best-looking, smartest, and toughest rider in the group. Before he knows it, John is happy, in love, and afraid. Like the bull that would like to stomp him into the ground, these feelings could take away his family, his friends, and his own self-respect. In the most dangerous summer of his life, John faces both physical and emotional annihilation—*Eight Seconds* at a time.

Related Activities

1. Pages 35 to 38 describe the history and operation of rodeos. Continue to research the history of the rodeo and share your information with the group.
2. *Eight Seconds* deals with stereotyping as well as sexuality. Define stereotyping. Then discuss the part it plays in the novel.
3. Kit rejects John after the fight in the Dairy Queen. Was Kit's decision a fair one?
4. The novels *Eight Seconds*, *Simon Says* (Related Work 1), *The Year They Burned the Books* (Related Work 5), *Ironman* (Related Work 4), and *True Believer* (Related Work 6), as well as the short stories

"The Magician" (Related Work 2) and "The Secret Life, According to Aunt Gladys" (Related Work 3), all present being gay in the context of other issues such as integrity, friendship, and ability. After reading each work, list each issue discussed and explain how it is discussed. Then explain how each issue relates to sexual identity.

5. *Eight Seconds* and *Simon Says* (Related Work 1) are both coming-of-age novels in which young men discover they have feelings they might hide or reject. Compare and contrast how each author develops the discovery and conclusion. Discuss which novel seems more realistic and why.

Related Works

1. Alphin, Elaine Marie. **Simon Says.** New York: Harcourt Brace and Company, 2002. 272p. $17.00. ISBN 0-15-216355-7. Charles Weston enrolls in Whitman High School for the Arts so he can meet Graeme Brandt, a teenager who has already published a novel. Charles, a talented but alienated artist, hopes Brandt will help him share his art. Their relationship leads to Brandt's suicide and Charles's commitment to be himself even if that means accepting his gay feelings.

2. Canales, Viola. "The Magician." In **Orange Candy Slices and Other Secret Tales.** Houston, TX: Piñata Books, 2001. 122p. $9.95. ISBN 1-55885-332-4. A young boy attends his uncle's bizarre carnival funeral and later realizes that the funeral was staged so the uncle could come back to life as a woman and marry the carnival clown. The story appears on pages 103 to 109.

3. Coville, Bruce. "The Secret Life, According to Aunt Gladys." In **Dirty Laundry: Stories About Family Secrets,** edited by Lisa Rowe Fraustino. New York: Viking Press, 1998. 181p. $16.99. ISBN 0-670-87911-8. Uncle George/Aunt Gladys comes to stay at the narrator's house while going through a sex change surgery. The uncle's sister tries to hide him, but her son, the narrator, persuades him to come to the living room when a neighbor is there and reveal all the family secrets. The story appears on pages 1 to 17.

4. Crutcher, Chris. **Ironman.** New York: Greenwillow Books, 1995. 181p. $15.00. ISBN 0-688-13503-X. A young man assigned to anger management class discovers while working through his problems that the teacher he admires and trusts the most is gay.

5. Garden, Nancy. **The Year They Burned the Books.** New York: Farrar Straus Giroux, 1999. 247p. $17.00. ISBN 0-374-38667-6. After the school paper runs an editorial suggesting that the school nurse should dispense condoms, two teenagers find themselves fighting a censorship battle and dealing with their homosexual feelings.

6.   Wolff, Virginia Euwer. **True Believer.** New York: Atheneum Books,
     2001. 264p. $17.00. ISBN 0-689-82827-6. In this sequel to *Make
     Lemonade*, LaVaughn falls in love with her former playmate, who is
     gay, and learns to accept him as a good friend.

のや

Newth, Mette. The Transformation.
New York: Farrar Straus Giroux, 2000. 195p. $16.00. ISBN 0-374-37752-9.

Summary/Description

Set in fifteenth century Greenland, *The Transformation* tells about the
journey of Navarana, a native of Greenland (a Human Being), and
Brendan, an Augustine brother (a stranger) sent to convert the heathens.
Navarana's mother was killed by jealous members of her community, and
Navarana's father was carried away on an ice flow. The Old One of the village is training Navarana to be a shaman. Navarana struggles to support
her orphaned sisters by hunting. Her hunt takes her to the deserted village of the strangers, where she saves Brendan, starving and freezing to
death in a church. Brendan, born on the Irish coast, was kidnapped at six
and sold to the Augustine monastery. He has been taught that his life
should center on guilt, penance, and suffering.

When they return to Navarana's village, Brendan's presence is a dis-
ruption, so Navarana, Brendan, the Old One, and the little sisters leave
to find Navarana's vision and a new home. Navarana and Brendan blend
their spiritual and physical lives. Navarana completes her shaman quest
and reveals to Brendan her vision of the Raven. As they marry and wait
for their daughter's birth, Brendan writes the story of his transformation
from a monastic stranger to a Human Being.

The Transformation requires a mature reader. It challenges traditional religious beliefs and alludes to Navarana and Brendan's sexual relationship. The rejection of Brendan's harsh religious training and his
sexual awakening define him as a Human Being.

Booktalk

The Transformation answers the question "Can a girl who carries a bear's
snout and a boy who carries a saint's bone joint find happiness together?"

Living in fifteenth century Greenland, orphaned Navarana sets out
to hunt food for her starving sisters. She discovers a bear to eat and saves
a man, an Augustine monk, who has been sent to save people like her:
heathens. He is starving and freezing to death. Navarana interrupts nature's plan and saves this Brendan. Now does she own his life? Can he

control her soul? Will their harsh gods dictate both their destinies? Fighting their gods, ghosts, the endless winter, and each other, Navarana and Brendan must live *The Transformation.*

Related Activities

1. On pages 31 and 32, Navarana and the Old One talk about blaming, dreaming, and accepting fate. Read the passage that begins "Navarana had asked..." and ends with "her quest was important to them all." Discuss how this passage relates to the rest of the novel and to your own experiences.
2. Navarana's father told her that "curiosity and caution are brother and sister," and he dies because he ignores that advice. Discuss the value of the advice and the difficulty in following it.
3. Brendan's mother's gift of the "butterfly in the golden egg" is an important image throughout the story. Find where the image appears and what it contributes to the novel.
4. Begin reading on page 126 with "He was awakened..." and continue to the end of the last full paragraph on page 129, "Watch your tongue, Brother Gareth, or you may lose it." Discuss what is happening to Brendan.
5. Find the passages in *The Transformation* that characterize the Raven. Describe the Raven in your own words.
6. Brendan writes about his transformation for future generations. What other transformations have taken place in the story? In your discussion include the labels of Human Being and stranger.
7. Using *Choose the Right Word: A Contemporary Guide to Selecting the Precise Word for Every Situation* (Related Work 2), find the definition of heathen and words related to it. Further research the history of the word and its role in historical movements. Share the information you find with the group and discuss it in relation to *The Transformation* and negative words used in schools or churches that separate people.

Related Works

1. Avi. "Oswin's Millennium" in **Second Sight: Stories for a New Millennium.** (See a full booktalk in chapter 2.) Living as a slave in the Abbey of St. Benedict, Oswin discovers a new life when he realizes the monks' vision of life and death is incorrect. He runs away from the Abbey. The story appears on pages 1 to 18.
2. Hayakawa, S. I. and Eugene Ehrlich (revising editor). **Choose the Right Word: A Contemporary Guide to Selecting the Precise Word for Every Situation, 2nd ed.** New York: HarperCollins

    Publishers, 1994. 532p. $20.00pa. ISBN: 0062731319. **NF** This source lists and explains synonyms in relation to each other.

3.   Jordon, Sherryl. **The Raging Quiet.** (See full booktalk in chapter 1.) Marnie and Raven find love with each other after being rejected by society.

4.   Pullman, Philip. **His Dark Materials Trilogy**. (See full booktalk in chapter 3.) **The Golden Compass**, **The Subtle Knife**, and **The Amber Spyglass** trace the journey of the new Adam and Eve as they battle the evil that has infected the universe. Good and bad are translated as freedom and control.

5.   Schimel, Lawrence. "how to make a human." In **half-human,** compiled and edited by Bruce Coville. (See full booktalk in chapter 2.) **NF** The poem, on pages 94 and 95, implies that man is a negative influence on the world and has lost contact with nature. It would be an excellent poem to read and discuss while reading *The Transformation.*

࿇ ࿇

Bertrand, Diane Gonzales. **Trino's Choice.**

Houston, TX: Piñata Books, 1999. 124p. $9.95pa. ISBN 1-55885-268-9.

Summary/Description

Twelve-year-old Trino Olivares lives in a trailer with his mother and three younger brothers. His own father is dead. His mother receives little or no financial support from the two fathers of her other children. With a mother who must constantly work to support her family and no positive father figure, Trino becomes involved with street boys. After he sees them beat and rob an elderly storeowner, they threaten him so he won't tell the police. Running and hiding, he ducks into a bookstore and meets a group of "school types." Attracted to Lisana, one of the girls, he returns to the bookstore for a poetry reading. He encounters the poet Montoya, an ex-convict and son of migrant workers whose poetry speaks to Trino's experience and who encourages Trino to learn all he can. Trino's mother throws out the alcoholic live-in and begins dating Nick, who provides a good role model for Trino and encourages him in school. Then Trino's mother loses her job. Trino, worried and upset, decides to get money by working with the gang. He arrives at the car wash they plan to rob and vandalize in time to see his friend killed. Nick understands why Trino was there and offers to hire him on Saturdays for his tree business. Realizing how close he came to death or jail, working with Nick, and making friends with Lisana, Trino begins to develop positive goals.

Booktalk

Trino is in big trouble. Rosca, the toughest kid in the school, is after him. Trino's father is dead. Garces, the slob his mother lets live in their trailer, isn't sober long enough to help anybody. His mother is always working, and his three brothers are too little to back him up. He is on his own, and he'd better find a good place to hide—fast. He does: a bookstore. Rosca and his gang will never look there. They would never go into one and, like the rest of his family, neither would Trino. But this store has more than books: food, a beautiful girl, and a poet who grew up in a world just like Trino's. Running away from one world, Trino stumbles into another. Soon both worlds will push him to make one of the biggest decisions of his life. It's all up to him. It's *Trino's Choice*.

✿✿

Bertrand, Diane Gonzales. **Trino's Time.**
Houston, TX: Piñata Books, 2001. 171p. $9.95pa. ISBN 1-55885-317-0.

Summary/Description

This sequel to *Trino's Choice* begins two weeks after that story ends. Hired by Nick to cut trees and separated from his old group of street friends, Trino learns to make his own opportunities. He gives his mother his earnings from the tree jobs but secretly takes a job with the grocer who was beaten up. Paid a couple of dollars per day and the food the store cannot sell, Trino starts to provide for his family. Nick, who is unsuccessfully encouraging Trino's mother to help herself by getting a job at the college, no longer comes to the house but gives Trino advice and support. Trino's new friends, "school types," encourage him to come with them to the college library to research their reports on Latin Heroes of the Texas Revolution. Trino identifies with the hero he researches, begins to believe in his own academic abilities, and through Nick's example and Lisana's encouragement, develops social skills that give him friends and self-respect. His efforts encourage his mother to work at the college after all. A storm that destroys the family's trailer proves Trino is a hero when he saves his mother and their belongings, reunites Nick permanently with the family, and demonstrates that Trino can overcome problems with good thinking.

Booktalk

Trino is starting to be a take-charge kind of guy. Nick, his mother's sometimes boyfriend, hires him to trim trees. Now Trino can help his mother out with some money. Then he gets another job at the local grocery.

Perk? Free food for the family. Trino is still hanging with the school types too—he's even going to the college library. It's *Trino's Time!* Then everything collapses. Will Trino collapse too? He works hard, but he knows he's no hero—yet!

Related Activities

1.   Read Montoya's poems on pages 40, 41, and 66 of *Trino's Choice*. When Trino reads each poem, he knows that Montoya and he have much in common. Discuss whether these poems appeal only to people of a Latin heritage. Explain your opinions.

2.   On pages 46 to 49 of *Trino's Choice*, Montoya confronts Trino about books and reading. When Montoya gives Trino his own book to keep and read, the poet emphasizes that Trino can use the book or throw it into the garbage. How does this confrontation and challenge affect Trino and the rest of the novel?

3.   Discuss Trino's friendships in both *Trino's Choice* and *Trino's Time*. How do Trino and his perception of friendship change in the two novels?

4.   The male characters are a significant part of both novels. Identify each male character and the influence that character has on Trino.

5.   In researching their history report, Trino and Hector find the sentence "Time will speak for everything." Discuss the meaning of that statement. Explain how it applies to *Trino's Time*. List three situations in your own life to which it might apply. Explain its application.

6.   Trino's mother is a rather confusing character. Discuss the choices she makes and what you believe influences those choices. What kind of role model is she for her sons?

7.   In *When Zachary Beaver Came to Town* (Related Work 3), Cal discovers that Juan, a character he dislikes and fears, is a completely different person than he thought. Discuss the character of Juan in relation to the characters presented in *Trino's Choice* and *Trino's Time*.

8.   In the nonfiction account *In My Hands: Memories of a Holocaust Rescuer* (Related Work 6) Irene Gut Opdyke explains how small choices she made each day made her the person many consider a heroine. From her essay "Amber," read the paragraph that begins with "But now I look back as an old woman...." Discuss how that paragraph applies to *Trino's Choice* and *Trino's Time*.

9.   In the Trino novels and *You Don't Know Me* (Related Work 4), the mothers' boyfriends, school experiences, and special girls have a great impact on the main characters. Compare the two novels and how the authors use those elements for very different purposes.

10. Heroism is a central theme in *Trino's Time*. After reading the novel, discuss what makes and creates a hero, both in everyday life and in history. Research the heroes mentioned in Trino's history class and more that your librarian might help you identify.

Related Works

1. Bauer, Joan. **Hope Was Here.** (See full booktalk in chapter 4.) Like Trino, the main character discovers that learning how to do a job well helps her cope with life.
2. Eickhoff, Randy Lee and Leonard C. Lewis. **Bowie.** New York: Forge, 1998. 304p. $23.95. ISBN 0-312-86619-4. A. J. Sowell, the narrator, tells the stories he has gathered from family, letters, and interviews and presents Jim Bowie the hero, the scoundrel, the lover, the dedicated husband, the gentleman, and the bully. He leaves the reader with the impression that the larger-than-life legends of any historical event are more important than the real men in it.
3. Holt, Kimberly Willis. **When Zachary Beaver Came to Town.** (See full booktalk in chapter 2.) Cal, the main character, discovers that the boyfriend of the girl he would like to date is someone to like rather than fear.
4. Klass, David. **You Don't Know Me.** (See full booktalk in chapter 1.) Almost killed by his mother's abusive boyfriend, the main character realizes he never understood how much his mother loved him.
5. Nickles, Greg. **The Hispanics.** New York: Crabtree Publishing Co., 2001. 32p. (We Came to North America). $15.96. ISBN 0-7787-0186-7. **NF** An overview of Spanish migration in North America, this book includes first-hand accounts of immigration and conflict as well as descriptions of culture and heroes.
6. Opdyke, Irene Gut with Jennifer Armstrong. **In My Hands: Memories of a Holocaust Rescuer.** (See full booktalk in chapter 4.) **NF** In this nonfiction account, Opdyke tells how she aids Jews and works for the Polish resistance during World War II.

Cⁿⁿ

Rinaldi, Ann. **The Second Bend in the River.**
New York: Scholastic Press, 1997. 279p. $15.95. ISBN 0-590-74258-2.

Summary/Description

This historical novel, based on the friendship and eventual romance between Rebecca Galloway and the Shawnee Chief Tecumseh spans the years 1798 to 1813. In 1798, Rebecca is seven. By the end of the novel, she is a wife and mother who learns about Tecumseh's death and heroism from her friend Molly Kiser, a white woman who lives with and interprets for the Shawnee people. Centering on this relationship between Rebecca and Tecumseh, Rinaldi tells about life in pioneer Ohio as the Galloways and their neighbors celebrate marriages, suffer sorrows, and bring the civilization of ministers, teachers, and newspapers to Chillicothe. The large Galloway family has come to Ohio to get away from slavery and make their "improvement" on the site of Tecumseh's old village. When Tecumseh returns to see his old home, he establishes a friendship with the Galloways. In each of his subsequent visits, they exchange gifts or knowledge. Tecumseh asks for Rebecca's hand when she is seventeen. Neither can live in the culture of the other and they agree not to marry, but both promise to respect the other's people. Rebecca knows Tecumseh has kept his promise when Molly tells her about his stopping the massacre of soldiers at Fort Meigs in the War of 1812. And because Molly's arrival parallels the events of her first meeting with Tecumseh, she believes that even in death he is with her. An author's note explains the story's blend of fact and fiction, and an extensive bibliography lists the works Rinaldi has used in her research.

Booktalk

Rebecca Galloway knows Indians smash babies against trees. Her best friend Mrs. Maxwell told her. When seven years old, she comes face to face with Tecumseh, a Shawnee warrior. He wishes to visit his old village, and her family is living on it. Surely he will kill them all. But her parents welcome him, and he returns many times to visit the "straw-hair" girl. Rebecca gives him the power to read and write the "talking leaves." He gives her the knowledge of healing and a belief in herself. Then Rebecca becomes a woman, and their most important exchange is a love that can ensure peace or cause war. Tecumseh takes her to *The Second Bend in the River*, the place of Shawnee secrets, but can he make her the wife of a chief?

Related Activities

1. Read *Tecumseh and the Shawnee Confederation* (Related Work 8) by Rebecca Stefoff. List the facts of Stefoff's account that support Rinaldi's novel.
2. Both *The Second Bend in the River* and *Tecumseh and the Shawnee Confederation* (Related Work 8) include extensive bibliographies. Using these resources, continue to research the life of Tecumseh. Share the information you find with the group.
3. *Echohawk* (Related Work 2), *The Turtle Clan Journey* (Related Work 3), *Standing in the Light* (Related Work 6), and *The Second*

Bend in the River all deal with encounters and subsequent relationships between the worlds of white people and Native Americans. After each person in the group has read all four of these books, discuss the positives and negatives the authors present about such relationships.

4. Define Manifest Destiny. Trace its development in the history of the United States. Define assimilation. Find examples of ethnic assimilation.

5. In *Stick and Whittle* (Related Work 4), Slender Thomas refers to Manifest Destiny as "man-infested-destiny," a disease responsible for killing Native Americans. Both *The Second Bend in the River* and *Stick and Whittle*, like *Tecumseh and the Shawnee Confederation* (Related Work 8), also make the point that assimilation was just as great a threat to Native American culture as annihilation. Discuss how each author presents the issues of Manifest Destiny and assimilation.

Related Works

1. Alder, Elizabeth. **Crossing the Panther's Path.** New York: Farrar Straus Giroux, 2002. 230p. $18.00. ISBN 0-374-31662-7. Fifteen-year-old Billy Calder, born to a Mohawk mother and a British soldier, becomes the translator for Tecumseh in the War of 1812.

2. Durrant, Lynda. **Echohawk.** New York: Clarion Books, 1996. 181p. $14.95. ISBN 0-395-74430-X. This is the first book about the life of Jonathan Starr, who was captured by the Lenape tribe.

3. Durrant, Lynda. **The Turtle Clan Journey.** (See full booktalk in chapter 3.) In this book, Jonathan Starr and his adopted Lenape family must move farther west to escape the pressure of the white world.

4. Hite, Sid. **Stick and Whittle.** New York: Scholastic Press, 2000. 209p. $16.95. ISBN 0-439-09828-9. In this story, set in the post-Civil War time period, a Civil War veteran, a refugee from the Chicago fire, and Native Americans looking for a burial ground team up to defeat the bad guys.

5. McGlinn, Jeanne M. **Ann Rinaldi: Historian & Storyteller.** Lanham, MD: The Scarecrow Press, 2000. 94p. (Scarecrow Studies in Young Adult Literature, No. 2). $29.50. ISBN 0-8108-3678-5. **NF** In chapter 5, pages 73 to 75, McGlinn uses the section "Exploring Who You Can Be" to analyze *The Second Bend in the River* and what it says about blending Native American and white cultures.

6. Osborne, Mary Pope. **Standing in the Light: The Captive Diary of Catherine Carey Logan.** New York: Scholastic Incorporated, 1998. 184p. (Dear America). $10.95. ISBN 0-590-13462-0. Catherine Carey Logan describes her capture by the Lenape tribe and her grad-

ual assimilation into their culture. She then describes her "rescue" by white soldiers and her difficult return to the Quaker community.

7. Schmidt, Thomas and Jeremy Schmidt. **The Saga of Lewis & Clark: Into the Uncharted West.** (See full booktalk in chapter 4.) **NF** This describes the expedition that established the Manifest Destiny mindset that helped destroy the Native American way of life. In chapter 8 of *The Second Bend in the River*, Rebecca's brother Sam runs away to join the expedition.

8. Stefoff, Rebecca. **Tecumseh and the Shawnee Confederation.** New York: Facts on File, 1998. 138p. (Library of American Indians). $25.00. ISBN 0-8160-3648-9. **NF** Tecumseh's story is told in the context of Westward Expansion. A central issue is each culture's perception of land and ownership and how the differences led to war and the destruction of the Native American world.

Teaching and Leading

෬෪

Aronson, Marc. Sir Walter Ralegh and the Quest for El Dorado.

New York: Clarion Books, 2000. 222p. $20.00. ISBN 0-395-84827-X. **NF**

Summary/Description

Living in Queen Elizabeth's Court, Ralegh understood the importance of drama and persona. Aronson tells Ralegh's life of courtly love, intrigue, exploration, upward mobility, literature, and even his failures and death in the context of a life-is-a-stage performance. Ralegh oppressed the Irish, courted the queen, helped defeat the Spanish Armada, explored the New World, and wrote about his love and adventures. Overconfident and ambitious, he attracted enemies. Questioning and loyal, he supported his country. Acknowledging that Ralegh was neither completely saint nor sinner, Aronson calls him the first modern man. A Cast of Characters lists all the persons mentioned and their relationships. The Prologue explains Ralegh's life dream of finding El Dorado. Pictures, maps, and portraits give a strong feel of the man and his time. The Endnotes and Bibliography provide a chapter-by-chapter list of sources and an explanation of their application. The Time Line begins one hundred years before Ralegh's birth and ends in 1618, the year Ralegh died. It includes four columns of events: Ralegh, England/Europe, Arts/Sciences, New World/Asia.

Booktalk

He wore a white pearl drop earring in his ear, and he wrote poetry. He massacred Irish people in the name of his queen and in hopes of a personal fortune. He created a market for tobacco and a home for the potato. He helped defeat the Spanish Armada and upend the justice system of the Western World. Who was this man who had so many roles? The larger-than-life character, Sir Walter Ralegh. In the age of Queen Bess and Shakespeare, Ralegh lives each day as a drama. His costume, lines, stage, and roles reflect, entertain, and shape his world. His own search for a new world and a golden city shapes his life. *Sir Walter Ralegh and the Quest for El Dorado* gives a glimpse of the man no one ever really knew.

Related Activities

1. On page 86, Aronson refers to Christopher Marlowe's "The Passionate Shepherd to His Love" and Sir Walter Ralegh's "The Nymph's Reply to the Shepherd." Read *Sir Walter Ralegh and the Quest for El Dorado* and the poems (Related Work 1). Then discuss how each reflects the appearance and the reality of Elizabeth's court and Ralegh's life.

2. Aronson cites several Shakespearean plays that relate to Ralegh's life. Shakespeare's themes, such as justice and mercy or the public and private face, reflect the struggles and ponderings of the Renaissance period. Choose one of these two themes or one that you yourself identify. As you read the Shakespearean plays to which Aronson alludes, keep a reading diary in which you record and react to each statement, action, or character illustrating your chosen theme.

3. On page 118, Aronson uses the first five lines of "All the world's a stage…" to illustrate the Elizabethan challenge of playing many roles. Read Jaques's complete speech in Act 2, Scene 7, from *As You Like It* (Related Work 5). Then read the passage on page 119 that begins "The seven ages of Man…" and ends with the sentence "We can become what we need to be." Discuss how the passage from Shakespeare and the paragraph from Aronson apply to Ralegh's life in Elizabeth's court.

4. Read the three versions of Sir Walter Ralegh's poem about life on pages 69 and 70 in *The Poems of Sir Walter Ralegh* (Related Work 4). Compare the three versions to Jaques's speech cited in activity 3. Be sure to note the stage metaphor Ralegh employs.

5. On page 65 of *Sir Walter Ralegh and the Quest for El Dorado*, Aronson describes the major participants in the Roanoke expedition. Read the paragraph that begins with "Scattered on the other boats…" Discuss what this combination of men and skills says about

Ralegh's judgment. Describe a group, perhaps a school or a church, in which you participate. Identify the talents and skills that different parts of the group contribute.

6. In *Thomas Harriot: Science Pioneer* (Related Work 6) and *Behind the Mask: The Life of Queen Elizabeth I* (Related Work 7), Ralegh is mentioned consistently. After reading all three books, compare the authors' treatments of Ralegh. Continue to research Ralegh's life and share your findings with the group.

Related Works

1. Harmon, William, ed. **The Classic Hundred Poems: All-Time Favorites, 2nd ed.** New York: Columbia University Press, 1998. 360p. $19.95pa. ISBN 0-231-11259-9. **NF** "The Passionate Shepherd to His Love" appears on page 19 and "The Nymph's Reply to the Shepherd" appears on page 13. Marlowe's poem reveals a wish for beauty and romance. Ralegh's poem presents life's cruel realities.

2. **Lost Colony of Roanoke.** Produced by A&E Television Networks, 1996. 50 min. Videocassette. Color. (In Search of History). $19.95. AAE-40320. This documentary reenacts what might have happened in the Roanoke colony that Ralegh backed.

3. Naylor, Phyllis Reynolds. **Sang Spell.** New York: Atheneum Publishers, 1998. 176p. $16.00. ISBN 0-689-82007-0. (See full booktalk in *Booktalks Plus*, 2001, pages 187 to 189.) Joshua Vardy becomes trapped in a world of indeterminable time called Canara that was founded by the Melungeons, people left behind by Captain Drake. See pages 72 and 73 of *Sir Walter Ralegh and the Quest for El Dorado.*

4. Rudick, Michael, ed. **The Poems of Sir Walter Ralegh: A Historical Edition.** Tempe, AZ: Arizona Center for Medieval and Renaissance Studies in conjunction with Renaissance English Text Society, 1999. 237p. (Medieval and Renaissance Texts and Studies, Volume 209). $25.00. ISBN 0-86698-251-5. **NF** On pages 164 to 166, a commentary discusses the discrepancies among the three versions referred to in activity 4.

5. Shakespeare, William. **As You Like It,** edited by Michael Hattaway. Cambridge: Cambridge University Press, 2000. 219p. $44.95. ISBN 0-521-22232-X. In Jaques's speech from *As You Like It*, the melancholy Jaques reduces man's life to specific and fixed stages.

6. Staiger, Ralph C. **Thomas Harriot: Science Pioneer.** New York: Clarion Books, 1998. 128p. $19.00. ISBN 0-395-67296-1. **NF** Staiger's book, aimed at a younger audience, explains the importance of Harriot's life and talents in the Elizabethan world.

7. Thomas, Jane Resh. **Behind the Mask: The Life of Queen Eliza-beth I.** (See full booktalk in chapter 4.) **NF** Like Ralegh, the queen used appearance and stagecraft to secure her power.

ℭℑℌ

Schmidt, Thomas and Jeremy Schmidt. The Saga of Lewis and Clark: Into the Uncharted West.

New York: DK Publishing, Inc., 1999. 210p. (A Tehabi Book). $35.00.
ISBN 0-7894-4638-3. **NF**

Summary/Description

This multi-layered volume combines the text with extensive maps, photographs, paintings, and sketches to tell the story of Lewis and Clark, the two explorers who mapped the American West and reinforced the concept of Manifest Destiny. The authors retraced the explorers' steps from the Mississippi to the Pacific and thoroughly studied their journals. The result is a very personal, lively, and graphic account that pulls Lewis and Clark from the pages of history and into the modern world. An Expedition Roster in the Log, which also includes an index, lists of plants and animals, and a glossary, reinforces the first chapter, "Members of the Expedition." Subsequent chapters describe different sections of the journey—interaction among expedition members, discoveries, and relationships with Native American populations. Captions, sidebars, pictures (some full-page and fold-out), and maps can be read and examined in sequence, separate from the text. Individual articles—such as "A Mandan Winter" and "Keen Observers"—highlight the more important or entertaining parts of the expedition.

Booktalks

Ask how many people walk or run every day. Compare the distances. Ask how many people camp out. Compare how long they camp out at a time. Show the fold-out on pages 27 and 28. Then continue randomly turning pages while speaking.

From 1804 to 1806, Meriwether Lewis and William Clark completed one of the longest wilderness explorations in history—over eighteen months and four thousand miles. President Thomas Jefferson had asked them to find a western route to the Pacific Ocean so America would have a claim to the land before the British. No one thought of the land belonging to the people who lived on it: the Native Americans. So the legendary Lewis and Clark, with thirty-eight others, including a slave, a Native American woman, and the woman's baby, explored a 4,000-mile trail and described its flowers, animals, and inhabitants to their President and the rest of the world. In pages of notes and journals, they fashioned a promise of an endless West, a West that Americans began to consider their destiny. Thomas Jefferson, the Louisiana Purchase, and Lewis and Clark came together to fire the American imagination. Read about their adventures in this wonderful, colorful *Saga of Lewis and Clark.*

Related Activities

1. After reading *The Saga of Lewis and Clark* and *The Journal of Augustus Pelletier* (Related Work 2), discuss how the historical information from *The Saga of Lewis and Clark* supports the fictional journal of Augustus Pelletier.
2. Augustus Pelletier, a fictional character with the Lewis and Clark Expedition, becomes good friends with Sacagawea because neither person "belongs" anywhere. Using specific details from *The Saga of Lewis and Clark,* write three journal entries Sacagawea might have written on the journey.
3. The Lewis and Clark expedition described and drew wildlife others had never seen. Choose one plant or animal. Observe it. Then describe it or draw it so someone who has never seen it might understand what you are observing.
4. Much earlier than Lewis and Clark, Sir Walter Ralegh sponsored exploration of the New World. Compare the participants of the Lewis and Clark expedition and Ralegh's Roanoke expedition. Discuss the similarities and differences between the two groups and each participant's contribution to each expedition.
5. In *Over the Top of the World: Explorer Will Steger's Trek Across the Arctic* (Related Work 6), Will Steger describes a successful high-tech exploration. Even though the two are separated by over one hundred years, compare the preparation and execution of the Arctic journey with the preparation and execution of the Lewis and Clark journey. Discuss the results of your comparison with the group.
6. Continue to research Manifest Destiny. Create a map or a series of maps that indicate the movement west and the historical events that encouraged that movement.

Related Works

1. Aronson, Marc. **Sir Walter Ralegh and the Quest for El Dorado.** (See full booktalk in chapter 4.) **NF** The diversity of the Roanoke expedition shows that Ralegh was interested in more than just riches.
2. Lasky, Kathryn. **The Journal of Augustus Pelletier: The Lewis and Clark Expedition.** New York: Scholastic Incorporated, 2000.

176p. (My Name is America). $10.95. ISBN 0-590-68489-2. Half French and half Omaha Indian, fourteen-year-old Gus has learned to live in the wilderness as well as read and write. When his stepfather tries to cut off Gus's ear, Gus runs away and volunteers his services to the Lewis and Clark Expedition.

3. **Lewis & Clark: Explorers of the New Frontier.** Produced by A&E Television Networks, 1993. 50 min. Videocassette. Color. (Men of Distinction). $14.95. AAE 14021. This documentary includes more of the interaction and viewpoint of the Native Americans with whom Lewis and Clark lived and bargained. Some of the cultural mores might be controversial for younger groups.

4. Philip, Neil, ed. **In a Sacred Manner I Live: Native American Wisdom.** (See full booktalk in chapter 1.) **NF** These Native American poems, songs, and speeches reveal an Indian culture in which private land ownership did not exist.

5. Severance, John B. **Thomas Jefferson: Architect of Democracy.** New York: Clarion Books, 1998. 192p. $18.00. ISBN 0-395-84513-0. (See full booktalk in *Booktalks Plus*, 2001, on pages 245 to 247.) **NF** This biography describes the irony that Jefferson shrewdly negotiated the Louisiana Purchase while his personal financial matters were in shambles.

6. Steger, Will and Jon Bowermaster. **Over the Top of the World: Explorer Will Steger's Trek Across the Arctic.** New York: Scholastic Press, 1997. 63p. $5.99pa. ISBN 0-590-84861-5. (See full booktalk in *Booktalks Plus*, 2001 on pages 32 to 34.) **NF** This description of an Arctic exploration, like the description of the Lewis and Clark expedition, shows the careful planning and the unpredictable natural challenges that might destroy those plans.

Fradin, Dennis Brindell. **The Planet Hunters: The Search for Other Worlds.**

New York: Margaret K. McElderry Books, 1997. 147p. $19.95.
ISBN 0-689-81323-6. **NF**

Summary/Description

The Planet Hunters is a history of planet discoveries. The first chapter tells about Aristarchus, a Greek astronomer who was accused of false teachings because he said the sun was the center of the universe, how planets differ from stars, and how they have fascinated cultures throughout time and the world. Each subsequent chapter centers on a significant discovery, misconception, or astronomer. When discussing the progress and persecution associated with the study of astronomy, Fradin also illustrates how closed minds, fears, and jealousies have impeded our knowledge of the universe but true scholars have continued to study regardless of the obstacles. Consequently, the reader can understand how one discovery depends on a previous one. Now planet discovery is common, and Fradin points out that modern technology has enabled us to peer into the solar system next door. The next challenge will be finding life on other planets, not necessarily within our own solar system.

Fradin begins with useful lists of Numbers Used in This Book and Metric Measurements. Throughout the book, he includes photographs and drawings of astronomers and planets. The center section is a collection of color photographs and drawings of planets and artists' perceptions. A chart, The Nine Known Planets of the Solar System, appears at the end of the book. Fradin includes a bibliography and index.

Booktalk

Ask how many people own or have used telescopes. Discuss what they have seen and what they know about the stars and planets.

Show Figure 31, just before page 61. Read the explanation under the picture. Discuss what this picture and explanation suggest about the study of the stars. If anyone needs clarification on light-years, read the explanation on page xi in Metric Measurements or the explanation of light-years on pages 58 and 59.

Have you ever gazed at the stars in the night sky? When you stargaze and then talk about or study what you have seen, you share in one of the oldest sciences: astronomy. To be a stargazer or "planet hunter," you don't have to be ancient or educated. Monks, farm boys, and even an eleven-year-old girl have contributed to our knowledge of the stars and planets. Planet hunters must only have the courage and patience to look up, watch, and discover for themselves. Why do some people spend almost every night with the stars and even risk their lives to gaze at them? Maybe they believe that as they look up, someone on another planet is looking back. Maybe they hope to be the first to say hello. According to *The Planet Hunters*, the chances of meeting our extra-terrestrial neighbors are getting better every day.

Related Activities

1. Create a timeline from the information in *The Planet Hunters*. Explain how these discoveries affected history.
2. Using the library's resources and the Internet, research and define astronomy and astrology. Explain your findings to the group.

3. Read *Thomas Harriot: Science Pioneer* (Related Work 4). Explain how his life and study relate to *The Planet Hunters*.
4. On pages 29 to 32 of *The Joy of Pi* (Related Work 1), David Blatner discusses how the attitudes of the Dark Ages affected the study of pi. Compare this discussion with the information about censorship in *The Planet Hunters* and *Thomas Harriot: Science Pioneer* (Related Work 4).
5. Fradin points out that naming the planets has been a complicated task. He notes that Venetia Burney's suggestion of Pluto was accepted because of the new planet's darkness. Research the names of each of the planets. Discuss if there is any relationship between the names and the characteristics of the planets.
6. Using the library's resources, research the myth of Prometheus. Discuss how his story might serve as a metaphor for the life of the scientist.
7. Using the bibliography at the end of *The Planet Hunters*, research further information about the planets. Your librarian might help you find additional sources.

Related Works

1. Blatner, David. **The Joy of Pi.** New York: Walker, 1997. 130p. $18.00. ISBN 0-8027-1332-7. (See full booktalk in *Booktalks Plus*, 2001, on pages 232 to 234.) **NF** Blatner's book discusses the Dark Ages and shows relationships between astronomy and mathematics.
2. Hamilton, Edith (text) and Steele Savage (illus.). **Mythology.** New York: Little, Brown, 1998. 497p. $13.00pa. ISBN: 0-316-19152-3. **NF** This reference will be useful in learning about the planet names and the myth of Prometheus.
3. Litwin, Laura Baskes. **Benjamin Banneker: Astronomer and Mathematician.** Berkeley Heights, NJ: Enslow Publishers, Inc., 1999. 121 p. (African-American Biographies). $20.95. ISBN 0-7660-1208-5. **NF** Studying independently for many years, Banneker became a skilled astronomer who helped survey the Federal Territory.
4. Staiger, Ralph C. **Thomas Harriot: Science Pioneer.** New York: Clarion Books, 1998. 128p. $19.00. ISBN 0-395-67296-1. **NF** *The Planet Hunters* does not mention this mysterious figure's contributions to the study of math and astronomy.
5. Turiel, Isaac. **How Do We Know the Size of the Solar System?** New York: Rosen Publishing Group, 2001. 109p. (Great Scientific Questions and the Scientists Who Answered Them). $19.95. ISBN 0-8239-3386-5. **NF** Turiel gives a factual report about the relationship between the development of measurement and space exploration. He briefly describes the planets and projects and makes inferences about future space exploration.

ↁↂ

Stewart, Melissa. Life Without Light: A Journey to Earth's Dark Ecosystems.

New York: Franklin Watts, 1999. 128p. $ 22.00. ISBN 0-531-11529-1. ⓃⒻ

Summary/Description

*L*ife *Without Light* begins by reviewing the relationship of light to life as we know it. Then it explains the surprise man experienced when he descended to the ocean floor. Deep-sea ecosystems contain creatures that have adapted to a dark world and, in some cases, have created their own light and survived through symbiotic relationships and chemosynthesis rather than photosynthesis. The book explores ocean geography that includes hydrothermal vent communities, the midocean ridge, and rift valleys. Stewart describes the ecosystems that live in caves, aquifers, and even rocks. Finally, she focuses on archaebacteria that might have come from another planet and might hold the key to the secret of life.

Pictures and diagrams, including sixteen pages of color photos, show the natural phenomena and illustrate the ideas discussed. A Glossary defines all the technical terms used in the text. The topic and title index provides easy access to the text's information. Source Notes and a resource list provide sources for further research.

Booktalk

In darkness, luminescent fish lure their prey with lights they can turn on and off as easily as flashlights. In darkness, the white, blind troglobites glow pinkish as blood rushes through their bodies; in darkness, oozing methane feeds rich tubeworm colonies; and in darkness, marvelous, dangerous bacteria, older than the earth, grow and change by the minute. These creatures, dwelling deep in darkness, surprise us, fascinate us, and warn us that undiscovered worlds exist even on our own planet. If life can exist here, why not on the planets we once thought too harsh for life? New questions, new fears, and new challenges come all at once when we start to study *Life Without Light*.

Related Activities

1. Melissa Stewart provides Source Notes and Resources for further research. Further research the topic of *Life Without Light*. Ask your librarian to help you find even more sources. Share your findings with the group.
2. Provide a display that illustrates and explains chemosynthesis.

3. Read *Plague and Pestilence* (Related Work 1). Discuss how exploring life in the dark areas of the world might threaten life dependent on photosynthesis.
4. Read *A Deepness in the Sky* (Related Work 5). Discuss how this science fiction world relates to the real world described in *Life Without Light*.
5. Read about troglobites on pages 68 to page 71. Note the type of information Melissa Stewart provides in her explanation: history, habitat, appearance, habits, and so on. Choose a creature with which you are more familiar but about which you would like to learn more. Ask the librarian to help you gather similar types of information. Then prepare a written or oral presentation.

Related Works

1. Altman, Linda Jacobs. **Plague and Pestilence.** (See full booktalk in chapter 3.) **NF** Altman describes the history of disease in relation to man's exploration.
2. Caes, Charles J. **How Do We Know the Age of the Earth?** New York: Rosen Publishing Group, 2001. 111p. (Great Scientific Questions and the Scientists Who Answered Them). $19.95. ISBN 0-8239-3381-4. **NF** This book traces the scientific efforts to figure out the earth's age and emphasizes the role of adaptation in developing new species.
3. Jenkins, Steve. **Hottest Coldest Highest Deepest.** Boston: Houghton Mifflin Company, 1998. 30p. $16.00. ISBN 0-395-89999-0. **NF** This series of collages explains geographical statistics with pictures and concrete comparisons.
4. Tyson, Neil de Grasse. **Just Visiting This Planet.** New York: Doubleday, 1998. 336p. $12.95pa. ISBN 0-385-48837-8. **NF** In a question-and-answer format, Tyson discusses issues of the planet and the larger universe it inhabits. He also includes the scientific, the pseudo-scientific, and the fantastic.
5. Vinge, Vernor. **A Deepness in the Sky.** New York: Tor Books, 1999. 606p. $27.95. ISBN 0-312-85683-0. This adult/young-adult science fiction novel centers on a colony of spiders with human minds and feelings. Their planet's environment has forced them to adjust to long periods of light and dark.

Landau, Elaine. **Heroine of the Titanic: The Real Unsinkable Molly Brown.**
New York: Clarion Books, 2001. 132p. $18.00. ISBN 0-395-93912-7. **NF**

Summary/Description

Landau tells the story of Margaret Brown, christened Molly Brown by the press. A working class woman who remained loyal to her humble beginnings after she and her husband realized a lucrative gold strike, Margaret Brown educated herself, raised a family, and socialized with the rich and famous of her time. Known to enjoy the best hotels and most popular resorts, she accompanied the controversial Astors on the Titanic. With extensive financial resources and education, Brown maintained a devotion to social causes that included women's and workers' rights. She fought the mining companies even though their labor practices provided her fortune. Her mastery of languages allowed her to help the immigrant wives and mothers who survived the Titanic. With her strong personality, she dominated her children's lives. Margaret Brown became the folk hero Molly Brown because her choices in crisis epitomized her practical, independent, generous, and flamboyant life. Landau emphasizes that Margaret Brown was unsinkable socially and emotionally as well as physically.

Suitable for students interested in the time period, women's rights, or the Titanic tragedy, this biography provides a chronology of Margaret Brown's life and a bibliography of books, periodicals, letters, films, places, and Web sites. The many photographs throughout the biography portray an active and ambitious woman with the courage to embrace a tumultuous time. The name and topic index makes information easy to access.

Booktalk

The Unsinkable Molly Brown—who was this lady who saved so many lives when the Titanic, the unsinkable ship, sank? She wasn't a saloon girl who struck it rich. She wasn't a frantic wife who, by mistake, burned her husband's money in the kitchen stove. Those were just the stories made up by a press wanting to sell newspapers. The real Molly Brown or Margaret Brown story is even better. Margaret Brown *decided* to live in the West when respectable single women wouldn't even consider a trip. She wanted to marry a wealthy man to take care of her and her family, fell in love with a poor one who became wealthy, and then decided she didn't need a man to help her at all. When Margaret Brown met the Titanic, she already had overcome disasters and made tough choices. She became the *Heroine of the Titanic* because she did what came naturally—thinking ahead and taking control.

Related Activities

1. Read Joan W. Blos's *The Heroine of the Titanic: A Tale Both True and Otherwise of the Life of Molly Brown* (Related Work 2). Compare

Blos's portrayal of Brown to Landau's. According to Landau, what parts of Blos's account are true and which parts are "otherwise"?

2. Choose a fictional account of another historic character. Ask your librarian to help you research the accuracy of that account against factual information.

3. Read *Titanic* (Related Work 1) by Simon Adams. Report on any additional information you find about Molly Brown. Then, on the basis of Landau's biography and Adams's description of the Titanic, discuss how Brown's reaction to the Titanic accident epitomized her contradictory and controversial life.

4. Margaret Tobin (Molly Brown) was born in 1867. Ida B. Wells, champion of civil rights, was born in 1862 (Related Work 3). Both of these very independent women were social activists. Compare their lives and discuss how the historical events of their time period affected them.

5. Molly Brown's reaction on the Titanic was consistent with her personality and other choices she made in her life. Compare her life story and her reaction to crisis with those of two other heroes: Shane Osborn (Related Work 6) and Irene Gut Opdyke (Related Work 5). Discuss the elements that produce true heroes and acts of heroism.

Related Works

1. Adams, Simon. **Titanic.** (See full booktalk in chapter 1.) **NF** Part of the Eyewitness series, *Titanic* describes the Titanic and its passengers in relation to other ships of the time. The color illustrations and captions pack a tremendous amount of highly motivating information in a few pages.

2. Blos, Joan W. (text) and Tennessee Dixon (illus.). **The Heroine of the Titanic: A Tale Both True and Otherwise of the Life of Molly Brown.** New York: Morrow Junior Books, 1991. 38p. $16.95. ISBN 0-688-07546-0. This children's book is a romantic account of the life of Molly Brown. Both the text and the illustrations serve as a marked contrast to Landau's biography.

3. Fradin, Dennis Brindell and Judith Bloom Fradin. **Ida B. Wells: Mother of the Civil Rights Movement.** (See full booktalk in chapter 4.) **NF** Wells, an investigative reporter and civil rights activist, fought for civil rights for women and African-Americans.

4. **Molly Brown: An American Legend.** Produced by A&E Television Networks, 1997. 50 min. Videocassette. Color. (Biography). $14.95. AAE-14284. This documentary emphasizes that Molly Brown's work for women's and workers' rights far outweighed the

fame she received through the Titanic. She epitomized the emerging modern woman.

5. Opdyke, Irene Gut with Jennifer Armstrong. **In My Hands: Memories of a Holocaust Rescuer.** (See full booktalk in chapter 4.) **NF** Faced with the Germans' persecution of Jews, Opdyke, a Catholic, gradually performs more dangerous acts to help them.

6. Osborn, Shane with Malcolm McConnell. **Born to Fly: The Heroic Story of Downed U.S. Navy Pilot Lt. Shane Osborn.** (See full booktalk in chapter 1.) **NF** In telling about his life and the events that led to his plane's encounter with a Chinese pilot, Osborn emphasizes the importance of dedication and preparation.

7. **Titanic.** Produced by A&E Television Networks, HEARST/ABC /NBC, 1994. 200 min. Videocassette. Color. $19.95. AAE-12900. Molly Brown is discussed in the third videocassette of this four-videocassette documentary.

ርჟየጋ

Schmidt, Gary D. **William Bradford: Plymouth's Faithful Pilgrim.**

Grand Rapids, MI: Eerdmans Books for Young Readers, 1999. 200p. $18.00.
ISBN 0-8028-5151-7. **NF**

Summary/Description

William Bradford began his quest for the new world as an orphaned shepherd boy. Moved from one house to another within his prosperous family, he had financial security but little love. His family expected him to work, contribute, and achieve. A frail, sick Bradford spent his time reading the Bible and began to question Queen Elizabeth's church. At twelve, he encountered Richard Clyfton, a charismatic leader who preached church reform. Although Bradford's family opposed reform, Bradford gained support from William Brewster, a reformer and a father figure to the young man. King James I escalated the persecution of the Separatists. Bradford, Brewster, and Clyfton, with the Separatists, fled to Holland. They discovered new lives and religious tolerance but found they were being absorbed into the Dutch community. Consequently, they decided to establish a community in the New World. After another harrowing and dangerous journey, Bradford's group arrived in Plymouth, a harsh and demanding land. Here Bradford and his fellow passengers signed the Mayflower Compact and established the basis for democracy in the New World. They negotiated with the Indians, learned to live off the land, and helped other communities start their lives. Becoming governor of his community at thirty-two, Bradford guided the Plymouth community for the rest of his life. *William Bradford: Plymouth's Faithful Pilgrim* provides pictures, maps, and diagrams, including a cross section of the Mayflower on page 56. A Preface sets the scene and communicates Bradford's mindset. Schmidt explains the major sources for the book and provides an annotated list of sources for further reading.

Booktalk

Imagine stepping into a wilderness filled with tribal peoples, unfamiliar vegetation, and wild animals. You might not have enough food to survive. Your ship might never return. Would you get off the boat? When William Bradford stood on the shore of the New World, he had already faced many adversities. He had lost his parents, he had changed his religion against his uncles' wishes, he had continued his beliefs in spite of government persecution, and he was about to start a new life in a new land. But Bradford was more than willing to embrace change and hardship. With hard work and struggle, he established the mindset of democracy. Joining in the Mayflower Compact, keeping his promises to the Native Americans who helped him, and faithfully shepherding the Plymouth community, *William Bradford; Plymouth's Faithful Pilgrim* teaches us that mutual respect, hard work, and faith can conquer a wilderness and build a community of trust.

Related Activities

1. Read the first three full paragraphs of the Preface of *William Bradford: Plymouth's Faithful Pilgrim.* The passage begins with "November 1620" and ends with "One of the very first ashore." These two paragraphs set the scene for William Bradford's mindset and the overwhelming task he faces. State what Schmidt accomplishes in each paragraph and how he accomplishes it. Using similar techniques, write a setting-the-scene description about a person embarking on a new enterprise.
2. In *The Journal of Jasper Jonathan Pierce: A Pilgrim Boy* (Related Work 3), Jasper records his reactions to the New World. What does Jasper share with Bradford in reaction and background?
3. Using the Suggestions for Further Reading, continue to research Bradford's life and the life of the pilgrim community. Report your findings to the group.
4. With the help of the librarian, research the conditions that led to the Separatist movement and the eventual colonization of the New World. Share your findings with the group.
5. *Thomas Harriot: Science Pioneer* (Related Work 5) and *Sir Walter Ralegh and the Quest for El Dorado* (Related Work 1) describe the

English exploration of Roanoke Island that resulted in unsuccessful colonization. Compare the motivation, discoveries, procedures, and results of that colonization with those of the Plymouth colony.

6. *The Journal of Jasper Jonathan Pierce: A Pilgrim Boy* (Related Work 3) tells about the pilgrim journey from the perspective of a young indentured servant. In his November 10 entry, he describes the motivation and composition for the Mayflower Compact. Starting with the information in *William Bradford: Plymouth's Faithful Pilgrim*, continue to research the Compact and its implications for American government.

7. Choose another member of the Separatists mentioned in *William Bradford: Plymouth's Faithful Pilgrim*. Write diary entries for three days of that person's life.

Related Works

1. Aronson, Marc. **Sir Walter Ralegh and the Quest for El Dorado.** (See full booktalk in chapter 4.) **NF** This biography of the flamboyant and dramatic Sir Walter Ralegh presents a great contrast in method and purpose to the picture of William Bradford in *William Bradford: Plymouth's Faithful Pilgrim.*

2. Erickson, Paul. **Daily Life in the Pilgrim Colony, 1636.** New York: Clarion Books, 2001. 48p. $9.95pa. ISBN 0-395-98841-1. **NF** This analysis of pilgrim life describes how a fictional pilgrim family conducts daily living in an established colonial community. It includes extensive pictures and sketches, a timeline, and an index.

3. Rinaldi, Ann. **The Journal of Jasper Jonathan Pierce: A Pilgrim Boy.** New York: Scholastic Incorporated, 2000. 156p. $10.95. ISBN 0-590-48531-8. Fourteen-year-old Jasper Jonathan Pierce tells the pilgrims' story from the point of view of an orphaned boy now serving as William Brewster's servant.

4. **San Antonio College LitWeb William Bradford Page.** Available: www.accd.edu/sac/english/bailey/bradford.htm (Accessed June 2002). This Web page includes a brief biography, a passenger list, references to additional books and videos, and a description of the expedition in the context of the time period.

5. Staiger, Ralph C. **Thomas Harriot: Science Pioneer.** New York: Clarion Books, 1998. 128p. $19.00. ISBN 0-395-67296-1. **NF** Harriot was part of the expedition to Roanoke in the New World. His records show much different motivations for discovery and much different results than for the Bradford colony.

ᘓᘔ

Thomas, Jane Resh. **Behind the Mask: The Life of Queen Elizabeth I.**

New York: Clarion Books, 1998. 196p. $19.00. ISBN 0-395-69120-6. **NF**

Summary/Description

In *Behind the Mask: The Life of Queen Elizabeth I*, Resh explains how Elizabeth shapes and is shaped by her times. As the daughter of a man and woman who contribute to a religious revolution, Elizabeth learns to assess her personal situation. Isolated as a child, sexually abused by her guardian, imprisoned by her sister, and plotted against by her cousin, Elizabeth never fully trusts or loves anyone. With a shrewd intelligence that serves her country's needs, she uses her court and personal presentations to create the myths of Good Queen Bess, Gloriana, and the Virgin Queen. Elizabeth brings a poorly managed and almost bankrupt England to a victorious world position. Although vain and petty, she encourages and inspires exploration, wit, and scholarship and gives an entire age her name.

The book includes pictures of Henry VIII's six wives, a Cast of Characters that explains the relationships surrounding Elizabeth, a chronology from the birth of Henry VIII (1491) to Elizabeth's death (1603), sources for each chapter, pictures and etchings of the times, and Queen Elizabeth's life in full-color portraits.

Booktalk

In the rich and flamboyant Elizabethan Age, the arts, science, and exploration flourished. Humanity was learning to direct its existence, and England grew into a world power, all because of a woman. *Behind the Mask* of Good Queen Bess, the magnificent Gloriana, or the self-sacrificing, pristine Virgin Queen, Queen Elizabeth I schemed, lied, and killed to protect her country and herself. She was a "spin doctor," an intellectual, and a shrewd money manager who outwitted popes, foreign princes, and her own parliament. In a man's world, Elizabeth was queen, and *Behind the Mask* tells the story of her daring, magnificent life.

Related Activities

1. *Anna of Byzantium* (Related Work 2) begins with Anna, a virtual prisoner in a convent, thinking about her life in a palace. In *Mary, Bloody Mary* (Related Work 7), Queen Mary reflects on growing up in a palace. In chapter 3 of *Behind the Mask*, Thomas describes Elizabeth's imprisonment and includes a short letter that Elizabeth sends to Mary. Choose one day described in Elizabeth's imprison-

ment. Write the journal entry you feel Elizabeth would have written as she reflects on her former life.

2. Using your library's resources, research exploration, art, religion, politics, and scholarship from 1491 to 1603. Organize the information you find in a timeline. Share the timeline and any explanations with the group.

3. After reading *Behind the Mask* and *Sir Walter Ralegh and the Quest for El Dorado* (Related Work 1), discuss how Elizabeth uses courtly love and its stereotypes to her advantage.

4. Read "We Wear the Mask" by Paul Laurence Dunbar on page 40 of *I, Too, Sing America* (Related Work 3). Discuss how the poem might apply to Elizabeth I. Could Elizabeth I have shared the feelings of people persecuted because of race?

5. After viewing *Elizabeth I: The Virgin Queen* (Related Work 4) and reading *Behind the Mask,* note the differing perceptions of Elizabeth that the two works present. Then discuss what this contrast suggests about studying and researching history.

Related Works

1. Aronson, Marc. **Sir Walter Ralegh and the Quest for El Dorado.** (See full booktalk in chapter 4.) **NF** Aronson approaches Ralegh's life as a drama he was forced to write and act out for a queen who controlled his prosperity. Part of the drama is the game of courtly love.

2. Barrett, Tracy. **Anna of Byzantium.** (See full booktalk in chapter 3.) Anna expects she will be the empress of Byzantium, but through royal intrigue, the crown falls to her brother.

3. Dunbar, Paul Laurence. "We Wear the Mask." In **I, Too, Sing America: Three Centuries of African American Poetry.** By Catherine Clinton (text) and Stephen Alcorn (illus.). New York: Houghton Mifflin Company, 1998. 128p. $20.00. ISBN 0-395-89599-5. (See full booktalk in *Booktalks Plus,* 2001, pages 219 to 221.) **NF** This poem, written in the 1890s, deals with hiding true feelings from a threatening world (page 40).

4. **Elizabeth I: The Virgin Queen.** Produced by A&E Television Networks, 1996. 50 min. Videocassette. Color. (Biography). $14.95. AAE-14201.X. The documentary portrays an indecisive woman who waits for events and other people to make things happen.

5. **Henry VIII: Scandals of a King**. Produced by A&E Television Networks, 1996. 100 min. Videocassette. Color. (Biography). AAE-18285. This documentary presents Henry as a corrupt and bullying force in Elizabeth's life.

6. Lasky, Kathryn. **Mary, Queen of Scots: Queen Without a Country.** New York: Scholastic Incorporated, 2002. 224p. (The Royal Diaries). $10.95. ISBN 0-439-19404-0. The young Mary, growing up in France, reflects on her position as queen, her family in Scotland, the importance of her marriage, and her cousins Mary and Elizabeth in England.

7. Meyer, Carolyn. **Mary, Bloody Mary.** New York: Gulliver Books, 1999. 227p. $16.00. ISBN 0-15-201906-5. Mary, as queen, reflects on a childhood haunted by rejection and intrigue. The novel suggests that Mary's leniency toward Elizabeth in adulthood stems from the bond developed between them when Mary was forced to care for Elizabeth.

ぐぬ

Fradin, Dennis Brindell, and Judith Bloom Fradin.
Ida B. Wells: Mother of the Civil
Rights Movement.
New York: Clarion Books, 2000. 178p. $18.00. ISBN 0-395-89898-6. **NF**

Summary/Description

Born a slave in 1862, Ida B. Wells became one of the first African-American investigative reporters. She maintained her civil rights activism throughout her life. Coming of age during Reconstruction, Wells took on the Chesapeake & Ohio Railroad in 1884 when she was ordered, under newly passed Jim Crow laws, to ride in the "colored" train car. Her five-hundred-dollar award symbolized her first victorious challenge to a racist system. Orphaned at sixteen, Wells supported herself and five siblings with teaching jobs, but her writing and speaking talents drew her to journalism. Dubbed "The Princess of the Press," Wells's daring reporting for newspapers she partially owned focused on lynching. Wells often questioned whether the victims' "crimes" centered on rape or interracial love. The challenge endangered her life but ultimately ended a notorious period of twisted vigilante justice. After raising six children, Wells also fought for women's rights and helped found organizations to support livelihood, education, and political activism for women and African-Americans.

Pictures, documents, and sketches provide a vivid sense of Wells's life and times. An extensive bibliography suggests additional sources. A topic and name index that includes bold numbers indicating illustrations makes information easily accessible.

Booktalk

Ask how many in the group have heard of Martin Luther King. Ask how many have heard of Susan B. Anthony. Ask how many have heard of Ida B. Wells.

Ida B. Wells isn't exactly a household name. When she was born in 1862, not many people noticed the birth of this black slave girl. And after Emancipation, few paid attention to this poor black free girl trying to grow up. Poor, female, and black wasn't a potent combination when it came to fame and fortune. But when Ida B. Wells refused to give up her seat in a "Whites Only" train car, the Chesapeake & Ohio Railroad noticed her. They removed her from the car, and she sued them. She won. When Ida B. Wells bought part of a newspaper business and started to write about the lynching of black men, the city of Memphis noticed her. In fact, they tried to kill her. Ida B. Wells learned that being noticed could be pretty dangerous. This Princess of the Press tackled women's rights, education, workers' rights—even a prejudiced United States President. Why? Because, as her son pointed out, "Nobody else will!" Ida B. Wells did get noticed, and she should be remembered. Rarely mentioned when all the fathers of civil rights are praised, here is the mother of the civil rights movement: *Ida B. Wells.*

Related Activities

1. *Color Me Dark: The Diary of Nellie Lee Love* (Related Work 4) describes events in the time period of Ida B. Wells. On page 153 of *Ida B. Wells: Mother of the Civil Rights Movement*, the paragraph beginning "By the end of World War I" outlines the political situation in which Nellie Lee Love grows up. Read the two books. Then discuss how the facts of the Wells biography support the fictional diary of Nellie Lee Love.

2. In *Adventures of Huckleberry Finn* (Related Work 6), chapter 22, Huck describes the attempted lynching of Colonel Sherburn. Begin reading with "They swarmed up towards Sherburn's house..." and end with "I could 'a' stayed if I wanted to but I didn't want to." Discuss what Sherburn reveals about himself and about lynching. Then discuss Twain's placement of this incident in the same chapter with Huck's circus experience and the introduction of what Huck refers to as *"our* show."

3. Choose one book from the bibliography on pages 169 and 170 of *Ida B. Wells*. Ask your librarian to help you find other sources. Share any additional information you find with the group.

4. Ida B. Wells disagreed with some of the most prominent leaders of her time: Booker T. Washington, Frederick Douglass, and Susan B.

Anthony. Ask three people to choose one of those three leaders. Ask them to find out as much as possible about their beliefs and leadership. Then ask them to share with the group how each might agree and disagree with Ida B. Wells. Choose one of the issues and organize a class debate.

5. After viewing *Vigilantes* (Related Work 7) and reading chapters 1 and 2 of *Kids and Guns* (Related Work 5), discuss the violence mentality in the United States in relation to racism and other social problems.

Related Works

1. Bacho, Peter. **Boxing in Black and White.** New York: Henry Holt and Company, 1999. 122p. $18.95. ISBN 0-8050-5779-X. **NF** Bacho suggests that boxing helped handle much of the racial frustration felt in the first half of the twentieth century.
2. Ellis, Rex M. **With a Banjo on My Knee: A Musical Journey from Slavery to Freedom.** New York: Franklin Watts, 2001. 160p. $26.00. ISBN 0-531-11747-2. **NF** In tracing the history of the banjo, Ellis tells the prejudice and oppression and particularly the lynching that placed the instrument in disfavor with African-Americans.
3. Haegele, Katie. **Monte Irvin.** New York: Rosen Central, 2002. 112p. (Baseball Hall of Famers of the Negro Leagues). $29.95. ISBN 0-8239-3477-2. **NF** On pages 75 and 76, a brief profile of Effa Manley, co-owner of the Newark Eagles and social activist, explains how the Manleys held "Anti-Lynching Days" at the ballpark and directed those funds to the movement.
4. McKissack, Patricia. **Color Me Dark: The Diary of Nellie Lee Love.** (See full booktalk in chapter 1.) When Nellie Lee Love is eleven years old, a gang of local white men kills her uncle. The family leaves Tennessee and moves to Chicago. Her mother joins the Ida B. Wells club, a group working to end lynching and improve the lives of colored women.
5. Schwarz, Ted. **Kids and Guns.** New York: Franklin Watts, 1999.128p. $24.00. ISBN 0-531-11723-5. **NF** Schwartz presents a balanced discussion about guns in the hands of young people. Chapters 1 and 2 review recent shootings and the history of gun use in the United States.
6. Twain, Mark. **Adventures of Huckleberry Finn.** In **The Portable Mark Twain.** New York: Random House, 1996. 418p. $25.00. ISBN 0-679-44889-6. In the Colonel's monologue about lynching, he describes the traditional Southern way of lynching. By placing the lynching next to the circus, Twain implies that the lynching was more entertainment than justice. The videocassette, *Vigi-*

lantes, corroborates that view. *The Adventures of Huckleberry Finn* was originally published in a different form in 1885 by Charles L. Webster and Company.

7. **Vigilantes.** Produced by A&E Television Networks, 1999. 50 min. Videocassette. Color. (History's Mysteries). $19.95. AAE-42602. This documentary talks about the sadism often accompanying the vigilante movement and distinguishes between the vigilantes of the West, who punished crimes, and the vigilantes of the South, who repressed people. Ida B. Wells is cited as a crusader against lynching.

ርን ᘛን

Burchard, Peter. **Lincoln and Slavery.**

New York: Atheneum Books for Young Readers, 1999. 196p. $17.00.
ISBN 0-689-81570-0. **NF**

Summary/Description

In simple language, Burchard traces Lincoln's intellectual and political journeys to the Emancipation Proclamation. He outlines the emotions and thinking of the times; Lincoln's boyhood, which included little contact with slaves; and the adult experiences that drew him into slavery court cases. As a politician, Lincoln wanted to stop the spread of slavery but preserve the Union. His double purpose sometimes led to contradiction and failure. Fearing that the Union would lose the Border States, Lincoln refused the help of African-American soldiers at the beginning of the war. When they finally entered as "contrabands," he applauded their courage and supported their cause. Still convinced that black and white could not live together, he advocated black colonization, but eventually saw his folly. Sometimes reflecting the prejudice of the period, he eventually counted Frederick Douglass as one of his closest friends. Burchard uses many pictures to reinforce his explanations. "Bibliographical Essay and Notes on Sources" begins with an essay explaining Burchard's overall use of primary and secondary sources. He includes a short essay for each chapter to "provide clear links between…text and…sources." These essays often recommend further reading. A three-page bibliography appears at the end of the book, and a name and topic index provides easy access to information.

Booktalk

Ask how many people in the group have heard of the Emancipation Proclamation. Ask someone to share what he or she knows.

Sadly, before the Emancipation Proclamation was written, our leaders worried about offending slave owners. Slave labor supported the nation's economy. So they talked about not extending slavery into new territories, and they talked about how a man could lose the right to slaves in wartime, and they talked about children born to slaves being free. And all this talking did nothing for slaves. At first, Lincoln felt that preserving the Union was more important than totally abolishing slavery. Then, as he saw the conditions of slavery, as he heard the pleas of former slaves, and as he let his feelings for others take control, he came to hate it. He decided to support the spirit of the Declaration of Independence over the compromises of the Constitution. Lincoln announced the Emancipation Proclamation and changed the United States forever. *Lincoln and Slavery* by Peter Burchard traces the careful and emotional journey that led Lincoln to both glory and death.

Related Activities

1. Burchard lists and discusses his sources. Using the bibliography he provides, continue reading about Lincoln's life and times. Share your findings with the group.
2. Choose another historical figure or time period. Prepare a report for the group. Following Burchard's example of listing and discussing his sources, explain the relative usefulness and value of each source in accomplishing the purpose of your report.
3. In *Letters from Vinnie* (Related Work 8), Vinnie Ream records her own personal growth throughout the Civil War but also her observations of Lincoln, the man whose statue she creates. Find more information about artists, writers, and photographers who recorded and interpreted the events and people of the Civil War. You might wish to start your nonfiction search with Duane Damon's *When this Cruel War is Over* (Related Work 2).
4. In *An Acquaintance with Darkness* (Related Work 7), Emily Bransby Pigbush discovers that her uncle is a body snatcher. After reading both *An Acquaintance with Darkness* and *Lincoln and Slavery,* discuss what Emily's uncle, a fictional character, might have in common with President Lincoln.
5. Both *Lincoln and Slavery* and *Black, Blue, and Gray: African Americans in the Civil War* (Related Work 6) discuss the role of slaves and African-American soldiers during the Civil War. Compare the two nonfiction accounts. Discuss how they complement and contradict each other.

Related Works

1. **Abraham Lincoln: Preserving the Union.** Produced by A&E Home Video, 1996. 100 min. Videocassette. Color. (American Presi-

dents). $14.95. AAE 14175. Tracing Lincoln's Civil War journey, the film points out that Lincoln's opposition to slavery grew from his personal contact with black soldiers.

2. Damon, Duane. **When This Cruel War Is Over.** Minneapolis, MN: Lerner Publishing Group, 1996. 88p. $19.95. ISBN 0-8225-1731-0. **NF** "Voices of Home," on pages 62 to 71, discusses photographers, artists, and writers whose talents recorded and influenced the Civil War.

3. Fradin, Dennis Brindell. **Bound for the North Star: True Stories of Fugitive Slaves.** New York: Clarion Books, 2000. 205p. $20.00. ISBN 0-395-97017-2. **NF** In twelve chapters, Fradin tells the stories of slaves struggling for freedom and the people and organizations that helped them. The narratives clearly illustrate the horrors of slavery and the strength of the human spirit.

4. Fraser, Mary Ann. **Vicksburg: The Battle that Won the Civil War.** New York: Henry Holt and Company, 1999. 100p. $16.95. ISBN 0-8050-6106-1. **NF** Known as the "Gibraltar of the Confederacy," "the key," and the "nailhead that held the South's two halves together," the battle also illustrated how the Civil War split loyalties within a single state.

5. Freedman, Russell. **Give Me Liberty! The Story of the Declaration of Independence.** New York: Holiday House, 2000. 90p. $12.95. ISBN 0-8234-1753-0. **NF** Freedman explains the Declaration of Independence by describing the events that created it. Chapter 9 explains Lincoln's interpretation that led to the Emancipation Proclamation and the modern perception of the Declaration.

6. Haskins, Jim. **Black, Blue, and Gray: African Americans in the Civil War.** New York: Simon & Schuster, 1998. 154p. $16.00. ISBN 0-689-80655-8. **NF** Haskins establishes that African-Americans were a central part of the Civil War despite the prejudice they had to face in both the Union and Confederate armies.

7. Rinaldi, Ann. **An Acquaintance with Darkness.** New York: Harcourt Brace and Company, 1997. 294p. $16.00. ISBN 0-15-201294-X. When Emily Bransby Pigbush discovers that her best friends are the center of President Lincoln's assassination and her physician uncle is rumored to be a body snatcher, she finds herself in two situations where she must support either prejudice or progress.

8. Sappey, Maureen Stack. **Letters from Vinnie.** Asheville, NC: Front Street, 1999. 248p. $16.95. ISBN 1-886910-31-6. In this historical novel, Vinnie Ream, the woman who sculpted the statue of Lincoln for the Capitol Rotunda, details the great sorrow she observes in Lincoln as she sculpts his face.

Looking Toward the Future

ꑞꑞ

Opdyke, Irene Gut with Jennifer Armstrong.
In My Hands: Memories of a Holocaust Rescuer.
New York: Alfred A. Knopf, 1999. 276p. $18.00. ISBN 0-679-89181-1.

Summary/Description

Opdyke describes how her family life and personal beliefs led her to help and hide Jews persecuted during the German occupation of Poland. A nursing student when Hitler invades Poland, Opdyke flees to Russian territory, where she is beaten and raped by soldiers. Then the head doctor of the hospital to which she is taken attacks her. Accused of spying, she manages to escape and find her way back home, where she performs forced labor in a munitions factory. She then serves in a restaurant with a kind German supervisor. She begins to put food under the fence surrounding the Jewish ghetto next to the restaurant, passes on military plans she overhears in her job, and hides Jews. The German major who helped her get her restaurant job takes a villa in town, and Opdyke becomes his housekeeper. He discovers the Jewish friends she is hiding in his home, and she agrees to be his mistress in exchange for his silence. When the Germans flee, Opdyke becomes part of the Polish resistance. After the war, Jews help her find a camp for displaced persons, and she eventually travels to the United States. A Postscript explains Opdyke's life in the United States, her motivation to speak out about the Holocaust, her selection as "one of the Righteous Among the Nations," and her reunion with her family. Pronunciation Guides for Polish and German help the reader pronounce the names and terms used in the text. "Some Historical Background" explains Germany's invasion of Poland and discusses how its military organizations sometimes worked against each other. Maps illustrate Poland's occupation and changing boundaries. "A Note on the Writing of This Book" explains the challenges Jennifer Armstrong met in writing the book.

Booktalk

Irene sees a bird thrown in the air and then shot by a German soldier. Suddenly she realizes that it's not a bird but a baby brutally killed in front of its mother—and then she sees the mother killed too. Scenes like this repeat each day in Irene's town, but Irene is just a girl, a young Catholic girl, not a Jew. How can she act against the Nazi war machine? Helping Jews could sentence her and her family to hang with other Poles who have helped the Jews.

But Irene decides to do a small thing, something no one will notice. She hides a little extra food under a ghetto fence. The next day it's gone. She tries again. Soon her days and deeds run together. Having the courage to say that some small things are *In My Hands*, she becomes a most wanted member of the Polish resistance and a heroic rescuer of the Holocaust, one step at a time.

Related Activities

1. The essays "Tears" and "Amber" frame Opdyke's story. Read these essays aloud. Discuss why Opdyke began and ended her book with these essays.
2. Opdyke emphasizes the importance of courage and free will. Explain how these two qualities interact. Compare Opdyke's experiences and choices with Oskar Schindler's. You might wish to view *Oskar Schindler: The Man Behind the List* (Related Work 6) or read *Oskar Schindler: Righteous Gentile* (Related Work 7).
3. *In My Hands* describes the Third Reich's persecution of the Jews and its aggression against Poland. *Stones in Water* (Italy) (Related Work 4), *Tomi: A Childhood Under the Nazis* (France) (Related Work 8), *A Traitor Among Us* (Holland) (Related Work 9), and *Darkness Over Denmark* (Related Work 3) show how the Reich acted against other European nations as well. Ask each person in a group of four to read one of these books and further research the German relationship with that country. Then discuss as a group the perception that the German leadership held of themselves and Germany.
4. *Torn Thread* (Related Work 2), *The Seamstress* (Related Work 1), *The Lost Childhood* (Related Work 5), *Darkness Over Denmark* (Related Work 3), and *In My Hands* all talk about the importance of fighting persecution and how practical skills, hard work, and planning help in resisting that persecution. Ask three people in a group to read one of the books and then discuss, speak, or write about how the three qualities are central to the main characters' struggles.
5. Make a list of small kindnesses that have been extended to you or to others. Explain how and why you feel each effort made a difference. Compare your list with that of someone else who has completed the same exercise. Then discuss the common elements in the acts and the reactions to them.

Related Works

1. Bernstein, Sara Tuvel. **The Seamstress: A Memoir of Survival.** New York: GP Putnam's Sons, 1997. 353p. $25.95. ISBN 0-399-

14322-X. **NF** Traveling and working throughout Europe to avoid the German advance, Sara Tuvel is finally sent to a forced labor camp and then a concentration camp.

2. Isaacs, Anne. **Torn Thread.** New York: Scholastic Press, 2000. 192p. $15.95. ISBN 0-590-60363-9. Twelve-year-old Eva joins her sister in a forced labor camp, where she learns to judge people as individuals not as members of a group and where she uses every skill, even candy making, to keep her sister and herself alive.

3. Levine, Ellen. **Darkness over Denmark.** New York: Holiday House, 2000. 164p. $14.95. ISBN 0-8234-1755-7. Levine explains the abrupt invasion of Denmark, the subsequent resistance, and the Danish protection of the Jewish population.

4. Napoli, Donna Jo. **Stones in Water.** (See full booktalk in chapter 3). Two Italian boys, one Catholic and one Jewish, are taken by German soldiers to live in work camps. Roberto, the Catholic, must hide his friend's true identity or they will both be killed.

5. Nir, Yehuda. **The Lost Childhood: A World War II Memoir.** New York: Scholastic Press, 2002. 288p. $16.95. ISBN 0-439-16389-7. **NF** Nir tells how his family successfully disguised themselves as Catholics during the war. He explains the very complicated position of the Polish Jews in relation to the Poles, Russians, and Germans.

6. **Oskar Schindler: The Man Behind the List.** Produced by A&E Television Networks, 1998. 50 min. Videocassette. Color. $14.95. AAE-14319. A more controversial figure than Opdyke, Schindler also helped Polish Jews and was honored by Israel.

7. Roberts, Jeremy. **Oskar Schindler: Righteous Gentile.** New York: Rosen Publishing Group, 2000. 112p. (Holocaust Biographies). $19.95. ISBN 0-8239-3310-5. **NF** Like the A&E film, this biography portrays Schindler as a complicated and controversial figure.

8. Ungerer, Tomi. **Tomi: A Childhood Under the Nazis.** Niwot, CO: Roberts Rinehart Publishing Group, 1998. 175p. $29.95. ISBN 1-57098-163-9. (See full booktalk in *Booktalks Plus,* 2001.) **NF** Fourteen-year-old Tomi Ungerer uses his personal possessions and documents to illustrate life in Alsace during the German occupation.

9. Van Steenwyk, Elizabeth. **A Traitor Among Us.** Grand Rapids, MI: Eerdmans Books for Young Readers, 1998. 133p. $15.00. ISBN 0-8028-5150-9. (See full booktalk in *Booktalks Plus,* 2001.) Thirteen-year-old Pieter becomes a courier for the Dutch Resistance during the German occupation of Holland.

CʒʡϾ

Bauer, Joan. Hope Was Here.

New York: GP Putnam's Sons, 2000. 186p. $16.99. ISBN 0-399-23142-0.

Summary/Description

This is another Bauer feel-good story about an upbeat, confident young woman who confronts negative experiences and comes out a winner. Sixteen-year-old Hope and her Aunt Addie have been swindled out of their Brooklyn diner and are heading to jobs at the Welcome Stairways Diner in Mulhoney, Wisconsin. G.T. Stoop, the owner, who has leukemia, now needs help running his restaurant. Hope is an excellent waitress, and Addie, who has raised Hope since her mother deserted her, is an outstanding cook. Even though the chemotherapy treatments have weakened G.T., he decides to run for mayor against a corrupt incumbent. Hope and Addie become part of the campaign effort and find themselves and G.T.'s other supporters threatened, intimidated, and fighting. G.T. wins the election when Hope uncovers a voter fraud scheme. He reforms the government, helps the town, marries Addie, and becomes the father Hope has always wanted. Hope develops her own romantic interest when she starts dating Braverman, the assistant cook. Although G.T.'s cancer briefly goes into remission, he dies within two years of their arrival. In her grief, Hope realizes how lucky they were to have their time together, no matter how brief.

Booktalk

Ask how many people in the group have ever waited tables or knew someone who waited tables. Discuss what kinds of problems they encountered and what kinds of skills they needed to overcome them.

At sixteen, Hope Yancey is the waitress any diner would want to hire. She can see the bigger picture, handle the bad times, and still keep pouring the coffee. Now she and her Aunt Addie, a premier diner cook, have to leave Brooklyn, the best home they ever had. Swindled and two-timed by Gleason Beal, "Slime Scourge of the Earth," they are headed for the Welcome Stairways Diner in "Cowville." But Mulhoney, Wisconsin, doesn't dish out the "basic bovine boredom" that Hope anticipates. G.T. Stoop, who owns the Welcome Stairways, is fighting leukemia, but he also decides to fight the big business that's strangling Mulhoney and a corrupt mayor who is helping them do it. When Addie declares, "Lord in heaven, I've got my work cut out for me here," they all find themselves part of a recipe for living life that most people only dream about, and Mulhoney learns it is pretty important that *Hope Was Here.*

Related Activities

1. Reread the passage on page 8 in chapter 2 that begins "I looked in the backseat…" and ends with the words *"Be prepared"* on page 9. Discuss what Hope's possessions and her reasons for keeping them reveal about her.

2. Reread the back of the Welcome Stairways menu on page 13. What does that passage reveal about G.T. Stoop? What does Hope reveal about herself when she reads it?

3. When Hope is twelve, she changes her name from Tulip to Hope. Discuss the significance of names. If you had the choice, what name would you choose and why?

4. List the skills learned in the diner that would prepare someone for living a happy life or tackling another career. Continue to research the pluses and minuses of teenagers working. Share the information you find with the group.

5. Even though Hope and Braverman work every day in the diner, they choose to volunteer at the town's family shelter on Friday nights. Reread the passage on page 176 that begins with "And we learned…" and ends at the bottom of the page. Discuss Hope's conclusions about leadership and politics. Agree and or disagree and cite examples that support your thinking.

6. Hope does not know her biological father, and she rarely sees her mother, yet both people have a significant effect on her. Explain how each influences her life.

7. Write an epilogue to the story that explains what each of the characters is doing at the end of ten years.

Related Works

1. Bauer, Joan. **Rules of the Road.** New York: GP Putnam's Sons, 1998. 201p. $15.99. ISBN 0-39923140-4. (See full booktalk in *Booktalks Plus*, 2001, on pages 114 to 116.) Sixteen-year-old Jenna Boller, super shoe salesperson, learns about life and herself when she chauffeurs her boss, the owner of a national shoe business, across country.

2. Bauer, Joan. **Backwater.** New York: GP Putnam's Sons, 1999. 185p. $16.99. ISBN 0-399-23141-2. (See full booktalk in *Booktalks Plus*, 2001, on pages 28 to 30.) Sixteen-year-old Ivy Breedlow proves her resolve to be a historian when she braves the wilderness to interview her hermit aunt.

3. Hobbs, Valerie. **Tender.** New York: Farrar, Straus, and Giroux /Francis Foster Books, 2001. 256p. $18.00. ISBN 0-374-37397-3. After her grandmother dies, the main character must live with a fa-

ther she doesn't know. The girlfriend who helps her adjust discovers she has cancer.

4. Holubitsky, Katherine. **Alone at Ninety Foot.** (See full booktalk in chapter 3.) The main character discovers that her father's new girlfriend, like Hope's stepfather, is a person she likes and trusts.

5. Silvey, Anita (comp.). **Help Wanted: Short Stories About Young People Working.** New York: Little, Brown, 1997. 174p. $15.95. ISBN 0-316-79148-2. "The Original Recipe" by Michael Dorris, on pages 1 to 13, and the excerpt from "Dandelion Wine" by Ray Bradbury, on pages 149 to 156, illustrate how enthusiasm sells and saves.

6. Wynne-Jones, Tim. **Lord of the Fries and Other Stories.** New York: DK Publishing, Inc., 1999. 214p. $17.95. ISBN 0-7894-2623-4. In the title story on pages 1 to 44, two girls discover that a thorny French-fry personality is actually a sensitive man who wishes only to protect his privacy and those he loves.

ᘓᘔ

Fleischman, Paul and Judy Pedersen (illus.). Seedfolks.

New York: HarperCollins/Joanna Cotler Books, 1997. 69p. $13.95.
ISBN 0-06-027471-9.

Summary/Description

In a vacant lot in Cleveland, Ohio, Kim, a young Vietnamese-American decides to plant bean seeds to show her deceased father that she, too, is a farmer. Her act begins neighborhood involvement that crosses age, nationality, and race. People without focus find one. Whether their contributions are seeds, equipment, protection, or social action, all the *Seedfolks* watch their lives and their neighborhood, as well as their plants, grow. Each chapter centers on a person involved with or fascinated by the garden. The last chapter reflects on the sadness of its winter sleep and the excitement of its spring awakening.

Booktalk

Hold up a bean seed. Ask if anyone knows what it is. Discuss how much it is worth.

Beans aren't too expensive, because—like everyday people—there are a lot of them around. And, like ordinary people, they are often passed up for something or somebody prettier, stronger, or bigger. But nine-year-old Kim knows seeds are powerful, no matter what kind they are. When she plants a few for the father she has never met, she harvests more than beans. She grows *Seedfolks*, and here they tell their street stories—stories that might make you think about planting a few things yourself.

Related Activities

1. Seedfolk can be seen as a metaphor to describe someone who makes a positive move that catches on. List ways that you could become a Seedfolk. Write down the goal you wish to achieve with your actions. You might wish to refer to *Highs!* (Related Work 5) or *Any Girl Can Rule the World* (Related Work 1).
2. Read the book aloud in a group. Ask each person to choose a chapter. After each chapter, discuss the results of the garden.
3. Predict what will happen with next year's garden.
4. After reading *Seedfolks*, read the short story "Antaeus" in *Help Wanted* (Related Work 2). Both works deal with bringing green and cooperation to the city. Compare the purpose of each and how the author accomplishes that purpose.
5. With the help of your librarian, research volunteer organizations. Note their names, addresses, goals, and credibility. Create a display in your library or school or invite leaders from these organizations to speak to your group.

Related Works

1. Brooks, Susan M. **Any Girl Can Rule the World.** Minneapolis, MN: Fairview Press, 1998. 224p. $12.95. ISBN 1-57749-068-1. **NF** This self-help book emphasizes how small, positive acts can change the world around you.
2. Deal, Borden. "Antaeus." In **Help Wanted: Short Stories About Young People Working,** compiled by Anita Silvey. New York: Little, Brown, 1997. 174p. $15.95. ISBN 0-316-79148-2. T.J., a new boy in the development, leads a group of boys in building a rooftop garden but destroys his own work when the building's owner says the garden is illegal. The story appears on pages 95 to 107.
3. La Machia, John. **So What Is Tolerance Anyway?** New York: Rosen Publishing Group, 2000. 48p. (A Student's Guide to American Civics). $17.95. **NF** The book defines tolerance and includes several examples to clarify the definition.
4. Luthringer, Chelsea. **So What Is Citizenship Anyway?** New York: Rosen Publishing Group, 2000. 48p. (A Student's Guide to American Civics). ISBN 0-8239-3097-1. **NF** The book defines citizenship and emphasizes the importance of participation.

5.   Packer, Alex J. **Highs! Over 150 Ways to Feel Really, REALLY Good...Without Alcohol or Other Drugs.** Minneapolis, MN: Free Spirit, 2000. 251p. $14.95pa. ISBN 1-57542-074-0. **NF** Packer offers 150 ways teenagers can feel more connected to themselves and the rest of the world. Pages 230 and 231 present the "Theory of Exponential Kindness Contagion" in the section "Practice Kindness."

Nam, Vickie, ed. Yell-Oh Girls!

New York: HarperCollins/Quill, 2001. 294p. $13.00pa. ISBN 0-06-095944-4. **NF**

Summary/Description

In this collection of essays and poetry, Asian-American females express their joy, frustration, and determination in relation to their ancestry. "Orientation: Finding the Way Home," focuses on the blending of two cultures and the final discovery of American identity. "Family Ties" addresses the universal problems and joys of family life as well as those rooted in Asian identity. "Dolly Rage" speaks to the tyrannical Asian expectations of body image and femininity. "Finding My Voice" expresses the determination of each speaker to accept herself. "Girlwind: Emerging Voices for Change" reveals a dedication to involvement in the world. Vickie Nam gathered these works to make Asian women a visible and cohesive force in the United States in spite of cultural mixed messages and prejudices. An editor's essay introduces each section, and a Mentor Piece written by a successful Asian woman concludes it.

Booktalk

Read "Who is Singing This Song" by Janice Mirikitani on pages xxxiii to xxxv. Then ask the audience to describe the speaker.

This speaker is intelligent, loving, determined, and dedicated. The speaker is like all of us. But the speaker is also different from some of us. The speaker is female and yellow—that is Asian. Do those differences separate her from others, or help her understand them even better? *Yell-Oh Girls!* is filled with voices of girls and women who worry about pimples, blue jeans, drinking Coke, difficult parents, getting through school, and helping the world. They know they come from a proud and demanding heritage and that the media stereotypes them and, still, they are truly Americans. Stand back and open the pages. These girls will show you their world, challenge yours, and then invite you to come along and build something better.

Related Activities

1. Read "Family Trip" by Debra Yoo on pages 23 to 24. Then read "Incident" by Countee Cullen on page 92 of *I, Too, Sing America* (Related Work 1). Compare the two poems, the speakers, and the time periods. Then discuss common threads of prejudice you find are independent of a particular group.

2. In the section "Orientation: Finding the Way Home," the speakers explain how they relate to a greater community or country. Explain your own relationship to your country of citizenship. In your explanation, consider the issues that affect that relationship.

3. In the essays "Tainted" on pages 57 and 58 by Belinda Wong and "I Love You Dad (An Unsent Letter)" on pages 99 to 103 by Grace Song, the speakers talk about their parents' expectations versus their own wishes. Much of each essay centers on cultural differences. Write your own essay or poem that explains how you perceive and handle the differences between your wishes and your parents' expectations.

4. "Dolly Rage" deals with expectations of appearance. After reading the selections, compare the attitudes expressed with those from "Media-Fed Images" in *Ophelia Speaks* (Related Work 5). Then write your own poem or essay about your perceptions of body image.

5. Research the contributions Asian-American women have made to the United States. You might wish to begin by reading the Mentor Piece at the end of each section. In a presentation or display, share the information you gather.

Related Works

1. Clinton, Catherine (prose text), and Stephen Alcorn (illus.). **I, Too, Sing America: Three Centuries of African American Poetry.** Boston: Houghton Mifflin Company, 1998. 128p. $20.00. ISBN 0-395-89599-5. (See full booktalk in *Booktalks Plus*, 2001, pages 219 to 221.) **NF** This collection of poems provides a three-century perception of the African-American experience.

2. Glenn, Mel. **Split Image: A Story in Poems.** New York: HarperCollins Publishers, 2000. 159p. $15.95. ISBN 0-688-16249-5. **NF** A series of poems describes how cultural conflict leads to an Asian girl's suicide.

3. Na, An. **A Step from Heaven.** (See full booktalk in chapter 1.) An eighteen-year-old Korean immigrant reflects on her life in the United States from the time she is three.

4. Namioka, Lensey. **Ties That Bind, Ties That Break.** (See full booktalk in chapter 1.) Nineteen-year-old Ailin relates the traditions and changes that influenced her move to and life in America.

5. Shandler, Sara. **Ophelia Speaks.** New York: Harper Perennial, 1999. 285p. $12.95pa. ISBN 0-06-095297-0. (See full booktalk in *Booktalks Plus,* 2001, pages 126 to 128.) **NF** Organized in a format similar to *Yell-Oh Girls!,* these essays and poems discuss problems of growth and adjustment for all girls in the United States.

Cฦฦ

Covey, Sean. **The 7 Habits of Highly Effective Teens: The Ultimate Teenage Success Guide.**
New York: Fireside, 1998. 268p. $14.00. ISBN 0-684-85609-3.

Summary/Description

Sean Covey, son of Stephen Covey, applies the 7 *Habits of Highly Effective People* to the lives of teenagers. Part I explains the importance of habits and how they relate to our perceptions and beliefs about the world. Part II includes the principle of The Personal Bank Account with which a person builds his or her own self-respect. It also deals with the first three habits: Be Proactive, Begin with the End in Mind, and Put First Things First. These three habits emphasize that the person must have a Private Victory or a strong sense of self before making an impact on the world. Part III, The Public Victory, first explains how a teenager builds a Relationship Bank Account to gain the respect and trust of others. It then details the next three habits, Think Win-Win; Seek First to Understand, Then to Be Understood; and Synergize. Part IV explains number seven, the renewal habit, Sharpen the Saw, and reflects on the spirit of the seven steps. Illustrations and testimonials from teenagers who have used the Covey seven steps show how the system has helped them become more aware of and successful in their behavior. "Baby Steps" suggests how the reader can apply the principles, and "Info Central," at the end of the book, gives 800-numbers and Web sites for information about Substance Abuse, Eating Disorders, Physical and Mental Health, Abuse, Gang Prevention, Education, General Youth Support Services, and Volunteerism. Page 252 lists 50 Great Books for Teens, and an additional bibliography includes the sources quoted or reprinted for each habit. A title and topic index makes information easily accessible.

Booktalk

Ask the group how they would define the word habit and how they think habits affect them. Discuss the responses. Then read "Who am I?," the definition of habit on the page following the table of contents for *The 7*

Habits of Highly Effective Teens. Discuss whether the group agrees or disagrees with the answer.

How do you control the world? You control yourself.

How do you control yourself? You develop good habits.

Sean Covey, like his father, gives us seven good habits, and no matter who you are, or who you think you are, you need them. You can achieve more and feel more comfortable about what you achieve if you spend only seven minutes per day reading and using *The 7 Habits of Highly Effective Teens.* Learn to build your own Personal Back Account with your family, friends, and the experiences that surround you.

Related Activities

1. Read the bold-print passage in *Zack* (Related Work 2) that begins "I am black....." How does this girl's statement of belief relate to the world that the main character Zack discovers when he searches for his heritage?
2. Read the bold-print passage on page 58 that begins "I was sexually abused..." as well as the bold print passage on pages 150 and 151 that begins "My problems with my mom..." in *The 7 Habits of Highly Effective Teens.* Discuss how these passages from *The 7 Habits of Highly Effective Teens* relate to *Speak* (Related Work 1).
3. Read the bold-print passage on page 78 of *The 7 Habits of Highly Effective Teens* that begins, "I had one bad year...." Discuss how the passage relates to the characters in *Bad* (Related Work 4).
4. Read the account on pages 42 to 44 of *The 7 Habits of Highly Effective Teens.* Discuss how Bryce's story relates to *Safe at Second* (Related Work 5).
5. Read "Win the Private Victory First" on page 154 of *The 7 Habits of Highly Effective Teens.* Discuss how the passage relates to *A Face in Every Window* (Related Work 6).
6. After reading each of the books referred to in activities 1 through 5, discuss how *The 7 Habits of Highly Effective Teens* would have helped the teenage characters.
7. Read "Shunner's Profile," "Tolerator's Profile," and "Celebrator's Profile." Classify the characters from *The Crusader* (Related Work 3) in terms of those profiles.
8. Read one of the books listed in "50 Great Books for Teens" in *The 7 Habits of Highly Effective Teens.* Explain why you think it was included and if you agree with its selection.
9. Continue to research self-help literature. Keep a journal as you read each book or pamphlet. Note the descriptions and advice that repeat. Record your experiences as you apply that advice. Compose your

own personal book for successful living, or share your advice and experiences with the group.

Related Works

1. Anderson, Laurie Halse. **Speak.** (See full booktalk in chapter 2.) A fourteen-year-old girl experiences date rape and is afraid to share the secret with her friends or busy family.
2. Bell, William. **Zack.** New York: Simon & Schuster, 1999. 192p. $16.95. ISBN 0-689-82248-0. Zack Lane searches for his intellectual, emotional, and racial identity.
3. Bloor, Edward. **Crusader.** (See full booktalk in chapter 2.) The people who work in a mall become family for a young girl whose mother has died and whose father has become distant.
4. Ferris, Jean. **Bad.** (See full booktalk in chapter 2.) A young girl, rebelling against her father, aids in a robbery and finds herself in a detention home.
5. Johnson, Scott. **Safe at Second.** New York: Philomel Books, 1999. 254p. $17.99. ISBN 0-399-23365-2. (See full booktalk in *Booktalks Plus*, 2001, pages 101 to 103). A star ballplayer learns to live with an injured eye that destroys his baseball career.
6. Nolan, Han. **A Face in Every Window.** (See full booktalk in chapter 1.) James Patrick O'Brian must adjust to an entirely new family after his grandmother dies.

ध् य

Bamford, Janet. Street Wise: A Guide for Teen Investors.
Princeton, NJ: Bloomberg Press, 2000. 223p. $16.95pa. ISBN 1-57660-039-4.

Summary/Description

Using clear, understandable language, Bamford explains basic terms and procedures for investing. She emphasizes the importance of compounding and investing for the long term and explores investment options such as individual stocks, bonds, and mutual funds. Credit buying is described as the negative investment. Custodial accounts are also considered. Descriptions of investment clubs, games, contests, investing, and research sources will help either a teenager or an adult connect with information and experiences to expand their knowledge of the market. The final chapter discusses possible internships and careers available and how a young person can prepare for them. A name and topic index makes information readily available.

Booktalk

Do you want to be a millionaire but you're too young to buy a lottery ticket, you can't book a flight to Las Vegas, and your ready cash isn't enough to rent a video? Take heart. You have a great deal of one thing that could make you very rich: time. If you save money and then let the returns compound, it will grow while you just study, hang out with your friends, or make plans for the big game. In fact, if you save ten percent of that babysitting or lawn mowing income (no matter how little), pay cash, and learn how to increase the rate of return, you might be a millionaire before you know it. Reading *Street Wise* will give you hints on how much to save, where to invest what you save, and even how long it will take you to double your money. By knowing what to do and how to do it, you can work smarter while your money works harder.

Related Activities

1. Using the Rule of 72, explained on page 12 of *Street Wise,* choose three separate investments, such as a savings account, a certificate of deposit, or a bond. Estimate how long it will take to double your money in each investment, based on the rate of return.
2. Track one stock daily for at least one year to see how its value increases, decreases, or stays the same. You might want to chart the rises and falls. Also record the events that seem to affect its price.
3. Throughout *Street Wise* and *TeenVestor* (Related Work 5), the authors refer to Web sites. Ask each person in the group to access one of the suggested Web sites and share a description of it with the group.
4. Keep a financial journal. In the left margin, list financial terms that are new to you or that are used in new ways. Define or expand the definition of each term by keeping track of the contexts in which you find it.
5. On page 198, the author lists several financial magazines. Ask each person in the group to choose one magazine. After reading several issues, ask each reader to share with the group the magazine's regular features, its format, and the position it takes on a particular aspect of financial news.
6. Ask your librarian to help you locate additional sources that give investing advice. In your financial journal, note which sources are most valuable to you and why.

Related Works

1. Benson, Peter L., Judy Galbraith, and Pamela Espeland. **What Teens Need to Succeed: Proven Ways to Shape Your Own Future.** Minneapolis, MN: Free Spirit, 1998. $14.95. ISBN 1-57542-027-9. **NF** Discussing assets in more general terms, this reference

helps teens see that each person has qualities, talents, and resources that are as important as or more important than financial investments.

2. Caes, Charles. **The Young Zillionaire's Guide to the Stock Market.** New York: Rosen Publishing Group, 2000. 48p. (Be a Zillionaire). $17.95. ISBN 0-8239-3256-6. **NF** Geared to middle school students, the *Guide to the Stock Market* gives brief explanations of exchanges, types of stock, dividends, stock quotations, and buying and selling.

3. Green, Meg. **The Young Zillionaire's Guide to Investments and Savings.** New York: Rosen Publishing Group, 2000. 48p. (Be a Zillionaire). $17.95. ISBN 0-8239-3261-3. **NF** Geared to middle school students, *Investments and Savings* talks about budgeting, saving, and investing as related habits.

4. Hettinga, Donald R. **The Brothers Grimm: Two Lives, One Legacy.** New York: Clarion Books, 2001. 180p. $22.00. ISBN 0-618-05599-1. **NF** On pages 48 and 49, Hettinga describes the value of nineteenth-century talers and how the term changed around the world, finally becoming dollars in America. On pages 21 and 22 is a letter showing how eleven-year-old Jacob handles financial matters for the family after his father dies. As a whole, the book relates the life and contributions of these two talented brothers.

5. Modu, Emmanuel and Andrea Walker. **TeenVestor: The Practical Investment Guide for Teens and Their Parents.** New York: Berkley Publishing Group/Perigee, 2002. 300p. $12.95. ISBN 0-399-52760-5. **NF** This family tutorial gives guidelines to help parents and children work together in managing money and building investments. A Web site supplements and updates the information presented in the text.

6. National Endowment for Financial Education in partnership with Cooperative Extension System. **NEFE High School Financial Planning Program: Instructor's Manual.** Greenwood Village, CO: National Endowment for Financial Education, 2001. 405p. Free, pa. **NF** This curriculum guide includes goals and objectives for each lesson; activities for diverse learning styles; instructions and exercises for goal setting, analyzing, and planning; overheads; grading rubrics; and full discussions of budgeting, saving, and investing. To order, contact National Endowment for Financial Education, High School Department, 5299 DTC Boulevard, Suite 1300, Greenwood Village, CO 80111. Phone: (303) 224-3511.

7. National Endowment for Financial Education in partnership with Cooperative Extension System. **NEFE High School Financial**

Planning Program: Student Guide. Greenwood Village, CO: National Endowment for Financial Education, 2001. 128p. Free, pa. **NF** The student guide is the companion to the Instructor's Manual listed in Related Work 6, which includes ordering information.

☙❧

Cart, Michael (comp.). Tomorrowland: 10 Stories About the Future.
New York: Scholastic Press, 1999. 224p. $15.95. ISBN 0-590-37678-0.

Summary/Description

*T*omorrowland includes ten stories that predict the future or reflect on the past. They deal with the following topics: the nature of mankind, the role of literature, disaster psychology, the value of machines in man's life, the threats that change creates, the importance of nature, donors replacing fathers, and the end of the world. After each story, the author explains the story's background. The collection's overall message is that human feelings such as love, empathy, and joy are more important than the technology people create. Rodman Philbrick has expanded his short story in this collection, "The Last Book in the Universe," into a novel of the same name.

Booktalk

The *Tomorrowland* stories talk about our questions about the future. Will machines be more important than people? Will animals still exist? Will people need to move to another planet? Will constant change drive all of us out of our minds? Or will the world just go on the same way, with the same feelings and conflicts and a few more buttons to push? *Tomorrowland* doesn't give any answers, but it proposes some interesting choices to think about.

Related Activities

1. "Homo…Sapiens?" (the opening story) and "Night of the Plague" deal with the past. Discuss why Cart chose to include these two stories in a collection about the future and especially why he chose to open with one of them.
2. The stories "What's the Point?," "Rage," "The Other Half of Me," and "Starry, Starry Night" deal with characters living in the present who think about the future. Discuss the part the future plays in each story and how thinking about the future can be both positive and negative.

3. "A Robot Doesn't Have a Curve Ball" and "The Last Dog" discuss how technology might decrease the quality of life. After reading the stories, discuss whether you agree or disagree and your own concerns about technology in the future.

4. "His Brother's Keeper" alludes to the story of Cain and Abel in the Bible. Read both and then discuss how the author's changes affect the story and reveal the author's vision of the future.

5. In your group, organize a *Tomorrowland* committee. Keep files of projected technologies. Periodically present these technologies to the group. Discuss the implications or write short stories and poems that incorporate them.

Related Works

1. Gallo, Donald R., ed. **Time Capsule: Short Stories About Teenagers Throughout the Twentieth Century.** New York: Delacorte Press, 1999. 221p. $16.95. ISBN 0-385-32675-0. This collection includes a story for each decade and presents possibilities for discussions about the past and future.

2. Haddis, Margaret Peterson. **Turnabout.** New York: Simon & Schuster, 2000. 223p. $17.00. ISBN 0-689-82187-5. In the year 2000, Melly and Anny Beth participate in an experiment that allows them to grow young and learn the challenges of living forever.

3. Levitin, Sonia. **The Cure.** New York: Harcourt Brace and Company, 1999. 184p. $16.00. ISBN 0-15-201827-1. Sixteen-year-old Gemm, who lives in a utopian community, is taught the dangers of dance, feelings, and music when he time-travels as a Jew to Strasbourg, Germany, in 1348, just before the Black Death.

4. Philbrick, Rodman. **The Last Book in the Universe.** (See full booktalk in chapter 2.) In this expansion of his short story, Ryter accompanies Spaz on a journey to save Spaz's sister. On the journey, Ryter's integrity and bravery motivate Spaz to become the next Ryter. He also helps a young feral child and begins to fall in love with a beautiful proov (genetically improved person).

5. Skurzynski, Gloria. **Virtual War.** New York: Simon & Schuster Books for Young Readers, 1997. 152p. $16.00. ISBN 0-689-81374-0. A fourteen-year-old boy raised in a box must wage a virtual war so his country will not experience destruction in a real one.

Index

271

About the Author

LUCY SCHALL, a retired English teacher with more than 30 years of experience, is a book reviewer for VOYA and lives in Meadville, Pennsylvania.